THE LOST
MASSEY LECTURES

D0964051

THE LOST MASSEY LECTURES

Recovered Classics from
Five Great Thinkers

JOHN KENNETH GALBRAITH
PAUL GOODMAN
JANE JACOBS
ERIC W. KIERANS
MARTIN LUTHER KING, JR.

ANANSI

Individual lectures copyright © 1965 John Kenneth Galbraith, 1966 Paul
Goodman, 1967 Martin Luther King, Jr., 1980 Jane Jacobs, 1984 Eric W. Kierans
Introduction copyright © 2007 Bernie Lucht

All rights reserved. No part of this publication may be reproduced or transmitted
in any form or by any means, electronic or mechanical, including photocopying,
recording, or any information storage and retrieval system, without permission
in writing from the publisher.

Published in 2007 by House of Anansi Press Inc.
110 Spadina Avenue, Suite 801, Toronto, ON, M5V 2K4
Tel. 416-363-4343 Fax 416-363-1017 www.anansi.ca

Distributed in Canada by	Distributed in the United States by
HarperCollins Canada Ltd.	Publishers Group West
1995 Markham Road	1700 Fourth Street
Scarborough, ON, M1B 5M8	Berkeley, CA 94710
Toll free tel. 1-800-387-0117	Toll free tel. 1-800-788-3123

Page 400 constitutes a continuation of this copyright page.

House of Anansi Press is committed to protecting our natural environment. As
part of our efforts, this book is printed on paper that contains 100% post-consumer
recycled fibres, is acid-free, and is processed chlorine-free.

11 10 09 08 07   1 2 3 4 5

Library and Archives Canada Cataloguing in Publication Data

The lost Massey lectures : recovered classics from five great thinkers /
John Kenneth Galbraith . . . [et al.].

(CBC Massey lectures series)
A collection of five Massey lectures are reprinted in their entirety.
The authors include: John Kenneth Galbraith, Paul Goodman, Jane Jacobs,
Eric W. Kierans, and Martin Luther King Jr.
Includes bibliographical references.
ISBN 978-0-88784-217-7 (pbk.)

1. United States — Social conditions — 1945–. 2. United States —
Civilization — 20th century. 3. United States — Moral conditions.
4. Developing countries — Economic conditions. 5. Industrial policy.
6. Corporate state. 7. National state. 8. Social policy. 9. Québec
(Province) — History — Autonomy and independence movements.
I. Galbraith, John Kenneth, 1908–2006. II Series.

JZ1242.L675 2007   909.82'5   C2007-903440-3

Library of Congress Control Number: 2007930189

CONTENTS

Introduction

The Massey Lectures were born in the winter of 1961. They were unveiled in late February by the vice-president and general manager of English networks at the Canadian Broadcasting Corporation (CBC), H. G. Walker. "Each year," he said in the press release announcing the series, "the CBC will invite a noted scholar to undertake study or original research in his field and present the results in a series of half-hour radio broadcasts." He continued, saying that he hoped the lectures would "make significant contributions to public awareness and understanding and . . . further development of the art of broadcasting."

The lectures were named for the Right Honourable Vincent Massey, who had recently completed a seven-year term as governor general of Canada. Massey is notable as the first Canadian-born person to hold the post, but it was work he did before becoming governor general that inspired the CBC to name the new lecture series after him.

In 1949, Vincent Massey had been appointed by the government of Prime Minister Louis St. Laurent to head a royal commission mandated to carry out a sweeping study of "the entire field of letters, the arts and sciences within the jurisdiction of the federal state." Grandly named the Royal Commission on National Development in the Arts, Letters and Sciences, it came to be known more simply as the Massey Commission. Its scope included science, literature, the arts, music, drama, film, and broadcasting. The commission held hearings across the country. It listened to testimony from more than a thousand witnesses and received 462 written submissions. It took two years to do its work and issued its final report in 1951.

The Massey Report was enormously influential. It led to, among other things, the establishment of the National Library of Canada and the Canada Council. But more broadly, the report was instrumental in modernizing the role of the federal government in cultural activity. Naming a prestigious lecture series after Vincent Massey was the CBC's way of giving him special recognition for the work he had done to promote culture and the humanities in Canada.

The first set of Massey Lectures was broadcast in the spring of 1961. It consisted of six half-hour talks by Barbara Ward, a British expert in economics and international affairs. Her lectures were called *The Rich Nations and the Poor Nations*, and in them she examined the causes of poverty in what were then known as the "underdeveloped nations." The lectures were broadcast once a week, on Thursday nights at 8:30. Vincent Massey himself introduced the first broadcast. The CBC later published the lectures as a book, and so began a tradition in public broadcasting and publishing that has continued for forty-six years, a tradition that has evolved and expanded with the times.

Most, but not all, of the Massey Lectures are still in print. The lectures today are the product of a happy collaboration of three partners — CBC Radio, House of Anansi Press, and Massey College in the University of Toronto. For most of their history, the Massey Lectures were recorded within the austere confines of a CBC radio studio in Toronto. But since 2002, they have been delivered each fall before large audiences on university campuses in cities across Canada. The recorded public lectures are then broadcast to listeners in Canada on CBC Radio One, and to all of North America on Sirius Satellite radio. They are also streamed worldwide on the Internet and available as podcasts. Simultaneously with the broadcasts, the lectures are published as a trade paperback that garners international attention and usually makes the bestseller lists. The Massey Lectures have established their place as a truly Canadian institution and are an annual highlight of our national intellectual life.

The CBC Radio program *Ideas* is assigned the task of producing the Massey Lectures. As executive producer of *Ideas*, I have been directly involved in the selection of Massey Lecturers since 1985, but my connection to the series goes back much earlier, to 1971. In September of that year, I was looking for work, having just returned to Canada from a two-year posting as a Canadian University Service Overseas (CUSO) volunteer in Nigeria. I applied to the CBC, where I had worked before. The program *Ideas* was looking for a production assistant, and against all odds I got the job.

My first assignment was to edit the raw studio recordings of that year's Massey lecturer, James A. Corry, one of Canada's most distinguished political scientists and a former principal of Queen's University. His topic was *The Power of the Law*.

Professor Corry was a naturally slow and thoughtful speaker. As I listened to the tape of him talking, I thought it would have been nice if he had spoken just a little bit faster. I wanted to speed him up and puzzled over whether or not I could. Technically, it could be done, but actually doing it seemed presumptuous. Speed up a distinguished and respected scholar? Who was I, a junior staff member of the CBC, to do that? But I couldn't resist. I set aside any reservations and started in. I set myself up in a tiny, fluorescent-lit editing room, armed with the tools of the trade — an ancient, floor-mounted Ampex reel-to-reel editing machine, a notepad, a stopwatch, a yellow grease pencil, a razor blade, and a little roll of special white adhesive tape.

The way to get Corry to speak more quickly was to take out the pauses in his speech. There were pauses everywhere — between paragraphs, between sentences, between clauses and phrases, and even between individual words. Cutting them out was laborious work that required making thousands of edits on the audiotape. These days we edit digitally, on computers, but until the late 1990s it was all done by hand. You physically marked the tape with the grease pencil and sliced out the bits you didn't want with the razor blade. Then you stuck the ends back together with the adhesive tape. You had to make sure the edit was undetectable to the ear. It was a good idea to save the bits that were cut out, including breaths and pauses, in case you needed to put them back in.

After Corry's Massey Lectures were broadcast, we received a lot of comments. Many came from people who said that they had enjoyed the lectures, but were somewhat puzzled: they had never heard Corry speak so quickly. This episode was my introduction to the Massey Lectures and the start of a decades-long association with them.

The Masseys have been graced by some of the greatest minds in the world. In this book, House of Anansi Press and the CBC have gathered together some early sets of lectures we are calling "the lost Massey Lectures." All of them have been out of print for years. The CBC had published the Massey Lectures as part of its own publishing program until the end of the 1980s, when Anansi took over that role. By then, some of the lectures had gone out of print, and we thought it was time to give the public an opportunity to rediscover them.

The lost Massey Lectures are about the complex of ideas that link our political, social, and moral worlds — how we live together in modern societies and define our responsibilities towards each other as global citizens. There are five sets of Massey Lectures in this collection. The first three — by John Kenneth Galbraith, Paul Goodman, and Martin Luther King, Jr. — were written during the heat and turmoil of the 1960s, the decade of "sex, drugs, and rock and roll," the escalating Vietnam War, political protest, civil rights struggles, cultural upheaval, and the assault on the staid certainties of the '50s.

In the 1965 Massey Lectures, the distinguished liberal economist and diplomat John Kenneth Galbraith returned to the theme Barbara Ward had introduced five years before. He called his lectures *The Underdeveloped Country*. The expression "underdeveloped countries" was coined in the late 1950s and is no longer in general use. Thought to be patronizing, it was replaced by other, more congenial descriptions — developing countries, less developed countries, the Third World, the South — but while the vocabulary may have changed, the issues Galbraith talked about more than four decades ago are depressingly familiar.

Galbraith analyzed the causes of poverty in different parts of the world. The barriers to advancement, he wrote, were not the same everywhere. In some areas, the main barrier was lack of education; in others, it was social structure or the way resources were distributed. To help poor nations move forward, aid was necessary, but one size would not fit all. Different problems required different solutions. In particular, Galbraith was concerned that what worked in rich countries would not work in poor countries, which faced different pressures. He decried conservative thinkers who opposed foreign aid, saying, "I do not worry about these people. They have always been with us; they add variety to life."

Paul Goodman followed Galbraith as Massey lecturer in 1966. Trained in philosophy and literature, Goodman taught at several major universities in the United States. He described himself as an anarchist. In keeping with the spirit of his times, he also taught at the so-called "free university" organized by students at San Francisco State College. Goodman was a trenchant social critic. He wrote essays, novels, plays, and poetry. His Massey Lectures, *The Moral Ambiguity of America*, were strongly felt and often angry. He was both gloomy and optimistic as he pondered the ambiguities in American values. On one side, he saw the drive for efficiency and control by the institutions of politics, industry, and commerce, which he argued destroyed vitality and excluded human beings as useless; these values produced what he termed the "Empty Society." In contrast were the lives of real, flesh-and-blood people, organized in local communities, dynamic and socially inventive. Goodman described this upside of American values as "our beautiful libertarian, pluralist and populist experiment."

The world lost a great spirit when Martin Luther King, Jr. was assassinated in the early evening of April 4, 1968, on the balcony of a motel in Memphis, Tennessee. He had come to the city to lead a march to support black garbage workers who were striking for better pay and working conditions. As a campaigner for civil rights and an orator of extraordinary power, King was unequalled. Who can forget the eloquence of his "I Have a Dream" speech, delivered at the Lincoln Memorial in 1963?

The broadcasts of King's Massey Lectures, *Conscience for Change*, began in November 1967. They followed a summer of severe racial unrest. There had been major riots in Detroit and Newark. Scores of people had been killed. Hundreds had been injured. Many more were permanently traumatized by what had happened. In his lectures, King spoke of the causes of the violence. He said that everyone had underestimated the rage that black people had been suppressing. Most of the violence in the riots had not been directed against people, he noted, but against property, the symbols of white power and wealth. Despite this, he argued that the best strategy for improving the tragic living conditions of black people, and of poor people everywhere, was through massive campaigns of non-violent civil disobedience. People had to transcend the boundaries of race, tribe, class, and nation. "We must either learn to live together as brothers," he said, "or we're all going to perish together as fools." In his final lecture, King described non-violence as an "imperative for action." The lecture was broadcast on Christmas Eve. A little more than three months later, he was dead.

The final two sets of Massey Lectures in this collection are about familiar and enduring themes in Canada: national unity and Canadian sovereignty. In 1976, René Lévesque, leader of the Parti Québécois, was elected premier of Quebec. He pledged to pursue a new relationship between the province and the rest of Canada, an arrangement he called "sovereignty-association." When the influential thinker and urban activist Jane Jacobs delivered her Massey Lectures, *Canadian Cities and Sovereignty Association*, late in the fall of 1979, the first Quebec Referendum was only six months away and the possibility that the province might secede from Canada was high on the country's list of national anxieties.

In her lectures, Jacobs described a key dynamic in the sovereignty debate as "a tale of two cities" — Toronto and Montreal. For most of its history, Montreal had been the financial, industrial, and cultural capital of Canada. In the 1970s, it was surpassed by Toronto and relegated to the status of a regional city. This, noted Jacobs, was unprecedented in Canada: never before had a national city lost its position. The traditional role of Canadian regional cities, she wrote, was to exploit resources from their hinterlands; they were not economically creative. If Montreal became a typical regional city, it would stagnate economically and culturally, which would spell trouble, not only for the city but for the province of Quebec as a whole. Jacobs wondered whether Montreal and Quebec would be able solve their problems within the Canadian political framework.

Jane Jacobs analyzed Lévesque's proposals for sovereignty-association. She was largely sympathetic to them, not just because she thought that the prevalent approach to economic life in Canada might not work for Quebec, but for another, more compelling reason, which went to the heart of her political thought: she hated centralization. She thought centralized governments and bureaucracies were "stifling" and "wasteful" and would become a heavy burden on future generations. Sovereignty-association might combat centralization and lighten the burden. It would be a "presentable gift to the future."

If Jane Jacobs was concerned about centralization in Canada, Eric Kierans was concerned about a larger process, globalization. A businessman and economist, Kierans had taught at McGill University and later had a short-lived career in federal politics under Pierre Elliott Trudeau. Critical of the government's economic policies — Kierans thought they undermined Canada's sovereignty — he resigned and returned to teaching in 1972.

Introduction

In his Massey Lectures, *Globalism and the Nation State*, delivered in the fall of 1983, Kierans took as his starting point the Summit of Industrialized Nations held in Williamsburg, Virginia, earlier that year. Hosted by U.S. President Ronald Reagan, the conference took place in the wake of the second oil price shock, a period of rising inflation, growing unemployment, and declining world trade. Tensions between the West and the Soviet bloc were high. The purpose of the Williamsburg Summit was to counter the Soviet threat and formulate common economic, foreign, and defence policies among the seven advanced industrial nations. As part of a closing statement, President Reagan read what he called the "Williamsburg Declaration on Economic Recovery." It called upon member nations to pursue policies that would lead to reduced inflation, lower interest rates, and increased investment and employment opportunities. Reagan spoke of achieving a "convergence of economic performance." Kierans saw in this the emergence of a Western bloc that would override the interests of individual countries and harm their capacity to look after the welfare of their own citizens. In his lectures, Kierans pleaded for Canada to affirm its independence. "We are not an accident of geography," he wrote, "nor are our traditions, culture, and languages to be written off in the alleged efficiency of a global economy." He called the promise that globalization would improve the living standards of people everywhere "an illusion and thoroughly dishonest."

We live in an age that is said to be ahistorical. It is difficult to remember the past — or even acknowledge it — living as we do, focused on an "eternal present," driven by busy schedules and information overload, and wrapped up in anxieties about careers, family, health, the environment, terrorism, the future of the world.

INTRODUCTION

It can be both comforting and discouraging to know that many of the issues we confront today have been with us in different forms for a long time; people have thought about them and grappled with them for generations. I hope you find that these lost Massey Lectures are both a useful mirror of the times in which they were written and an insightful context for some our most pressing current dilemmas.

BERNIE LUCHT
Toronto
June 2007

THE UNDERDEVELOPED COUNTRY

by

JOHN KENNETH GALBRAITH

In a lecture series, in contrast with a novel, there is no harm in a premature disclosure of the plot. These five lectures have all to do with the same general theme—the economics and politics of what we have come to call, with some optimism, the developing countries. In the manner of a musical composition—and this I imagine is the only resemblance—the treatment has several distinct movements. The first two lectures deal with the common features of the poor countries and the problems that are common to them. They show how poverty tends to induce common patterns and modes of economic, political and also social and biological behavior and to justify our looking at the poor countries as a class.

The next two lectures are concerned with the causes of poverty. In contrast with the first two, they show the great differences between the poor countries. They show that although poverty enforces common patterns of behavior it proceeds from radically different causes. This I consider to be the most serious error now characterizing not all but a great deal of the discussion of economic development. In these lectures, I divide the developing countries into three distinct classes in accordance with the obstacles which principally oppose economic advance.

Inherent in this type of classification is a diagnosis—an identification of the causes of backwardness and poverty. In the last lecture, I go on from diagnosis to remedy—to consider what can be done to promote or insure advance in light of the causes previously identified.

I

UNDERDEVELOPMENT AND
SOCIAL BEHAVIOR

| 1 |

The first and most obvious consequence of poverty is political and social and civil instability. As I write these lectures, the world is anxiously watching the ominous course of conflict in Vietnam. We are occasionally reminded that there is also chronic warfare a little to the west in Laos. There have recently been riots over food in India and the Indians and Pakistanis continue to snarl—and at this writing are fighting—across their long and intricate frontier. Various of the Arab states are at odds with each other on all matters except their hostility to Israel. Algeria has recently undergone a convulsive change in government. In the Congo vast areas, in the words of today's *New York Times*, "are not being governed in any significant sense." In this hemisphere we have had until recently an armed truce in Santo Domingo and a good deal of tension in Colombia, Bolivia and other of the Latin American republics. Even in the countries I have not mentioned in Africa, Asia and Latin America one can count, from time to time, on window-breaking at the American Embassy, or the burning of a United States Information Service Library, these being the now accepted manifestations of discontent. It is said in Washington that the American diplomat, once characterized by his striped pants, cocktail glass and dignified bearing, can now be told by his putty knife.

By contrast, in recent years things have been peaceful in Western Europe and, by all outward evidence, in Eastern Europe and the Soviet Union. And similarly in Canada and the United States. We are having disorders associated with racial discontent, and will have more, and this is by no means unconnected with the poverty with which I am here concerned. This apart, the major manifestation of unsettlement in the United States in recent times has been the Free Speech movement at the University of California. And now all is quiet there. Either free speech is safe or interest in it was a passing fad.

A visitor from another planet, in these past years, would have been inclined to divide this one into two halves—into the troubled and the untroubled sector. The untroubled sector would be the comparatively well-to-do countries of Eastern and Western Europe and of North America. The troubled part would be the poor and contentious lands comprising most of the rest of the globe. Only after snatching a surreptitious look at the staff papers of the National Security Council, hearing a speech by a high State Department official on the intentions of the Sino-Soviet Bloc,[1] studying a thoughtful article in *Foreign Affairs* or seeing the newspapers of our two countries would he be aware that the proper distinction is not between the well-to-do and tranquil countries and the poor and troubled but between the Communist countries and the Free World.

The instinct of the man from outer space has a great deal to commend it; he might be given a minor advisory role in either the United States or Canadian government. The distinction between the Communist and the non-Communist world is firmly grounded in the tradition of conventional diplomacy, the wounding recollection of Josef Stalin and the desire to show a negative reaction in the event of any future saliva test for loyalty. There are, certainly, differences between the Communist and non-Communist states, and it seems certain that this is a matter where one's relation to the society induces a certain measure of both vehemence and subjectivity. High Communist office holders, one senses, are more likely to emphasize the unique blessings of socialism than the average toiler in a factory or on a collective farm. Whatever the system, he belongs to the group that ends up working eight hours a day. And no one celebrates the values of capitalism so eloquently as the oil millionaire who has his taxes reduced by depletion allowances and capital gains unless it be the department store man who lives effortlessly on the dividends earned by his grandfather. But the similar reactions of the comfortable are not my case. I wish to argue that as much, perhaps more, of the behavior of people and nations is explained by their poverty or their well-being as by their political systems. To fail to see this is increasingly to misunderstand the world in which we live.

| 2 |

The first and most elementary effect of poverty is to enforce attitudes and behavior that make it self-perpetuating. Similarly the first effect of wealth is to allow the freedom of action that permits of the creation of more wealth. It has often been observed that very poor communities are intensely conservative—that, far more than the more fortunate, these people resist the change that is in their own interest. Illiteracy, and the limited horizons it implies, is a partial cause of this; so is the inertia resulting from poor health and malnutrition. But poverty is an even more direct cause of conservatism. If there is no margin to spare, there is no margin for risk. One cannot try a new variety of wheat or rice that promises an additional twenty per cent yield if there is any chance that it is vulnerable to insect pests, disease or drought and thus in an occasional year might fail altogether. However welcome the extra twenty per cent, it is not worth the risk of not eating for a whole season, the consequences of which tend to be both painful and irreversible. Since there is a measure of risk in anything that is untried, it is better to stick with the proven methods—the methods that have justified themselves by the survival of the family to this time. The well-to-do farmer, by contrast, can accept some risk of loss if the prospect is for a greater gain. He is in no danger of starving whatever happens. Even within India the comparatively well-to-do Punjabis in the north are far more inclined to try new crops and new methods than the villagers in the poorer regions who live closer to subsistence. Needless to say, in the firm tradition of the fortunate, they attribute their progressiveness not to higher income but to higher intelligence.

But fear of loss is not the only cause of conservatism among the very poor. Any change is regarded with uneasiness—and also with reason. In our world, change is identified with new and better ways of producing things or of organizing production; it is an article of faith that the whole community benefits from the advance. If someone loses his job, he is told with great unction and some truth that his sacrifice is for the greater good of the greater number. As a result, to be against change is like being against God and perhaps worse for, of late, we have been more tolerant of religious than of economic heresy.

The experience of the poor community is with a very different kind of change. Technical innovation is unknown; change when it has occurred has usually meant that some rascal more powerful, more ruthless or more devious than the rest has succeeded in enriching himself at the public expense. Change is associated with someone seizing land, exacting rents, levying taxes, provisioning an army or exacting tribute for his own benefit. In the language of my colleague, Professor A. O. Hirschman, the image of change is *ego-focused*.[2] This being the view of change, the instinct of the community is to resist it and to suspect even beneficial change.

| 3 |

These are the psychological effects of poverty; the biological consequences are equally profound. In all well-to-do communities, there is a strong tendency to limit the number of children in order to protect the given standard of living. Population increases with increasing well-being but never so rapidly as to threaten the improvement itself. Education, emancipation of women, the knowledge of birth control methods and the widespread availability of contraceptives all contribute to this controlled birthrate. In such communities, moreover, the available knowledge on infant care, epidemiology and public health is extensively applied. The life span may gradually lengthen from the development of new knowledge. It is unlikely to increase suddenly from the rapid application of existing knowledge.

In the poor country, things are almost exactly in reverse. If the standard of living seems already as low as it can go, there is no reason to protect it from further decline. And children will share the burdens of manual toil and, since old age pensions cannot be afforded, they are also a man's only hope for care in his old age. It is prudent to have as many as possible for, infant mortality being high, not many will survive. Nor is there much choice for neither contraceptive knowledge nor contraceptives are available and—a somewhat neglected point—sexual intercourse plays a larger recreational role in the poor community than the rich. For the couple who come from the field to a hut devoid of newspapers, radio, light, even a comfortable chair, it may provide the day's only escape from a gray existence. To urge restraint is to leave very little in life.

But not only is poverty a strong inducement to procreation, modern medical science and public health research have provided a large reservoir of measures that reduce the death rate. Their application means a further sharp increase in population. This is one of the earliest effects of modernization. And in many countries this addition is to a population that is already massive. In this respect the problem of the countries now seeking development is unique. The industrial development of the United States and Western Europe was launched in countries of—by modern standards— almost negligible population. In 1770, on the eve of the Industrial Revolution, the population of England and Wales was not much over seven million. The United States seventy years later had fewer than twenty million. None of the western communities we now think of as developed had as many as thirty million when their industrialization began. India has now some 470 million and adds some ten or eleven millions—many more than the pre-industrial population of Britain—every year. Indonesia and Pakistan each have well over one hundred million. Poverty applies the greatest population pressure to those countries least able to absorb it.

| 4 |

I turn now to the effect of poverty on economics—on what is recognized by all right-thinking people as the queen of the social disciplines. One fact of economic life is common to capitalist, socialist and Communist societies, or for that matter Catholic,

Presbyterian, Pentecostal, Buddhist or Animist, and is not subject to controversy as between economists of any shade of color or opinion. This is that any purposeful increase in future production requires saving from current consumption. Only from such saving can the people be supported who are making the machines, building the factories, constructing the dams, digging the ditches or otherwise elaborating the capital which makes possible the increased future output. Saving can be by the highly regarded men of thrift who put a little something by for their children or their own rainy day, or by the rich who are under no great pressure to spend all they receive, or by corporations which plow back revenue before it ever gets into the hot and eager hands of those who might spend it and by governments which, by a variety of devices of which taxes are the most important, can restrict consumption and thus enforce saving by their otherwise profligate citizens.

But while there must be savings in all societies if there is to be economic advance, the difference in the degree of difficulty in getting savings as between the rich countries and the poor is so great as to be a difference in kind.

In the rich country, to refrain from consumption may be inconvenient, difficult or well beyond one's power of will. It rarely involves physical deprivation—hunger, exposure, pain. And a great deal of saving is automatic or a by-product of motives and preoccupations that have little to do with national progress. Thus, concern for personal security puts income into life insurance, pension funds, and the social security trust funds of governments. The business prestige that comes from heading a growing corporation pours earnings back into expansion. Recurrently our problem is to offset by sufficient investment (or by public or private spending) all that we are disposed to save from high levels of income; for if we fail to offset savings, income and output will decline and unemployment will rise. The reduction in taxes in the United States in 1964 was part of such a strategy to offset the high level of savings—some induced by taxation itself—which we now get at a high level of income and economic activity.

Thus, saving in the rich country not only comes easily; it may be excessive. The country must invest these savings (or offset them with increased consumption) if it is to avoid unemployment. Economic progress, it follows, is something it gets more or less automatically in the course of preventing unemployment. Unemployment is the ogre which stalks the politician and which he bends every effort to exorcise.

Here we have the explanation of the remarkable course of economic events in North America and Western Europe since World War II. Although there have been variations in detail, in all countries there has been a large and well-sustained increase in output. This has far exceeded anything in earlier experience. Faithful to the vanity of politicians, and the economists who advise them, this excellent showing has been attributed in each case to the remarkably astute economic policies being followed. This has been so even though the policies avowed in different countries have differed by at least 180 degrees. West Germany brought off her economic miracle by (it is alleged) rigid adherence to free private enterprise. Norway did almost equally well by an intelligent application of the principles of socialist planning. France has done yet better in recent years, some suggest, by eschewing commitment to any principle. In fact, in all of these countries, as in the United States, comparative wealth made saving easy. Given this, and a policy of maintaining full employment, growth came with comparative ease. It would have required considerable determination to have failed.

The situation of the poor countries is sadly different. Here to forego consumption, as I have said, is to suffer pain and the pain is not eased if the government enforces the saving through taxation. In the rich countries, the poor do little saving; in the United States only a negligible amount comes from those in the lower half of the income brackets. In the poor countries, nearly everyone is poor. And even the few who are rich may not be a very good source of savings. The landed feudal tradition of the well-to-do minority in South America and the Middle East is one of easygoing and often lavish expenditure. And finally, there is the exceptional visibility of the rich man. This, and his resulting insecurity, may cause him to invest his savings not in farms, factories and power plants, but in a numbered account in a Zurich bank.

This picture is not all black. India and Pakistan paid off and dispossessed their princes, rajas, zamindars and jagirdars—a company which had included some of the world's most conspicuous spenders. These spendthrift feudal classes were, in effect, put on a dole. And their industrialists, while they doubtless have some precautionary funds abroad, invest heavily at home.

Nonetheless the broad generalization stands. Saving in the poor country, on which progress depends, is painful to obtain and the amounts obtained, even painfully, are meager. As a result the economic advance which comes easily and automatically in the rich country comes at great cost and is wretchedly slow in the poor country.

On this somber note, I must end the first of these lectures. Next time I will begin with the obvious question which is whether, and to what extent, this painful shortage of savings can be eased by transfer from the countries where saving is easy and perhaps excessive.

II

UNDERDEVELOPMENT AND SOCIAL BEHAVIOR (CONTINUED)

| *1* |

In the last lecture I spoke of the effect of poverty on various facets of human behavior—of its effect in making people mistrustful of technological and social change and of its effect in making the savings, on which all economic advance depends, painful to obtain even in meager amounts. This latter is in striking contrast with the rich countries where modern economic policy consists, in very large measure, in designing policies that insure the use of all available savings. For if savings are not fully used, the result is unemployment. And unemployment, I noted, is the specter which haunts all modern governments and especially those that are taking a thoughtful view of an approaching election.

The obvious question, it follows, is whether savings cannot be transferred from the countries where they are abundant to those where they are so scarce. In the last century there was a substantial flow of savings from the relatively rich countries of Western Europe to the Americas and later on to parts of Africa and the Far East. This was largely under private auspices; Canada and the United States were major beneficiaries. The Pre-Cambrian shield and the Canadian prairie were partially bridged by such savings. At least until recently some Englishmen (or their descendants) who supplied money to that monument to the eternal optimism of investors, the Grand Trunk Railway, were still hoping to be paid. All prophets of the commonplace, a remarkably numerous group whenever economic development is discussed, continue to call for a new flow of private capital from the rich countries to the poor. The chances that it will take place are very slight.

Where there is a prospect for developing petroleum, bauxite, iron ore or other resources for supply to the United States or Europe, private capital continues to go abroad. This is related to the profits to be made in the U.S., Canada or Europe. A little capital also goes to develop additional markets—trucks, tires, soap, pharmaceuticals—for American or European firms. But almost none goes to build the power plants, railroads or factories which are designed to serve the people of the poor countries as British capital in the last century built railroads in the United States, Canada and the Argentine to serve Americans, Canadians or Argentineans. This is partly because the poor countries being poor are an unattractive market as compared with the rich countries. Capital goes where people have incomes and money to spend and where, accordingly, money can be made. And, as I shall suggest in the following lectures, there are other problems. Some of the poor countries lack the social institutions and manpower which enable them to make effective use of capital and hold out a reasonable promise of repayment. In others the social system is unfavorable to effective capital use; power lies with those for whom government is not an instrument of economic progress but a means to personal enrichment. But even the countries which can make effective and secure use of capital for power, irrigation, transportation and basic manufacturing are unlikely to get it from private sources. They compete badly for funds with the developed and high-income countries. They must, therefore, have help of other governments or such international organizations as the World Bank. Failing this, we shall leave them in a painful and perhaps losing struggle for progress. We shall go forward, meanwhile, with increasing ease. It takes a certain effort of mind to suppose that this will be the basis for easy relationship between ourselves and the poor lands. If we are to have a tolerable relationship with the poor lands, we shall need to supply the kind of assistance that is appropriate to their needs.

| 2 |

A scarcity of economic resources is not a purely passive matter. It deeply affects the economic policy of a country. We think of ideology as having a controlling influence on the way governments manage their economy. Ideology is not without importance. But the availability of capital, and the associated poverty or affluence, is a much greater influence than we imagine.

Thus, in the United States or Canada, where capital is abundant and privately mobilized through the capital markets, no one need give thought as to how it is used. It may go into steel mills, fertilizer plants, power stations or other good Calvinist employments. But equally it may go into a deadfall in Las Vegas, a racetrack in florida or a plant to manufacture electric golf carts and electric exercise machines so we can extirpate, once and finally, the remaining occasions for employing muscular energy. Capital may even be conscripted, on occasion, for wholly hypothetical mines deep in the Canadian wilderness. We recognize that there is some waste but we do not worry, if our own money is not involved.

The poor country has no such easygoing option. It must use its resources for the right things; if it fails to do so—if funds slip into fancy housing, a glittering airport or official Cadillacs—the cries of outrage and horror will come first of all from the most rugged American free enterprisers. If it is getting aid, such wasteful expenditure shows it is unworthy of help; if it is not getting help, this proves it is wholly undeserving. It must, in short, exercise firm control on the nature of its growth. It must use its capital in accordance with a well-considered, though not necessarily elaborate, plan. And conservative critics are among the first to insist on such planning. If private entrepreneurs are not around to undertake the investment, the government will be urged to take the initiative itself.

So we come to the fairly remarkable result that free enterprise—the practice of letting the market decide where we invest and what we produce—is in part the product of well-being. Planning, by contrast, is in some degree compelled by poverty. This, of course, is not the whole story. Many of the governments of the new countries have embraced socialism and planning as a matter of conviction—capitalism has come to mean the British, French, Dutch (or, for that matter, American) companies that were associated with colonial rule. Or, as in Africa, it denotes the merchants and traders—also usually foreigners—who are firmly identified in people's minds with high prices and high profits and a good deal of sanguinary swindling. Students from such backgrounds learned eagerly about socialism at the Sorbonne, Oxford and the University of London, though almost never at Moscow. They now are cabinet officers.

None of this, I might add, is the good fortune of the poor country. Socialism and planning are very demanding in the administrative apparatus that they require. An unplanned economy is infinitely easier to run than a planned one. And the rich countries that are not obliged to plan have the most highly developed systems of public administration. The United States or the United Kingdom could go in for fairly complete planning without undue difficulty—and did during World War II. But they have no great need or urge to do so. In Asia and Africa, where both the desire and the need for planning are far greater, the administrative structure is weaker and in some cases almost nonexistent. Whoever arranged matters in this way is open to serious criticism.

It follows further that we must be tolerant of different and far less efficient economic performance in the poor countries than in our own. Their task is both different and far more difficult. We are right to press for sensible use of funds that we supply and for economic policies that insure that they will be effective. But we cannot press for a carbon copy of western capitalism and we cannot hold others even to our sometimes imperfect standards of performance.

I turn now to the effect of wealth and poverty on national behavior. Here, also, a clear view will have a considerable effect on the wisdom with which western countries conduct their foreign policy.

| 3 |

In Europe in the last decade governments have been stable and secure because their people have been contented and secure. International cooperation, and most notably the creation of the Common Market, has been possible for the same reason. If unemployment is minimal and unfeared, then governments have freedom to reduce tariffs, lift quotas and arrange migration. Even now a bad depression in Europe would cause governments to concern themselves with their own people, if necessary, at the expense of their neighbors. If things got bad enough, politicians would be tempted to divert attention from economic problems to national concerns and grievances—to the German military threat, the nationalism of General de Gaulle, possibly even such ancient issues as the Sudetenland and the Saar.

In the poor countries nearly all governments are insecure. That is partly because people have little to lose from a change. Things are always bad. There is a certain uniformity in misfortune. The prerogatives and spoils of office also look attractive to those on the outside—not only is it good to throw the rascals out but you get a Mercedes as a reward. Meanwhile, the man who is clinging to office and who finds economic development hard going looks for a scapegoat for his failures or some object of popular antipathy which will engage passions and thus divert attention. The British, French or Dutch are at fault. Or the Yankees. Or the Indians, Pakistanis or Malaysians next door. Or the Muslims, Hindus, Christians or Jews. Or the Turks or Cypriots. As well-being is a solvent for tensions, so poverty is a principal cause. The poor countries are the focus of internal disturbance, insecurity, interracial friction and international conflict because these are intimately a part of the politics of privation.

We often have a simpler explanation for disorder in these lands. It is the Communists who are at fault. There is a fine, simple, hard-boiled quality about this explanation which economizes thought and goes down well with the modern American conservative. An official never arouses the men from the intellectual boondocks by blaming things on the Bolsheviks. It is the more or less automatic reaction of one type of older State Department official. (George Kennan once said that in the making of American foreign policy it is not the American interest that is consulted but the American right.) There is no better test

of sophistication than mistrust of the man who attributes everything that goes wrong to the reds.

| 4 |

Obviously, differences in income have a penetrating effect on
national behavior. Let us reflect on what they explain. Poverty
or well-being affect attitudes toward technical change. They
have a controlling effect on the ease or difficulty of economic
progress and affect the nature of the country's economic organization. They determine political behavior and international
attitudes. They have a profound effect on human reproduction
and demography.

We have only to look a little further to see why they are more
comprehensive than the differences associated with ideological
preference or commitment. I have spoken of the effect of privation on the behavior of the countries of the non-Communist
world. Its effects as between China and the Soviets form an almost
exact parallel. China, under the pressure of need and ambition, has
tried different and more radical (although not for that reason
more successful) forms of economic organization than the Soviet
Union. These the Soviets have thought wrong. The Chinese have
taken this ill. They have accused the Soviets of being unfaithful to
Marx and his prophets. But clearly the Soviets in their more
comfortable situation were not as hard pressed. What served in a
comparatively affluent country such as Russia could hardly be
expected to serve in a poor one such as China. The parallel
between the United States and India is evident.

The Soviets have also used economic aid as a political lever.
When the Chinese failed to follow their lead it was withdrawn.
The Chinese have bitterly resented this and, given the pride of the
poor country and the importance of aid, one can see how this

could be a source of contention. Finally, the Soviets have criticized the Chinese for chauvinism and adventurist foreign policy. We have seen that these are also at least partly the products of poverty—of the need to fix people's eyes on non-economic goals and to divert them from domestic failure. Thus the main points of contention between the two Communist countries are immediately explicable in terms of the conflicting interests of rich and poor. However, I did not come here to Canada to instruct the Soviets on how to get along with China or vice versa. We may perhaps better reflect for a moment on some of the lessons for our own relations with the poor countries.

There are several. We must, for example, be braced for the resistance to change and react to it with sympathy and understanding. It is not irrational; rather it reflects an experience different from our own. We must also be scrupulously careful that the change we advocate is sufficiently riskless to be acceptable to people who cannot afford risk. More than one eloquent American agricultural specialist in these last fifteen years has converted villagers to techniques, which, however impeccable in Michigan or Missouri, did not pay off in a distant clime. The price was paid by the villagers and not by our man who by then was back home.

We must be aware of the difficulty which the poor countries have in finding savings and resulting capital. We must encourage them to conserve and husband their resources; we must be exceedingly cautious about urging expenditure for anything but the highest priority. On occasion we have allowed our much more easygoing standards of spending to influence our recommendations as to what the poor countries should do. Educational luxuries are a case in point. More important, we certainly have not been sufficiently sensitive to the very great burden that is imposed on these countries by military expenditure. I venture to think that Mr. Dulles's military alliances and their concomitant military expenditures will eventually be shown to have done more to promote than to prevent Communism by the burdens they imposed on people who could ill afford them.

Most important, we must not waver on the importance of aid. It is not a luxury of modern foreign policy. It is, in fact, the obvious accommodation between countries where saving is easy and automatic and those where it is difficult and painful. It is the principal basis for harmonious coexistence between the rich countries and the poor.

And it has been serving this purpose very well. In the last fifteen years, errors and setbacks notwithstanding, the United States has won a position of influence and esteem in the poor lands. We are regarded not as remote, self-interested and selfish, as well we might be. On the whole, we are considered a friend with a concern for the less fortunate. This is a great achievement for a nation that is both economically and geographically as far removed from the experience of the poor countries as we are. There should be no doubt as to what accomplished it. It was not our military power. It was not the acuity of our propaganda. It was not the exceptional deftness of our intelligence organization. It was not even the skill or eloquence of our diplomats, political or professional. It was the American aid program. One type of modern conservative opposes the aid program because he imagines all change, including that which conserves peace and stability, to be a conspiracy against the American form of government or, at a minimum, his pocketbook. I do not worry about these people. They have always been with us; they add variety to life. Their ancestors opposed steam navigation, fire and the wheel. Their fathers opposed the cream separator and the National Banking System. But I confess to some discouragement over the tendency of more thoughtful conservatives, as well as men of liberal goodwill, to become apologetic about foreign aid. We need to adjust the form of aid much more closely to the circumstances of the poor lands—as I will argue in the next two lectures. But we must also bear in mind that it is our most distinctive contribution to the comity of nations.

| 5 |

Next it is evident that we should be cautious about urging forms of organization that are commonplace in the rich countries upon the poor. We have always mistrusted the man who mounts the rostrum to demand that the world commit itself here and now to free enterprise as it is uniquely revealed to the orator. There is a suspicion that he is not so much interested in spreading free enterprise as in provoking applause. But we also see that the imperatives of the poor country, as regards economic organization, are very different from our own. The notion that a moderately well-to-do country and a poor one can have a common economic policy has been a prime source of friction between the Soviets and China. It would be equally a source of friction between the United States and the Indians were we to insist that they do precisely as we do. We should not be above imitating the accomplishments of the Communist countries. We need not imitate their errors.

It is also evident that relations between the rich and the poor countries are likely to be touchy—as also the relations between the poor lands themselves. We must bear in mind that the governments of these countries are subject to pressures, growing out of their poverty, from which we are exempt. Our more tranquil reactions are not the mark of superior patience but of superior fortune. To realize this is to be more tolerant and more painstaking in the never-finished tasks of mediation, negotiation and compromise.

There are other lessons ranging from those that grow out of the relation of poverty to the birthrate and the bearing of this on birth control techniques to the prospects, given the difficulties I have cited, for development itself. But I should like to postpone further discussion of remedies until we have had a closer look at the poor lands. We have seen that poverty produces much that is common in behavior. We must now see that it has many differences as to cause.

III

CAUSE AND CLASSIFICATION

| *1* |

We have seen that poverty enforces strongly common patterns of behavior. If one had to settle on the distinction between nations of greatest descriptive importance in our time it would certainly be the difference between the rich and the poor.

And this, with some exceptions, has come to be the distinction employed by those who deal professionally with the problems of economic development. Excluding the Communist countries, their discussion has tended to divide the world into the developed and the underdeveloped sector and these terms generally reflect differences in incomes.[1] The underdeveloped countries are assumed to have enough in common so that as "the descriptive literature on such countries suggests . . . we may confidently describe 'a representative underdeveloped country'".[2]

To this tendency there are exceptions and the one that comes first to mind is that adumbrated by Professor W. W. Rostow in his *The Stages of Economic Growth*[3] with its not wholly reticent claim of being an answer to *The Communist Manifesto*. Professor Rostow regards all countries as passing in rather measured fashion from a traditional mold; into preparation for take-off into sustained growth; on to "the great watershed" of modern societies, the take-off; and finally on to maturity and then an age of high mass consumption.

There are several difficulties with Professor Rostow's scheme and his critics have not been lacking in either vigor or material. The take-off period he has assigned to various countries—Great Britain 1783-1802, France 1830-1860, Canada 1896-1914, Russia, putting Lenin and Stalin neatly where they belong, 1890-1914[4]—differs only marginally in rate and character of change from that before and after.[5] The notion of a take-off, a comparatively brief period when there is technical change, the building of railways and other social capital and the appearance of a political group devoted to modernization, radically minimizes the obstacles that the poor country encounters. As a consequence, the notion of development has become associated in the popular mind with an ease and certainty, and a rate of possible improvement, which is unfortunately at odds with the reality.[6]

But the most serious fault of Professor Rostow is that, on closer examination, he is seen also to deal with the underdeveloped countries as a class. His countries are at different way stations along the same path; they differ from each other only as a child from an adolescent and an adolescent from someone in early maturity. The broad prescription for growth is the same for all; differentiation is required only in accordance with the stage of the country as with the age of the individual. Should it be that the path is different for different countries, the common prescription will obviously be inadequate or in error for some. This is the case.

It must be said in defense of Professor Rostow, in this respect, that his dereliction is considerably more mild than those who, forswearing even his distinctions, speak of all underdeveloped countries as one. The dangers here require a special word.

| 2 |

Once some years ago I visited Bhutan, a lovely pastoral country in the Himalayas with rich forests, clear streams and—unique in Asia—a declining population. It is indubitably underdeveloped. It has no industry, airport, railroad, post office, television, department store, diplomacy, bureaucracy, air pollution, outdoor advertising, or settled capital city. It occurred to me that a fence should be built around it to protect it from development. But I quickly recovered my senses. Economic development is an intrinsically normative subject. To talk about underdevelopment is to consider, *pro tanto*, the steps that will overcome economic backwardness. It follows that, so long as we speak of underdeveloped countries as a class, we will tend to assume a common therapy applicable to the whole class. We will devise programs that are meant to be applicable generally to underdeveloped countries; we will continue to say, as we often do now: "This is what an underdeveloped country should do."

Or this will be the tendency. But, in fact, there is now considerable differentiation in our prescription for the poor countries. India, in per capita income, is almost as poor as any country in Africa. Yet we recognize that her capacity to use capital is much greater. So is her ability to plan the use of her resources. And with mention of India, the problem of population comes almost immediately to mind.

The African countries, for their part, are strongly interested in education. And gradually a design for development is emerging which places primary emphasis on this. And this is in contrast, in turn, with the seeming requirements of many of the Latin American countries where social reform occupies a place of particular urgency. Though in analysis, we still speak of the underdeveloped country, for purposes of prescription we make important distinctions. There is need, evidently, for bringing the analysis abreast of the differentiation that practical judgment requires.

| *3* |

In recent years at Harvard, we have been experimenting with a classification of underdeveloped countries that is based on the obstacle or combination of obstacles which, in the given case, is the effective barrier to economic advance.[7] The identification of these obstacles or barriers is not a highly scientific exercise. It involves observation and judgment, and those who assess truth in accordance with whether it depends on precise measurement will find much in the classification to which they can object. However, the classification is not based on small distinctions. For selecting the largest tree from among those of similar size, there is no substitute for measurement. But if one tree towers over the others, much can be accomplished by inspection. And all scientific method must be seen in context. Imperfect classification is better than the aggregation of unlike cases. It still remains the first step toward science, however short the step or intractable the material.

The classification is a four-fold one. Three classes are important for present purposes; the fourth embraces the countries where there is no strongly operative obstacle to development and where, accordingly, it proceeds at a more or less rapid pace. It is useful to give each of the classes or models not only a number but an identification with the part of the world to which they are the most applicable. Their application is not, however, confined to the geographical or other area in the designation. The three models of underdevelopment are:

Model I.   The Sub-Sahara African Model.
Model II.   The Latin American Model.
Model III.   The South Asian Model.

As noted, the Models are set apart from each other by the barrier or combination of barriers to development which are operative in each case. In some instances, the barriers which characterize one Model are also operative in another. There are, as might be expected, intermediate or mixed cases. And the geographical designations do not include all of the countries of the area. Ceylon is not typical of the South Asian Model; Ghana, Nigeria and Kenya are not characteristic of the Sub-Sahara African Model; Mexico and Costa Rica do not conform to the Latin American Model; and Brazil, a notably difficult case, conforms more closely to that Model in the northern than in the southern states.

| 4 |

In the Model I or Sub-Sahara countries, the principal barrier to development is the absence of what I shall call a minimum cultural base. It is important, both for reasons of tact and precision, that this be not misinterpreted; the problem is not absence of aptitude but absence of opportunity. Most of the countries that are described by this Model have recently emerged from colonialism, sometimes of the more regressive sort. More fortunate countries have had decades and centuries of preparation for the tasks of economic development. These have had only a few years. "To an extent unmatched in most of the underdeveloped world, positions of skill and responsibility (in Africa) were until recently in the hands of non-Africans. . . . As late as 1958 there were only about 8,000 Africans graduated from all the academic secondary schools below the Sahara, and only about 10,000 others were studying in universities—more than half of these in Ghana and Nigeria. . . . in 1962 there were still few African countries where more than two hundred Africans received full secondary diplomas."[8] When the Republic of the Congo gained independence, there were fewer than 25,000 Congolese with any secondary education and only about thirty Congolese university graduates. The first university, Lovanium, had opened only in 1954 and only thirteen Africans had graduated by 1960.[9]

Professors Harbison and Myers have classified numerous countries in accordance with their resources in educated and trained manpower. In their lowest class, primary and secondary teachers average 17 per 10,000 population. On the basis of limited data, there are 0.6 scientists and engineers per 10,000 population and 0.5 physicians and dentists.[10] Of the seventeen countries placed formally in their lowest class, all but three (Afghanistan, Saudi Arabia and Haiti) are in Africa. Another twelve African countries were cited as probably falling in this class.

The consequences of an inadequate cultural base are comprehensive—on government, the economy, internal security, communications, even foreign policy. But the most visible manifestation is on the apparatus of government. People with the requisite education, training, and ethical standards for performing public tasks are unavailable. As a consequence, taxes are collected in haphazard or arbitrary fashion and public funds are spent inefficiently or for no particular purpose except the reward of the recipients. Where this is the case, government will ordinarily be unstable; those who do not have access to public income will have a strong incentive to seek the ouster of those who do. As a further consequence, law enforcement is unreliable; and so, at a minimum, are essential public services. In this context, in turn, there can be no economic development that involves any sophistication in technique or organization.[11] Primitive and local trade will flourish under almost any handicaps. But larger scale commerce and industry—the modern corporate enterprise—are demanding in their environment; their persons and property must be reasonably secure; their property cannot be hidden and must not be taxed merely because it is visible; profits cannot be readily concealed and must not be taxed simply because they are made; their business cannot be transacted in the absence of posts, telephones, and common carrier transportation. In the colonial era, firms were allowed to provide for their own security and establish services essential to their existence. With independence, such extraterritorial administration is not ordinarily permissible.

But the inadequacy of government is only one of the manifestations of an inadequate cultural base. And it reflects the absence of schools, colleges and cultural environment for producing or preparing people for public tasks. All discussion of economic development involves difficult problems of sequence and circularity. This is an example. How does a country get an educational system without an adequate government? How does it get a government without the qualified people that an educational system provides? There is no obvious answer. But it helps to have narrowed the problem to this point. For we then recognize that little is accomplished by action that does not break into this particular circle. Assistance in the form of capital funds will not be useful if there is no one with the technical competence to employ it, and if the environment is hostile to the resulting enterprises. Technical assistance will not be useful if there is no one to advise or assist. In the next Model, progress waits on reforms which reduce the power of a vested ruling elite. Here there is no such elite.

There is a measure of overstatement in any attempt to establish categories. No country is without some small group of honest and competent people in some area of economic activity or government. But in those countries where colonialism was exploitive and regressive—where there was no liberalizing urge that sought to prepare people for some role other than that of primitive agriculture and unskilled industrial labor—this group is very small. This Model, as a result—as in the classic case of Haiti and possibly the more recent one of the Congo (Leopoldville)—can readily become one not of advance but of disintegration with eventual reversion to tribalism or anarchy. All that is needed is for the perilously small group of competent and honest people to be overwhelmed by those who see government in predatory and personal terms. Once the latter are in possession of the available instruments of power—the army, government payroll, police—it is not clear when (or even whether) the process of disintegration can be reversed by internal influences. This disintegration, not Communism for which these countries are as little prepared as for capitalism, is the form of failure in this Model.

IV

CAUSE AND CLASSIFICATION
(CONTINUED)

| 1 |

In the first two lectures, I spoke of the homogenizing influence of poverty on individual and social behavior. I suggested that it might be more important in explaining how people react—biologically, socially and politically—than any other factor including their decision to be communists, socialists, free enterprisers or some judicious combination of all three. It is not easy walking through a South Asian jungle, or across the Andean *altiplano*, to determine whether the country is capitalist or communist. And the people themselves tend to be clear only on one principal point, which is that they are poor. The more sophisticated distinctions as to social structure acquire importance only as one approaches world capitals, including Washington.

But in the last lecture I argued that one must not mistake similarity in effect for similarity in cause. The causes of the poverty of different countries are, in fact, very different. I started in to make a rude classification of underdevelopment based on the principal barrier to advance. I dealt last time with what I called the Sub-Sahara African Model where the obstacle to advance is the very narrow cultural base—the very small number of trained and educated people and the very limited capacity for getting more. I come now to Model II—what I have called the Latin American case.

| 2 |

The great mass of the people in these countries is also very poor. But in most of them there is also a sizable minority that is well-to-do. And associated with this well-to-do minority is a rather large number of people with a diverse assortment of qualifications and skills—lawyers, physicians, accountants, engineers, scientists, economists and managers. As compared, in other words, with the Model I countries, the cultural base is quite wide. And back of this group there is a limited, undemocratic and otherwise imperfect, but still substantial, educational system. Peru, Ecuador and Guatemala are, by any calculation of per capita income, very poor countries. Argentina, Brazil and Chile are well below North American and European levels. But all have trained and educated personnel and facilities for its replacement that are far better than those of the new African states. As a further aspect, they have a strong intellectual tradition. As is also true of the United States or Canada, they could use more people of the highest caliber and training. Public servants of high competence are rarely in surplus. But in these countries—as also in the Arab states and Iran where the pattern is similar—the absence of trained and educated people is not the obvious barrier to development.

The far more evident barrier to advance is the social structure.

The elite, though sizable, depends for its economic and social position on land ownership, or on a *comprador* role in the port or capital cities, or on government employment or sinecure, or on position in the armed forces. Beneath this elite is a large rural mass and, in some cases, an unskilled and often semi-employed urban proletariat. The rural worker, in the characteristic situation, either earns the right to cultivate a small plot of land by giving service to the estate on which he resides or he is part of the *mini-fundia*—a cultivator of a small plot on which he has some form of permanent tenure. In either case he has no effective economic incentive. He thoughtfully renders the landlord the minimum service that will earn him the right to cultivate his own plot. The latter plot was anciently arranged to be the minimum size consistent with survival. The same tends to be true of any holding to which he has title. So any possibility that he might improve his position by increasing output is excluded by what amounts to a systematic denial of incentives.[1] In a number of countries—Peru, Guatemala and Ecuador for example—the fact that most of the rural mass is Indian adds a sense of racial exclusion to this denial.

But the elimination of economic incentives is not confined to the rural masses. Beginning, at least in time sequence, with them, it tends to become comprehensive. The landlord, since he has a labor force that is devoid of incentive, cannot do much to increase production. Often he lives in the capital city and does not try. Instead of the revenues of a small area farmed efficiently, he enjoys those of a large area that is inefficiently farmed. (It is strongly characteristic of this Model that agriculture, some plantation operations apart, is labor intensive and technologically stagnant.)[2]

Income derived from government position or the armed forces is also unrelated to economic service. It depends, rather, on distribution of power, and this leads to the further likelihood of struggle over the division of power. Feudal agriculture is so constituted as to survive unstable or avaricious government. Modern industry—again unless under external protection—is much more vulnerable. So instability in government and its use as a source of personal income has a further adverse effect on industrial incentives. In this Model, substantial rewards accrue to traders. But this, also, is at least as dependent on a strong monopoly position—the franchise for the sale of a North American or European branded product or the strong position in financing and procurement of some local product—as on efficient economic service.

It is the normal working assumption of economists in advanced communities that income rewards economic effort. Since it induces that effort, it is functional. There has been ample dispute over whether particular functions are over- or under-rewarded, and this is the foundation of the ancient quarrel between Marxians and non-Marxians. But the problem of the adequacy of reward for service is not the issue in this Model; the problem is that numerous claimants—landlords, members of the armed services, government functionaries, pensioners—render no economic service.[3] And the best rewarded businessman is not the one who performs the best service but whose political position or franchise accords him the most secure monopoly. It is useful to have a term for the income which is so divorced from economic function and one is readily at hand. It may be called non-functional income.

Not only is this income large but strong forces act to limit the amount of functional income. The rural worker gets the maximum established by custom; greater endeavor brings him no more. The landlord, as noted, is confined by a labor force that is without incentive. The efficient urban entrepreneur risks being regarded as a better milch cow by those who live on the state. He can protect himself only by developing the requisite political power; this means that his income comes to depend not alone on economic performance but also on political power. His return, or that part of it which derives from political influence, thus also becomes economically non-functional.

| *3* |

The position of the controlling elite is commonly associated with the ownership of land. And this, certainly, has been the traditional source of power. But, in its modern manifestation, it is a mistake to identify it exclusively or even predominantly with land. The armed forces, hierarchical wealth other than land, the bureaucracy and shifting of permanent coalitions between these groups can provide the requisite sources of power. Government will then be in the interest of the controlling group or groups; and since these groups are economically non-functional, it will not be in the interest of economic development.[4]

In a number of countries of this Model, most notably Argentina, Brazil and Chile, the non-functional groups are in competition with each other and more recently franchised economic groups for the available income. (In each of these countries an incomplete revolution accorded political power to urban white collar and working classes without disestablishing the old non-functional groups. Chileans often speak of the "'struggle' or even 'civil war' between the country's major economic interest groups.")[5] The total of these claims bears no necessary relationship to the income that is available. Since productivity is low, the tendency is for claims to exceed what is available, and invariably they do. The easiest way of reconciling competing claims is to meet that of each group in money terms and allow them to bid against each other for real product in the market. As a result, in these countries inflation is endemic. In countries such as Ecuador and the Central American countries where the urban white collar and working classes are weak, inflationary pressures are much less strong. This, however, reflects the weakness of these classes, not their better position under non-inflationary conditions.

| 4 |

With variations as to the composition of the non-functional elite, and its source of power, Model II has general application in Central and South America and in Iran, Iraq and Syria. In few if any of these countries—and one or two Central American countries are possible exceptions—is the cultural base the decisive factor; in none would economic advance appear to be barred by the absence of trained and educated people. A shortage of capital is assumed almost intuitively by economists to be the normal barrier to advance. Iran and Iraq have rich sources of income from oil and Peru from oil and minerals. This has not rescued them from backwardness and some of the oil-rich countries are among the poorest in the world.[6]

In Latin America two countries do break decisively with this pattern. One is Mexico and the other is Costa Rica. Mexico, by revolution, destroyed its old power structure based on land ownership. Costa Rica was always, in the main, a country of modest land holdings. Costa Rica has no army; the Mexican army is insignificant in size, cost and influence. Neither has any other strongly vested non-functional group which combines power with a claim on income. In consequence, income in both countries is— by all outward evidences—far more closely related to economic performance than in the remainder of Latin America. They are the two countries which enjoy the most favorable rate of economic development.

For purposes of identification, I have associated Model III with South Asia. The clearest prototypes are, indeed, India and Pakistan, although it has application to the United Arab Republic, in limited measure to Indonesia, and, since its characteristics transcend political organization, to China.

In this Model, the cultural base is very wide. India and Pakistan have systems of primary and secondary education that are far superior to those of Latin America. There are at least as many full-time professors in the University of Delhi alone as in all Latin America. Both countries tend to a surplus rather than a shortage of teachers,[7] administrators, scientists and entrepreneurs. In recent years, these countries have been substantial, if inadvertent, exporters of medical and scientific talent to the United States and the United Kingdom. Without the doctors provided by this informal educational exchange, the hospitals of both countries would be in even worse shape.

In both India and Pakistan, there is a substantial volume of non-functional income. But it is not, as in Latin America, associated with political power. In India the political power and non-functional claims on land revenues of the princes, jagirdars, zamindars and large landlords were terminated or greatly curtailed at the time of independence or in ensuing reforms. The armed forces, though costly, do not have decisive political power.[8] In consequence, producers can generally count on receiving much of the return to their efforts. Economic incentive is thus reasonably operative. The endemic inflation which characterizes many of the Model II countries is absent. The social structure in these countries is not at the highest level of compatibility with economic advance. But it is clearly not the operative barrier.

The barrier in this Model is drastically bad proportioning of the factors of production. Demographic forces which extend deeply into the past have given these countries a large and dense population. The supply of arable land in India, Pakistan and Egypt has been subject to repeated and very great increases through irrigation. But this increase has been followed, as harvest follows planting, by a relentless increase in population. As a result, per capita agricultural production and incomes have remained small and, as a further consequence, savings are limited and so consequently is the supply of capital. Capital shortage, in turn, has retarded and continues to retard industrial development. The small land and capital base provides effective employment for only part of the available labor force. People who live close to the margin of subsistence, as I have noted, cannot afford any risk that they might fall below subsistence levels. This is a further inducement to backwardness.

The Model III countries are, in some respects, the most comprehensible in their backwardness. They conform most closely to the standard explanations of the economists; because of their education and cultural sophistication, their people tend to speak for all of the underdeveloped lands. Their case, in consequence, is regularly generalized to all instances of underdevelopment.

| 6 |

I come in the next lecture to the question of policy—to what is called for by way of action, given the various obstacles to advance. But already it will be evident, I think, how dangerous it is to treat the poor countries as a class. The poverty that produces so many common tendencies in behavior—and which also gives such stark uniformity to the village hut or urban slum—proceeds from very different causes. For purposes of prescribing economic policy, it is at least as unwise to associate a country with a narrow cultural base such as the Congo, Niger, Ethiopia, Nyasaland, Somalia, Afghanistan or Saudi Arabia with a culturally advanced country such as India as to prescribe a common policy for India and the United States. There is at least equal error in associating for purposes of policy countries with a regressive social structure such as Ecuador, Iran or Peru with the African countries where social structure is not a primary obstacle to advance.

In recent years, economists have prided themselves on the progress that they have made in refining the concept of economic growth and in developing the theory that explains it and the policies that promote it. We are inclined to believe that we are becoming much more scientific about the whole business although, in an established tradition of the discipline, there is some tendency to identify scientific precision with mechanical elegance rather than reality. But the claim to progress in these matters must also be viewed with some doubt so long as underdeveloped countries are treated as a class and one theory is assumed to cover all. The subject of economic development cannot be considered scientific so long as it involves highly unscientific generalization.

V

A DIFFERENTIAL PRESCRIPTION

| *1* |

In the last two lectures I suggested a classification of the poor countries of the world in accordance with the barriers that are principally operative in preventing their advance. In the Model I countries, which I identified broadly, but not exclusively, with sub-Sahara Africa, it is the narrowness of the cultural base—the shortage of trained and educated people and the absence of facilities for providing more. In the Model II countries, which I identified with much of Latin America, the principal barrier is a regressive social structure. This means that most people labor without much hope for increased reward from increased effort or superior intelligence. In the Model III countries, which I identified principally with India, Pakistan and Egypt, we have the classically impoverishing phenomenon of too many people struggling to make a living with insufficient land and capital. It is evident that if the obstacles to advance are different, the measures designed to remove those obstacles will be different. Any appropriate line of action for one Model will be quite inappropriate for another. It is time now to consider the policy appropriate to each of the three Models.

| 2 |

In the Model I countries, if the barrier to progress is the shortage of trained and educated people, the obvious first step is to widen the cultural base. Internal effort and external assistance must center on the provision of the trained and educated people without whom advance is impossible. It seems likely that this core must be substantial—large enough to dominate an adverse environment. Presumably, also, it must be pyramidal in shape—a small number with the highest administrative and technical skills, a larger number with the equivalent of secondary education, a yet larger number with basic literacy and companion preparation.

Here is the problem of the Model I countries. It requires a government of minimal competence, together with a nucleus of teachers to organize an educational system. In the more fortunate former colonial countries, this organization was provided by the colonial authority or the nucleus of teachers was provided by missionaries out of the sensible conviction that heaven has at least a marginal preference for the literate. In the less fortunate countries, comparable help from outside is still required.

This leads to the conclusion that, for Model I countries, organizations such as the American Peace Corps are a strategic form of aid. And, though originally regarded as an outlet for youthful idealism, the Peace Corps is coming to play this role. It is having its greatest success in Africa where it is primarily a teaching organization. In 1964, approximately one-third of the 9,000 Peace

Corps Volunteers were serving in sub-Sahara Africa; of these over 80 per cent were teaching in formal educational programs.[1]

External training of teachers, administrators and specialists on a generous scale is also important for the Model I countries. So is the need to supply administrators, teachers and specialists at a more advanced level than those supplied by the Peace Corps. In all instances, it should be noted, emphasis must be on active or primary participants as distinct from advice. Advisers are of little value when there are no effective institutions to advise, and real resources are more important than money. Pecuniary assistance, where provided, should carry with it the organization—provision of engineering, administration and training of local people—that insures its effective use.

Along with the requirements of the Model I countries, it is equally important to see what they do not need. Capital, by itself, is not of great value. It must be supplied in conjunction with the companion institutions that allow of its effective use. Otherwise it will be wasted and, additionally, it can have a corrupting influence on the society.[2, 3]

Public ownership is obviously to be discouraged in the Model I countries; if administrative resources are not sufficient for the basic tasks of government, they obviously should not be taxed with these further and more demanding responsibilities.[4] Elaborate planning of capital use is unnecessary and a drain on scarce talent. Social reform is not central to the problem of development in this Model.

All discussion of Model I countries must reckon with the possibility, and indeed the likelihood, that in some instances development will be impossible. Predatory and anarchic influence will overwhelm and submerge the small cultural legacy of the colonial period. Thereafter there will be disintegration without foreseeable end. The Republic of Haiti, where social fabric, political structure and living standards have deteriorated with slight interruption in the century and a half since the French were expelled, is a case in point. Instead of the efficient slavery of the plantations, there is the incompetency and arbitrary despotism of Dr. Duvalier. This is defended in the name of national sovereignty. One wonders if some form of international administration, designed to develop the requisites of self-sustaining political development, should not be available for countries caught by such self-perpetuating misfortune. Whatever the virtues of national sovereignty, they are not so absolute as to justify the degradation of a whole people for an indefinite period.

I venture to think that in most of the Model I countries, given ample assistance in widening the cultural base, the prospect is much better. But it is important that we take an ample and generous view of such aid. Because aid does not go into dams, airports, steel mills and other physical monuments, it should not, for that reason, be less in amount.

| 3 |

Coming to the Model II countries—the Latin-American case— we may again begin by discarding, or assigning a low priority to, what is least important.

These countries already have an educated elite; administrators, teachers, engineers, entrepreneurs and like talent are comparatively plentiful. However desirable it might be to have more, this is not the decisive obstacle. And if public administrators are given to larceny or idleness, it is not because their training and education are deficient, but because there is the tradition of using the government not as an instrument of service but as a source of unearned income. If it seems hard to argue against primary education as a first priority, it remains true that the poor state of such education is a reflection of the politically powerless position of those whom it would benefit. If the distribution of political power were different, the rural masses would have schools.

Nor is capital as such the decisive requirement for change. Many of the countries of this Model have considerable earnings from oil or—less frequently—other natural resources. These resources are now misused because the power structure channels them into non-functional employments. There is danger that this will happen to pecuniary aid; it will further enrich the functionless rich and further strengthen, or at least rigidify, the power structure which is the obstacle of progress.[5]

In recent years, it has unquestionably occurred to both Latin American and North American conservatives (abetted as always by the politically innocent) that economic aid can be a highly welcome support to the *status quo*.

| 4 |

There are other temptations to the pursuit of the forms rather than the substance of development in this Model of which the most prominent, in the past, has been the preoccupation with inflation.

Inflation is not the operative barrier to economic advance. As noted, it is the product of much more deeply-seated social and political factors—in particular, the political power of the non-functional groups, the low productivity which characterizes society which returns income to political power rather than economic performance, and the bidding between groups for the product that is available. But inflation has high visibility. And regularly in Latin America, it has been regarded not as the consequence of these deeper disorders, but as the disorder itself. As a result, men of self-described soundness of view, on coming into touch with Latin

American problems, have regularly prescribed not for the disorder but for the symptom.

To a certain extent, countries have been urged to treat whatever symptom they were displaying at the moment. Thus, if prices are rising rapidly, policy is directed toward arresting the inflation. This will include budget curtailment, restraint on wage and salary increases, efforts to reduce government employment and restriction on government and perhaps private investment. The non-functional income, as in the particularly clear case of the army, has political power. Thus, it can protect itself from any curtailment. Or, as in the case of landed income, by nature it is beyond the reach of any effective restriction. The burden of stabilization is thus borne by the urban proletariat, white collar workers or other vulnerable groups. It does not greatly affect *comprador* or trading enterprises or old and static industries which have no need for funds for expansion. It does force curtailment of developing industries which do need funds. So, as a broad rule, functional incomes and outlays are vulnerable to an anti-inflation policy; non-functional income is protected.

In consequence of this disparate effect, a stabilization policy is borne by the weakest groups and strikes at the expanding sectors of the economy. It becomes a source of social tension, possibly even social disorder, and a cause of economic stagnation. Those who arrive to advise the country at this stage are certain to urge relaxation. And, in the more common case, it is forced by political necessity—to continue the stabilization would be to jeopardize the position of those in power and also give further ammunition to the Communists and fidelistos. The result of the relaxation is a greater rate of inflation. This policy rhythm has now continued for many years in Brazil, Chile and Argentina.[6] It is obvious that both the stabilization and inflation phase are variants on a far more fundamental theme.

There can be no effective design for economic development in the Model II countries which does not disestablish the non-functional groups—which does not separate them from political power and, *pari passu*, reduce or eliminate their claim on income. This solution applies equally whether power derives from land, other hierarchical wealth, the army, the non-functional bureaucracy or some coalition of these. (The problem presented by the trader or *comprador* group is less clear, for it performs, however expensively, an economic function. Elimination of privileged or monopoly position is more important here.) There can be no *a priori* judgment that a particular non-functional group, for example landlords or the army, is more regressive than another. Any non-functional group which governs in its own interest will govern at the expense of economic incentives.

The problem is that the disestablishment of non-functional groups is a task not of reform but of revolution. A country does not redistribute land or eliminate an army by passing a law. Certainly it will not do so if landowners or the military are in control of the government. Nor is compensation an answer; men will sell property but they will not sell power. Such change in recent times has usually involved some violence except where it has been under the *force majeure* of military occupation. General Douglas MacArthur's land reforms in Japan and Korea—one of the more remarkable achievements of an occupying army and one that would have provoked fascinating comment in conservative circles in the United States had anyone but MacArthur been responsible—were peaceful because any protest was futile. The disestablishment of the princes and other feudatories in India was peaceful (except for the police action in Hyderabad) only because those affected recognized that vast shifts in the power structure had made opposition futile. Bolivia and Cuba, the other two recent examples of land reform, did not escape violence.

Yet there must be change in the social structure if there is to be economic advance. And the pressures for advance, in a world where the demonstration effect of economic development is persuasive, are unlikely to abate. The choice may well be between earlier and later revolutionary change, a choice which may well coincide with that between liberal revolutionary change—which establishes conventional economic incentives—and Communism.[7]

Yet the chance for liberal revolutionary change in countries of this Model is by no means unfavorable. It accords with a profound instinct of the people. We make a great mistake in supposing, in the manner of American conservatives, that constitutional liberties are valued only by Anglo-Saxons of good character, some property, superior education and good personal hygiene. And although the surrender of non-functional power cannot be purchased, the surrender can be made less painful by payment. This is what was envisaged under the Alliance for Progress. It is by far the most desirable form of assistance for the Model II countries. This was the most progressive single policy of the Kennedy Administration. There should be no doubt as to why political conservatives and routine diplomats have regarded the policy with such suspicion.

One of the advantages of aid that is designed to facilitate social change is in showing that the United States is categorically on the side of such change and that reactionary or, more inimically, politically innocent officials in the United States will not act on the assumption that thrust toward change is Communist in inspiration.[8] Should they be allowed to continue to do so, there is a very good chance that the ultimate such thrust will be Communist.

It goes without saying that not only moral but material support should be denied to non-functional ruling groups. In particular, support to Latin American armed forces has been, as earlier noted, the most symmetrically self-defeating exercise in American foreign policy in the last half century. In the belief that power was being built up for resistance to Communism, a power was created that was strongly inimical to orderly political development and to economic progress. It helped make Communism increasingly attractive as a solution. Like most moderately well-paid and sedentary groups, members of these armies are averse to personal risk. So, as in Cuba, they are unlikely ever to interpose much physical opposition to the Communists. By surrender and possibly even by purchase, they are an excellent source of arms. One wonders if the Soviets have ever considered leaving the propagation of Communism to the more orthodox of our old-line Latin American hands and those who believe that wherever there is a soldier he should be given an American gun. If Communism must be encouraged, let it be done by proven talent.

| 6 |

In the Model III countries, prescription comes much closer to what we have come to consider the standard policy for underdevelopment. The cultural base in these countries being wide, this requires no urgent action. Education is important; no one would argue for a moment against its further development. But it does not remove the prime barrier to advance.[9] The social structure is, as everywhere, imperfect. But the claims of non-functional groups and the absence of reward for those who have function are also not the decisive barrier to advance. One is spared the delicate task of recommending the right kind of revolution.

In these countries the simple fact is that too many people struggle to make a living from too few resources. As a further consequence, little can be saved to enlarge the capital base—factories, power plants, transport—by which production is increased. The obvious remedy is to provide resources for immediate consumption if these are patently insufficient, to provide capital for expansion of existing agricultural and industrial plant, and, most urgently, to limit the number of people who must live from these perilously scarce resources.

Translated into specific measures, this means that all feasible steps must be taken—by encouraging individual savings, encouraging the retention and reinvestment of earnings, and by judicious use of taxation—to mobilize internal savings. The amount so made available will almost certainly be small. The country has the cultural resources to use considerable amounts. This is the meaning of the common statement that India, Pakistan and Egypt have large absorptive capacity for capital. So external capital assistance in generous amounts is of great importance in this Model.

The social structure of these countries makes poverty comparatively democratic. For a very large proportion of the population, accordingly, consumption will have a larger claim on resources than saving for capital formation, for this consumption is coordinate with life itself. This not only sets limits on what can be squeezed out of these economies for investment, but it also emphasizes the value, in these countries, of direct consumption assistance, such as the food provided by the United States under Public Law 480, provided, of course, that it is not a substitute for domestic effort to increase food production.

It is obviously important that capital, being scarce, be used effectively. This means that there must be a plan which establishes priorities and an administrative apparatus for carrying these priorities into effect. The administrative and technical resources from the wide cultural base make such planning feasible. It is both less essential and less feasible in the other two Models.

It is of the highest importance in this Model that the nexus between poverty and the birth rate be broken. A high birth rate is a common attribute of poverty, but it is in Model III countries that action is most urgent. For years, men of modest foresight have been warning that, in the future, the dense populations of these lands would press alarmingly on the means for supporting them. Now the future has come. This is the meaning of the food riots in these last years in India.

It would be wrong to wait on more studies or a better contraceptive. Research on population has already been used to the limit as an alternative to determined action on birth control. Whichever contraceptive is now most practical must be provided in adequate quantity at the earliest moment to every village and with every possible encouragement and incentive to its use. Results must be measured not, as now, by pamphlets issued, speeches delivered and conferences attended, but by what happens to the birth rate. The moral choice is no longer between contraception and children, but between contraception and starvation. The provision of food from abroad—and by a long supply line that might be cut with disastrous consequences—is justified if it enlarges consumption for an existing population. It is not so easy to justify if it induces a Malthusian increase in population with the result that people are as hungry as before but there are more people to be hungry.

| 7 |

This brings me to the end of these lectures. It will be evident that in all of these Models we face problems of the most formidable difficulty. There can be no talk of the poor countries catching up with the rich. Nor can we hope to keep the gap between those that grow easily and those that grow only with difficulty from widening. Our best hope is that the people of the poor countries, in comparing their position in the given year with that of the year before, will have a sense of improvement. This is not a negligible accomplishment; the basic comparison in economic affairs is with the position of very near neighbors and the year before. But to insure this improvement will require patience and great effort. It will also take a good deal of money. However, failure can surely be counted upon to cost more.

The Moral Ambiguity of America

by
Paul Goodman

I

THE EMPTY SOCIETY

| *1* |

During Eisenhower's second administration, I wrote a book describing how hard it was for young people to grow up in the corporate institutions of American society. Yet statistics at that time indicated that most were content to be secure as personnel of big corporations; a few deviated in impractical, and certainly unpolitical, ways, like being Beat or delinquent. The system itself, like its President, operated with a cheerful and righteous self-satisfaction. There were no signs of its being vulnerable, though a loud chorus of intellectual critics, like myself, were sounding off against it. We were spoil-sports.

Less than ten years later, the feeling is different; it turns out that we critics were not altogether unrealistic. The system of institutions is still grander and more computerized, but it seems to have lost its morale. The baronial corporations are making immense amounts of money and are more openly and heavily subsidized by the monarch in Washington. The processing of the young is extended for longer years and its tempo speeded up. More capital and management are exported, interlocking with international capital, and more of the world (including Canada) is brought under American control. When necessary, remarkable military technology is brought to bear. At home, there is no political check, for no matter what the currents of opinion, by and large the dominant system wreaks its will, managing the parliamentary machinery to look like consensus.

Nevertheless, the feeling of justification is gone. Sometimes we seem to be bulling it through only in order to save face. Often, enterprises seem to be expanding simply because the managers cannot think of any other use of energy and resources. The economy is turning into a war economy. There are warnings of ecological disaster, pollution, congestion, poisoning, mental disease, anomie. We have discovered that there is hard-core poverty at home that is not easy to liquidate. Unlike the success of the Marshall Plan in Europe in the Forties, it increasingly appears that poverty and unrest in Asia, Africa, and South America are not helped by our methods of assistance, but are perhaps made worse. There are flashes of suspicion, like flashes of lightning, that the entire system may be unviable. Influential senators refer to our foreign policy as "arrogant" and "lawless" but, in my opinion, our foreign and domestic system is all of a piece and is more innocent and deadly than that; it is mindless and morally insensitive. Its pretended purposes are window-dressing for purposeless expansion and a panicky need to keep things under control.

And now very many young people no longer want to co-operate with such a system. Indeed, a large and rapidly growing number—already more than 5% of college students—use language that is openly revolutionary and apocalyptic, as if in their generation they were going to make a French Revolution. More and more often, direct civil disobedience seems to make obvious sense.

We are exerting more power and feeling less right—what does that mean for the future? I have heard serious people argue for three plausible yet drastically incompatible predictions about America during the next generation, none of them happy:

(1) Some feel, with a kind of Virgilian despair, that the American empire will succeed and will impose for a long time, at home and abroad, its meaningless management and showy style of life. For instance, we will "win" in Vietnam, though such a victory of brute military technology will be a moral disaster. Clubbing together with the other nuclear powers, we will stave off the nuclear war and stop history with a new Congress of Vienna. American democracy will vanish into an establishment of promoters, mandarins, and technicians, though for a while maintaining an image of democracy as in the days of Augustus and Tiberius. And all this is probably the best possible outcome, given the complexities of high technology, urbanization, mass education, and over-population.

(2) Others believe, with dismay and horror, that our country is over-reaching and is bound for doom; but nothing can be done because policy cannot be influenced. Controlling communications, creating incidents that it then mistakes for history, deceived by its own Intelligence agents, our system is mesmerized. Like the Mikado, Washington is captive of its military-industrial complex. The way we manage the economy and technology must increase anomie and crime. Since the war-economy eats up brains and capital, we will soon be a fifth-rate economic power. With a few setbacks abroad—for instance, when we force a major South American country to become communist—and with the increasing disorder on the streets that is inevitable because our cities are

unworkable, there will be a police state. The atom bombs may then go off. Such being the forecast, the part of wisdom is escape, and those who cultivate LSD are on the right track.

(3) Others hold that the Americans are too decent to succumb to fascism, and too spirited to remain impotent clients of a managerial elite, and the tide of protest will continue to rise. The excluded poor are already refusing to remain excluded and they cannot be included without salutary changes. With the worst will in the world we cannot police the world. But the reality is that we are confused. We do not know how to cope with the new technology, the economy of surplus, the fact of One World that makes national boundaries obsolete, the unworkability of traditional democracy. We must invent new forms. To be sure, the present climate of emergency is bad for the social invention and experiment that are indispensable, and there is no doubt that our over-centralized and Establishment methods of organization make everybody stupid from top to bottom. But there is hope precisely in the young. They understand the problem in their bones. Of course, they don't know much and their disaffection both from tradition and from the adult world makes it hard for them to learn anything. Nevertheless, we will learn in the inevitable conflict, which will hopefully be mainly non-violent.

I myself hold this third view: American society is on a bad course, but there is hope for reconstruction through conflict. It is a wish. The evidence, so far, is stronger for either our empty success or for crack-up. My feeling is the same as about the atom bombs. Rationally, I must judge that the bombs are almost certain to go off in this generation; yet I cannot believe that they will go off, for I do not lead my life with that expectation.

Let me stop a moment and make another comparison. Thirty years ago the Jews in Germany believed that Hitler did not mean to exterminate them; "nobody," they said, "can be that stupid." So they drifted to the gas chambers, and went finally even without resistance. Now the nuclear powers continue stockpiling bombs and pouring new billions into missiles, anti-missile missiles, and armed platforms in orbit. You Canadians, like us Americans, do not prevent it. Afterwards, survivors, if there are any, will ask, "How did we let it happen?"

I am eager, as well as honored, to be talking to a Canadian audience on the state of American society, and especially to the Canadian young. You people are not yet so wrongly committed as we. Your land is less despoiled, your cities are more manageable, you are not yet so sold on mass mis-education. You are not in the trap of militarism. A large minority of you are deeply skeptical of American methods and oppose the unquestioned extension of American power. Some of us Americans have always wistfully hoped that you Canadians would teach us a lesson or two, though, to be frank, you have usually let us down.

| 2 |

In these lectures on our ambiguous position, I shall have to talk a good deal about style. To illustrate the current style of American enterprise, let me analyze a small, actual incident. It is perfectly typical, banal; no one would raise his eyebrows at it, it is business as usual.

Washington has allotted several billions of dollars to the schools. The schools are not teaching very well, but there is no chance that anybody will upset the apple-cart and ask if so much doing of lessons is the right way to educate the young altogether. Rather, there is a demand for new "methods" and mechanical equipment, which will disturb nobody, and electronics is the latest thing that every forward-looking local school board must be proud to buy. So to cut in on this melon, electronics corporations,

IBM, Xerox, etc., have hastened to combine with, or take over, text-book houses. My own publisher, Random House, has been bought up by the Radio Corporation of America.

Just now, General Electric and Time, Inc., that owns a textbook house, have put nearly 40 millions into a joint subsidiary called General Learning. And an editor of *Life* magazine has been relieved of his duties for five weeks, in order to prepare a prospectus on the broad educational needs of America and the world, to come up with exciting proposals, so that General Learning can move with purpose into this unaccustomed field. The editor has collected and is boning up on the latest High Thought on education, and in due course he invites me to lunch, to pick my brains for something new and radical. "The sky," he assures me, "is the limit." (I am known, let me explain, as a severe critic of the school establishment.) "Perhaps," he tells me at lunch, "there *is* no unique place for General Learning. They'll probably end up as prosaic makers of school hardware. But we ought to give it a try."

Consider the premises of this odd situation, where first they have the organization and the technology, and then they try to dream up a use for it. In the 18th century, Adam Smith thought that one started with the need and only then collected capital to satisfy it. In the 19th century there was already a lot of capital to invest, but by and large the market served as a check, to guarantee utility, competence, and relevance. Now, however, the subsidy removes the check of the market and a promotion can expand like weeds in a well-manured field. The competence required is to have a big organization and sales force, and to be *in*, to have the prestige and connections plausibly to get the subsidy. Usually it is good to have some minimal relation to the ostensible function, e.g. a textbook subsidiary related to schooling or *Time-Life* related to, let us say, learning. But indeed, when an expanding corporation becomes *very* grand, it generates an expertise of its own called Systems Development, applicable to anything. For example, as an expert in Systems Development, North American Aviation is hired to reform the penal system of California; there is no longer need to demonstrate acquaintance with any particular human function.

Naturally, with the divorce of enterprise from utility and competence, there goes a heavy emphasis on rhetoric and public relations to prove utility and competence. So an editor must be re-assigned for five weeks to write a rationale. It is his task to add ideas or talking points to the enterprise, like a wrapper. The personnel of expanding corporations, of course, are busy people and have not had time to think of many concrete ideas; they can, however, phone writers and concerned professionals. Way-out radicals, especially, do a lot of thinking, since they have little practical employment. And since the enterprise is free-floating anyway, it is dandy to include, in the prospectus, something daring, or even meaningful. (Incidentally, I received no fee, except the lunch and pleasant company; but I did pick up an illustration for these lectures.)

In an affluent society that can afford it, there is something jolly about such an adventure of the electronics giant, the mighty publisher, the National Science Foundation that has made curriculum studies, and local school boards that want to be in the swim. Somewhere down the line, however, this cabal of decision-makers is going to coerce the time of life of real children and control the activity of classroom teachers. These, who are directly engaged in the human function of learning and teaching, have no say in what goes on. This introduces a more sober note. Some of the product of the burst of corporate activity and technological virtuosity will be useful, some not—the pedagogical evidence is mixed and not extensive—but the brute fact is that the children are quite incidental to the massive intervention of the giant combinations.

I have chosen a wry example. But I could have chosen the leader of the American economy, the complex of cars, oil, and roads. This outgrew its proper size perhaps thirty years ago; now it is destroying both the cities and the countryside, and has been shown to be careless of even elementary safety.

Rather, let me turn abruptly to the Vietnam War. We notice the same family traits. Whatever made us embark on this adventure, by now we can define the Vietnam War as a commitment looking for a reason, or at least a rationalization. There has been no lack of policy-statements, rhetorical gestures, (it seems) manufactured incidents, and (certainly) plain lies; but as the war has dragged on and grown, all these have proved to be mere talking-points. Ringing true, however, has been the fanfare about the superb military technology that we have deployed. The theme is used as a chief morale-builder for the troops. In the absence of adequate political reasons, some have even said that the war is largely an occasion for testing new hardware and techniques. It is eerie to hear, on the TV, an airman enthusiastically praise the split-second scheduling of his missions to devastate rice-fields. Such appreciation of know-how is a cheerful American disposition, but it does not do much credit to him as a grown man.

Yet what emerges most strikingly from our thinking about and prosecution of the Vietnam War is, again, the input-output accounting, the systems development, and the purely incidental significance of the human beings involved. The *communiqués* are concerned mainly with the body-count of V.C. in ratio to our own losses, since there is a theory that in wars of this kind one must attain a ratio of 5 to 1 or 10 to 1. According to various estimates, it costs $50,000 to $250,000 to kill 1 Vietnamese, hopefully an enemy. Similarly, the bombing of civilians and the destruction of their livelihood occur as if no human beings were involved; they are officially spoken of as unfortunate but incidental. (The average indemnity for a civilian death is $34.) We claim that we have no imperialist aims in Vietnam—though we are building air-bases of some very heavy concrete and steel—but evidently old-fashioned imperialism was preferable, since it tried to keep the subjugated population in existence, for taxes and labor.

At home, correspondingly, college students are deferred from the draft because they will be necessary to man the professions and scientific technology, while farm boys, Negroes, and Spanish Americans are drafted because they are otherwise good for nothing. That is to say, war is not regarded as a dread emergency, in which each one does his bit, but as part of the on-going business of society, in which fighting and dying are usual categories of the division of labor. But this is bound to be the case when 20% of the Gross National Product is spent on war (using a multiplier of 2); when more than half of the gross new investment since 1945 has been in war industry; and when much of higher education and science is devoted to war technology.

The Americans are not a warlike or bloodthirsty people, though violent. The dehumanizing of war is part of a general style of enterprise and control in which human utility and even the existence of particular human beings are simply not a paramount consideration. Great armaments manufacturers have said that they are willing and ready to convert their capital and skill to peaceful production when given the signal; this seems to mean that it is *indifferent* to them what they enterprise. Studies of American workmen have shown that they take their moral and esthetic standards not from family, church, friends, or personal interests, but from the organization and style of work at the plant; and I think that this explains the present peculiar situation that other nations of the world regard our behavior in the Vietnam War with a kind of horror, whereas Americans sincerely talk as if it were a messy job to be done as efficiently as possible.

———————

This brings us to a broader question: What do we mean by technical efficiency in our system?

| 3 |

Corporate and bureaucratic societies, whether ruled by priests, mandarins, generals, or business managers, have always tended to diminish the importance of personal needs and human feeling, in the interest of abstractions and systemic necessities. And where there has been no check by strong community ties, effective democracy, or a free market, it has not been rare for the business of society to be largely without utility or common sense. Nevertheless, modern corporate societies that can wield a high technology are liable to an unique temptation: since they do not exploit common labor, they may tend to exclude the majority of human beings altogether, as useless for the needs of the system and therefore as not quite persons.

This has been the steady tendency in America. The aged are ruled out at an earlier age, the young until a later age. We have liquidated most small farmers. There is no place for the poor, e.g., more than 20 million Negroes and Latin Americans. A rapidly increasing number are certified as insane or otherwise incompetent. These groups already comprise more than a majority of the population. Some authorities say (though others deny) that with full automation most of the rest will also be useless.

There is nothing malevolent or heartless in the exclusion. The tone is not like that of the old exploitative society when people were thrown out of work during the lows of the business cycle. For humane and political reasons, even extraordinary efforts are made to shape the excluded into the dominant style, so they can belong. Even though the system is going to need only a few percent with elaborate academic training, all the young are subjected to twelve years of schooling and 40% go to college. There is every kind of training and social service to upgrade the poor and to make the handicapped productive members of society. At high cost of effort and suffering, mentally retarded children must be taught to read, if only "cat" and "rat."

But a frank look shows, I think, that, for most, the long schooling is a way of keeping the young on ice; the job training is busywork; and the social services turn people into "community dependents" for generations. Much of the anxiety about the "handicapped" and the "underprivileged" is suburban squeamishness that cannot tolerate difference. What is *never* done, however, is to change the rules of the system, to re-define usefulness in terms of how people are, and to shape the dominant style to people. This cannot be done because it would be inefficient and, indeed, degrading, for there is only one right way to exist. Do it our way or else you are not quite a person.

Inevitably, such self-righteous inflexibility is self-mesmerizing and self-proving, for other methods and values are not allowed to breathe and prove themselves. Often it would be cheaper to help people to be in their own way or at least to let them be; but anything in a different or outmoded style has "deviant" or "underprivileged" written on it, and no expense is spared to root it out, in the name of efficiency. Thus, it would have been cheaper to pay the small farmers to stay put if they wished. (Anyway, I shall try to show in a subsequent lecture, it is not the case in many situations that small farming and local distribution are less efficient than the plantations and national chain-grocers that have supplanted them with the connivance of government policy.) It would be far cheaper to give money directly to the urban poor to design their own lives, rather than to try to make them shape up; it has been estimated that, in one area of poverty in New York City, the cost per family in special services is more than $10,000 a year; and anyway, to a candid observer, the culture of poverty is not inferior to that of the middle class, if it were allowed to be decent, if it could be, in Péguy's distinction, *pauvreté* rather than *misère*. Very many of the young would get a better education and grow up usefully to themselves and society if the school-money were used for real apprenticeships, or even if they were given the school-money to follow their own interests, ambitions, and even fancies, rather than penning them for lengthening years in increasingly regimented institutions; anyway, many young people could enter many professions without most of the schooling if we changed the rules for licensing and hiring. But none of these simpler and cheaper ways would be "efficient"; the clinching proof is that they would be hard to administer.

Also, *are* the people useless? The concept of efficiency is largely, maybe mainly, systemic. It depends on the goals of the *system*, which may be too narrowly and inflexibly conceived; it depends on the ease of administration, which is considered as more important than economic or social costs; but it depends also on the method of calculating costs, which may create a false image of efficiency by ruling out "intangibles" that do not suit the method. This source of error becomes very important in advanced urban economies where the provision of personal and social services grows rapidly in proportion to hardware and food production and distribution. In providing services, whether giving information, selling, teaching children, admitting to college, assigning jobs, serving food, or advising on welfare, standardization and punch-cards may seem to fulfill the functions, but they may do so at the expense of frayed nerves, waiting in line, bad mistakes, misfitting, and cold soup. In modern conditions, the tailor-made improvisations of fallible but responsive human beings may be increasingly indispensable rather than useless. In the jargon of Frank Riessman, there is a need for "sub-professionals." Yet the mass-production and business-machine style, well adapted to manufacturing hardware and calculating logistics, will decide that people are useless anyway, since they can theoretically be dispensed with. It is a curious experience to hear a gentleman from the Bureau of the Budget explain the budget of the War on Poverty according to cost-benefit computation. He can demonstrate that the participation of the poor in administering a program is disadvantageous; he can show you the flow chart; he cannot understand why poor people make a fuss on this point. It is useless to explain to him that they do not trust the program (nor the director) but would like to get the money for their own purposes.

Abroad, the Americans still engage in plenty of old-fashioned exploitation of human labor, as in Latin America; yet the tendency is again to regard the underdeveloped peoples as not quite persons, and to try to shape them up by (sometimes) generous assistance in our own style. For example, one of the radical ideas of General Learning, the subsidiary of General Electric and Time, Inc., is to concentrate on electronic devices to teach literacy to the masses of children in poor countries; we must export our Great Society. Our enterprisers are eager to build highways and pipelines through the jungle, to multiply bases for our aeroplanes, and to provide other items of the American standard of living, for which the western-trained native political leaders have "rising aspirations." Unfortunately, this largesse must often result in disrupting age-old cultures, fomenting tribal wars, inflating prices and wages and reducing decent poverty to starvation, causing the abandonment of farms and disastrous instant urbanization, making dictatorships inevitable, and drawing simple peoples into Great Power conflicts. And woe if they do not then shape up, if they want to develop according to their local prejudices, for instance for land reform. They become an uncontrollable nuisance, surely therefore allied with our enemies, and better dead than Red. In his great speech in Montreal, Secretary McNamara informed us that since 1958, 87% of the very poor nations and 69% of the poor nations, but only 48% of the middle income nations, have had serious violent disturbances. The cure for it, he said, was development, according to the criteria of our cash economy, while protected from subversion by our bombers. How to explain to this arithmetically astute man that he is not taking these people seriously as existing?

A startlingly literal corollary of the principle that our system excludes human beings rather than exploits them is the agreement of all liberals and conservatives that there must be a check on population growth, more especially among backward peoples and the poor at home. We are definitely beyond the need for the labor of the "proletariat" ("producers of offspring") and the Iron Law of Wages to keep that labor cheap. Yet I am bemused by this unanimous recourse to a biological and mathematical etiology for our troubles. Probably there *is* a danger of world-overpopulation in the foreseeable future. (The United States, though, is supposed to level off at 300 millions in 2020, and this would not be a dense population for our area.) Certainly with the likelihood of nuclear war there is a danger of world-underpopulation. However, until we institute more human ecological, economic, and political arrangements, I doubt that population control is the first order of business; nor would I trust the Americans to set the rules.

| *4* |

In this lecture, I have singled out two trends of the dominant organization of American society, its increasing tendency to expand, meaninglessly, for its own sake, and its tendency to exclude human beings as useless. It is the Empty Society, the obverse face of the Affluent Society. When Adam Smith spoke of the Wealth of Nations, he did not mean anything like this.

The meaningless expansion and the excluding are different things, but in our society they are essentially related. Lack of meaning begins to occur when the immensely productive economy over-matures and lives by creating demand instead of meeting it; when the check of the free market gives way to monopolies, subsidies, and captive consumers; when the sense of community vanishes and public goods are neglected and resources despoiled; when there is made-work (or war) to reduce unemployment; and when the measure of economic health is not increasing well-being but abstractions like the Gross National Product and the rate of growth.

Human beings tend to be excluded when a logistic style becomes universally pervasive, so that values and data that cannot be standardized and programmed are disregarded; when function is adjusted to the technology rather than technology to function; when technology is confused with autonomous science, a good in itself, rather than being limited by political and moral prudence; when there develops an establishment of managers and experts who alone license and allot resources, and it deludes itself that it knows the only right method and is omnicompetent. Then common folk become docile clients, maintained by sufferance, or they are treated as deviant.

It is evident that, for us, these properties of the empty society are essentially related. If we did not exclude so many as not really persons, we would have to spend more of our substance on worthwhile goods, including subsistence goods, both at home and abroad; we would have to provide a more human environment for the children to grow up in; there would be more paths to grow up and more ways of being a person. On the other hand, if we seriously and efficiently tackled the problems of anomie, alienation, riot, pollution, congestion, urban blight, degenerative and mental disease, etc., we would find ourselves paying more particular attention to persons and neighborhoods, rather than treating them as standard items; we would have a quite different engineering and social science; and we would need all the human resources available.

Certainly we would stop talking presumptuously about The Great Society and find ourselves struggling, in the confusing conditions of modern times, for a decent society.

The chief danger to American society at present, and to the world from American society, is our mindlessness, induced by empty institutions. It is a kind of mesmerism, a self-delusion of formal rightness, that affects both leaders and people. We have all the talking-points but less and less content. The Americans are decent folk, generous and fairly compassionate. They are not demented and fanatical, like some other imperial powers of the past and present, but on the contrary rather skeptical and with a sense of humor. They are not properly called arrogant, though perhaps presumptuous. But we have lost our horse sense, for which we were once noted. This kind of intelligence was grounded not in history or learning, nor in finesse of sensibility and analysis, but in the habit of making independent judgments and in democratically rubbing shoulders with all kinds and conditions. We have lost it by becoming personnel of a mechanical system and exclusive suburbanites, by getting out of contact with real jobs and real people. We suddenly have developed an

Establishment, but our leaders do not have the tradition and self-restraint to come on like an establishment. Thus, we are likely to wreak havoc not because of greed, ideology, or arrogance, but because of a bright strategy of the theory of games and an impatient conviction that other people don't know what's good for them.

II

COUNTER-FORCES FOR
A DECENT SOCIETY

| *1* |

In the first lecture, I depicted my country as bound on a course that must lead either to an empty and immoral empire or to exhaustion and fascism. There is evidence for both gloomy pictures. Let me now mention some counter-forces and give evidence for a future of more decency. These forces seem weaker and, except for court decisions, they do not constitute official policy nor control technology. Yet they are wonderfully stubborn and show flashes of power. And of course the traditional American sentiment is that a decent society cannot be built by dominant official policy but only by grass-roots resistance, community development, social invention, and citizenly vigilance to protect liberty. These, surprisingly, are reviving. In any case, if, even with good intentions, the interlocking corporate style destroys vitality, an increasing ragged conflict (hopefully without much violence) might at present be our best hope.

The ambiguity of values in America is really striking. Often it is as if there were a line down the front page of *The New York Times*, with half of the stories making one despondent, afraid, or indignant and half cheerful, hopeful, and proud. Needless to say, the trends that please me are called un-American by some; but you will recognize them as classically American. *The question is whether or not our beautiful libertarian, pluralist, and populist experiment is viable in modern conditions.* If it's not, I don't know any other acceptable politics, and I'm a man without a country.

With a few exceptions, the Supreme Court has been extending liberty of publication, art, assembly, and political action. It has condoned flagrant examples of civil disobedience. Even more significant are its decisions limiting the police, forbidding wiretapping and forced confession, and tightening due process, for here the conflict with the system is evident. The trend of the government, the suburbs, etc., is toward more police, equipped with a powerful technology, and instant national and international connections; but the Court and a stubborn group of lawyers and sociologists seem determined to resist unchecked police power and draconian punishments. Capital punishment is being rather rapidly abolished, largely, I think, because of the general revulsion, well expressed by Camus, against the mechanical State snuffing out a life. New York and the District of Columbia have reformed the bail system, to rescue the poor from rotting in jail before trial, and other states will follow suit. These reforms are the reverse of the moral insensitivity I spoke of in my first lecture. It is not 1984. We are as yet unwilling to identify with the system in which we nevertheless act.

Some cities have adopted civilian boards to review complaints against the police. (But New York has just voted its board out of existence: these cases are touch and go.) Legislation is proposed for a Public Defender to offset the advantage of the State Attorney's staff and business machines. There is talk of an ombudsman to review complaints against government bureaucracy. Almost invariably, to be sure, such agencies, like the regulatory agencies in Washington, end up in coalition with what they are supposed to regulate; they cushion protest rather than remedy abuses; nevertheless, they do indicate an awakening alarm about total control. Unwilling to alter the framework, people hanker for a kind of Roman tribune to intervene with his drastic personal vote. A better proposal, in my opinion, is for disadvantaged groups, like Negroes, to police their own neighborhoods according to their own mores.

Puritanism persists, yet there is a remarkable shift away from moralism and hypocrisy, and toward plain inconsistency. For instance, narcotics laws are strengthened and extended to LSD and other non-addictives; but there is a strong campaign for the English system for the addictive drugs, and champions of LSD have a messianic fervor, claiming that the issue is between conformism and a personal or religious way of life. We have the odd situation that penalties become heavier while public opinion is more and more uncertain.

The continuing sexual revolution deserves special notice. Here the inconsistency between High Thought and the repressive laws and sexless schools is blatant. But the most practical change has been not the actual sexual behavior of the adolescents and adults, which so far has not produced much poetry or deep joy, though it is better than the sexual climate in which I grew up; rather, it is the now widely accepted freedom of the children, the relaxed toilet-training, permitted masturbation, nakedness, informal dress. A generation ago we were warned that this freedom would produce an unruly brood; it has, and I like the results. Correspondingly, counter to the gigantism and stepped up schedule, curriculum, and grading of the official schools, there is a revival of progressive schools, and inevitably these veer toward A. S. Neill's Summerhill, freeing the children from compulsory attendance and giving them a say in the school administration. Progressive education belongs, of course, to only a few middle class families; yet the Freedom Schools of the Negro revolution are pedagogically not so very different.

There is a revival in the churches. Long pillars of the establishment, they too have begun to take alarm that the establishment is becoming anti-human; and we find clergymen in the unlikely position of fighting for migrant farm-workers and against the drug and sex laws, and confessing that God is *not* on our side in Vietnam and in manufacturing nuclear bombs. The churches have latched onto non-directive community-development. Some of them have sponsored the most daring, and unofficious, protest organizations and legal defense for Negroes and Spanish-Americans. In New York City, the best community theaters—indeed the best theaters—are in churches; nor are the plays lacking in dirty words. And on many college campuses, the young existentialist chaplain—or even the Catholic—is the center of radical student activity.

There is an odd explosion in the arts, with an immense number of amateurs, of a kind of urban folk art in all genres. It is entirely inauthentic in style, combining misunderstood fragments of international culture with commercialized mountain music and stereotyped urban naturalism; yet it is authentic to the actual urban confusion. On a more intellectual level, there have been lovely sporadic attempts to enliven the cities with happenings in the park, spontaneous fence painting, and vest-pocket playgrounds laid out by adolescents. Unfortunately, since the urban folk have neither tradition nor resources and their art is largely an outcry of alienation, there is no popular effort to cope with the big horrors of urban ugliness and pollution; even so, what the folk do has more vitality than the synthetic culture-centers sponsored by government and foundations.

Economically, there is an increase in minimum wages and unionization of the most exploited groups, hospital attendants and migrant farmhands. More significantly, there is a growing sentiment, which I think will prevail, for a guaranteed minimum income, which would be far preferable, in the United States, to the present system of welfare payments and social services. It would be a giant step toward making decent poverty possible, reopening independent choice of how to live, and encouraging small businesses and rural reconstruction. It would loosen top-down control.

The most spectacular battle with American business-as-usual-and-more-so has been, of course, the belated movement for Negro emancipation. This has occurred, naturally, when the need to exploit field and unskilled labor has diminished and Negroes have joined the ranks of the simply excluded. Their refusal to be excluded has penetrated the moral obtuseness of some Americans, but the most far-reaching effect will be, in my opinion, the renewed political lesson, that people are taken seriously when they raise Cain and insist on managing in their own way. Any help given by government—it has been small—has been because of local pressure, threat of riot, and riot. And, at least in the South, the movement has given remarkable proof that decentralized grass-roots action, loosely co-ordinated, can exert political power.

The Negro movement is part of a tide of populist direct action rising throughout the nation. There are almost daily marches, boycotts, sit-ins, protest to the point of smashing chairs at City Council meetings, civil disobedience to the point of filling the jails. This populism is called lawless, but, as I shall argue in a later lecture, it is the alternative to anomie and crime. Most of the actions are not constructive, there is rarely a political program; but they are necessary counter-actions to actions of the dominant system that are absurd, presumptuous, and finally intolerable. The protest against poisoning the milk with nuclear tests and boycott of the bomb-shelters were archetypal, and the mothers, high-school students, and famous scientists took to the streets, the principal's office, and the pages of *The New York Times*. So, neighborhoods rally en masse to stop high-handed Urban Renewal and Highway commissioners. Housewives picket super-markets because of inflationary prices. The League for Sexual Freedom parades with floats and dirty words. The hustlers and waifs of the Tenderloin in San Francisco organize for self-help and a voice in the local Economic Opportunity Council. Negroes march against a police outrage and end with a riot. Resentment at not being taken seriously by municipal social workers easily consolidates into organization à la Saul Alinsky. Students sit down around an Administration spokesman on foreign policy because he will not answer their questions. Seven hundred students are arrested in Berkeley because the college administration has lied to them. It is a ferment of populism occurring, under urban conditions, because finally there is no other way to exist. Naturally, the Federal Bureau of Investigation has proved that it is all a Communist plot. The serious question, to which I shall return later, is a different one: will this urban populism succeed in reviving democracy, or will it be manipulated like the Roman mob in the time of Caesar?

With a populist sounding-board behind them, finally, muckraking intellectuals always sound more for real. Atomic scientists, Rachel Carson, or Ralph Nader write books, and there is a flurry of Congressional investigation. Ingenuous college students imagine that the social criticism that they read in paperbacks is supposed to lead to action as well as being entertainment.

| 2 |

The most portentous libertarian and populist counter-force is the youth movement, and I shall devote to it the remainder of this lecture, for it expresses with remarkable precision, point by point, the opposition to the over-centralized, interlocking, and empty society.

About half the Americans are under 26. Nearly 40% of the college age group go to college. Of the present collegians—there are now 6 million in 2,000 institutions—it is estimated that 5% are in some activity of the radical youth movement. This does not seem a great proportion, but it has increased at least tenfold in the last decade and it and the number of its alumni will certainly increase even more rapidly in the next years. More important, unlike the Negroes, the radical young are not only the middle-class collegians, graduate students, or graduates, but they are also disproportionately the best students and from the best schools. They are an economic force, looming large among the indispensable inheritors of the dominant power in society. And although—or perhaps because—they do not share a common ideology but rather a common sentiment and style, in showdown situations like the troubles in Berkeley they have shown a remarkable solidarity and a common detestation for the liberal Center, crossing even the apparent chasm between Extreme Right and Extreme Left.

A major reason for their solidarity and their increase is mass higher education itself. For most, this has little academic value, and one of the shared sentiments is resistance to being academically processed for the goals of the system; nevertheless, the colleges and universities are, in fact, many hundreds of physical and social communities of young people, with populations of a few thousand to 25,000, sharing a sub-culture, propagandizing one another, and learning to distrust anybody over 30. Such collections of youth are a social phenomenon unique in history. Consider some details from San Francisco State College, where I was hired by the Associated Students last spring. With 15,000 students, the Associated Students have $300,000 annually in student dues, more than half of which is free and clear and which they use for untraditional purposes including organizing a tenants' organization, helping delinquents in a reformatory, running a tutorial program for Negro and Mexican children (with 300 collegian tutors), sponsoring a weekly television program, running an "experimental college" with twenty offbeat courses, and hiring their own professor. They apply on their own for grants from the Ford Foundation and the Poverty program!

Or consider the college press, with its fairly captive audience of several million, often daily. In a few cases, e.g. Harvard and Columbia, publication has gone off campus and is not under the tutelage of "faculty advisers." Increasingly, the college papers subscribe to news services and print (and edit) national and international news, and they also use syndicated material, like Art Buchwald, Feiffer, Russell Baker. Occasionally, notably the Cornell *Sun*, the college paper is the chief daily of its town. More important, there is a national student press service that could be a powerfully effective liaison for mobilizing opinion on common issues. Last winter I wrote a fortnightly column on student matters for a tiny college in Vermont, which the enterprising editor at once syndicated to fifty other college papers. On this model there could spring up a system of direct support, and control, of the students' "own" authors, just as, of course, they now indirectly support them through magazines whose main circulation is collegiate.

Nor are these young people properly called "youth." The exigencies of the American system have kept them in tutelage, doing lessons, till 23 and 24 years of age, years past when young industrial workers used to walk union picket-lines or when farmers carried angry pitchforks, or soldiers are now drafted into the army. Another cause of their shared resentment is the foolish attempt to arrest their maturation and regulate their social, sexual, and political activity.

Unlike the suburban practice of making acquaintance by role, status, or caste, these young live a good deal by "interpersonal relations" and are unusually careless, in their friendships, about status or getting ahead. I do not mean by this that they are especially affectionate or compassionate—they are averagely so—but they have been soaked in modern psychology, group therapy, sensitivity training; and as a style they go in for direct confrontation and sometimes brutal frankness. Add to this the lack of embarrassment due to animally uninhibited childhood. They are the post-Freudian generation—their parents were analyzed from 1920-1940! The effect—for example, long sessions of mutual analysis or jabber about LSD trips—can be tiresome, but it is pretty fatal to suburban squeamishness, race and moral prejudice, and maintaining appearances. And still another cause of resentment at the colleges is the impersonality and distance of the teachers and the big classes that make dialogue impossible.

Middle-class privacy vanishes. An innovation of the Beats was the community use of one another's pads, and this spirit of sharing has persisted in off-campus university communities, which are very different from paternalistic dormitories or fraternity row. In big cities there are growing bohemian student neighborhoods, tending to be located in racially mixed sections; and such neighborhoods, with their own coffee-houses and headquarters for student political clubs, cannot be controlled by campus administration. In the famous insurrection of Berkeley, Telegraph Avenue could easily rally 3,000 students, ex-students, wives, and pals. The response of the administration of the University of California has been, characteristically, to try to root up the neighborhood with Federally financed Urban Renewal!

The community meaning of the widespread use of hallucinogenic drugs is ambiguous. (Few students use addictives.) I have heard students hotly defend the drugs as a means of spiritual and political freedom, or hotly condemn them as a quietist opium of the people, or indifferently dismiss them as a matter of taste. But they do not operate like the chummy alcoholism of the fraternities, suburbs, and Washington; and, of course, being illegal and hard to procure, they tend to create conspiracy.

The LSD cult especially must be understood as part of a wave of religiosity that has included Zen, Christian and Jewish existentialism, a kind of psychoanalytic yoga, and the *Book of Changes*. We have seen that on the campus the young chaplain is often the center of action. Certainly the calculating rationalism of modern times is losing its self-evidence; and it is not the end of the world to go crazy temporarily.

The shagginess and chosen poverty of the student communities have nuances that are immensely important. We must remember that these are the young of the affluent society, used to a high standard of living and confident that, if and when they want, they can fit in and make good money. Having suffered little pressure of insecurity, they have little psychological need to climb; just as, coming from impeccably respectable homes, they feel no disgrace about sitting a few nights in jail. By confidence they are aristocrats—en masse. At the same time, the affluent standard of living which they have seen is pretty synthetic and very much of it useless and phony, and the poverty of the students is not degraded or insecure but decent, natural, and in many ways more comfortable than their parents' standard, especially if they can always corral obvious goodies like hi-fi equipment and motorcycles. Typically, they tour Europe on nothing, sleeping under bridges;

but if they get really hungry, they can drop in at American Express. Most of the major satisfactions of life, sex, paperback books, guitars, roaming, conversation, and activist politics, need cost little. Thus, they are the first generation in America selective of the standard of living; if this attitude became general, it would be a disaster for the expanding GNP. And there is an unmistakable tone of policy and defiance in their poverty and shagginess. They have been influenced by the Voluntary Poverty of the Beat movement, signifying withdrawal from the trap of the affluent economy. Finally, by acquaintance they experience the harsher tone of the involuntary poverty of the Negroes and Spanish Americans whose neighborhoods they visit and with whom they are friends.

| 3 |

The chief (conscious) drive of the radical young is their morality. As Mike Harrington has put it, "They drive you crazy with their morality," since for it they disregard prudence and politics, and they mercilessly condemn legitimate casuistry as if it were utterly phony. When politically minded student leaders, like—sometimes—the Students for a Democratic Society, engage in "tactics" and the "art of the possible," they swiftly lose influence, whereas indignation or a point of honor will rally the young in droves.

Partly this drive to morality is the natural ingenuousness of youth, freed of the role-playing and status-seeking of our society. As aristocrats, not driven by material or ulterior motives, they will budge for ideals or not at all. Partly their absolutism is a disgusted reaction to cynicism and the prevalent adult conviction that "nothing can be done, you can't fight City Hall, modern life is too complex." But mostly, I think, it is the self-righteousness of an intelligent and innocent new generation in a world where my own generation is patently stupid and incompetent. They have been brought up on a literature of devastating criticism that has gone unanswered because there is no answer.

The philosophical words are "authenticity" and "commitment," from the existentialist vocabulary. And it cannot be denied that our dominant society is unusually inauthentic. Newspeak and double-talk are the *lingua franca* of administrators, politicians, advertisers, and mass media. These people are not even lying; rather, there is an unbridgeable chasm between the statements made for systemic reasons or the image of the corporation and what is intended and actually performed. I have seen mature graduate-students crack up in giggles of anxiety listening to the Secretary of State expound our foreign policy with his usual patient good humor; when I questioned them afterward, some said that he was like a mechanical man, others that he was demented. The trouble was that his personal aplomb was not related to his function and action; he was not engaged. And most campus blow-ups have been finally caused by administrators' animal inability to speak. The students have faithfully observed due process and manfully stated their case, but the administrators simply could not talk like human beings.

In principle, "commitment" proves authenticity. You must not merely talk but organize, collect money, burn your draft card, go South and be shot at, go to jail. And the young eagerly commit themselves. However, a lasting commitment is hard to achieve. There are a certain number of causes that are pretty authentic and warrant engaging in: give Negroes the vote, desegregate a hotel or bus, practice fair employment, commute Chessman's sentence to the gas chamber, abolish grading and get the CIA out of the university, get out of Vietnam, legalize marijuana and homosexuality, unionize the grape-pickers. But it is rarely the case that any particular authentic cause can really occupy the thought and energy of more than a few for more than a while. Students cool off and hop from issue to issue. Then some become angry at the backsliders; others foolishly try to prove that civil liberties, for instance, are not so "important" as Negro civil rights, for instance, or that university reform is not so "important" as stopping the bombing of Hanoi. Others, disillusioned, sink into despair of human nature. And committed causes vanish from view at the June vacation, when the community disperses.

Shrewder psychologists among the young advocate getting involved only in what you "enjoy" and gravitate to, but this is a weak motive compared with indignation or justice.

The bother is that, except with a few political or religious personalities, the students' commitments do not spring from their own vocations and life ambitions; and they are not related in a coherent program for the reconstruction of society. This is not the fault of the students. Most of the present young have unusually little sense of vocation—perhaps sixteen continuous years of doing lessons by compulsion is not a good way to find identity; and there *is* no acceptable program of reconstruction—nobody has spelled it out—only vague criteria. Pathetically, much "definite commitment" is a self-deceptive way of filling the void of sense of vocation and utopian politics. Negroes, who are perforce really committed to their emancipation, notice this and say that their white allies are spiritually exploiting them.

It is a terrible period for the young to find vocation and identity. For most of the abiding human vocations and professions, arts and sciences, seem to them, and are, corrupt; law, business, the physical sciences, social work—these constitute the hated System. And higher education, both curriculum and professors, which ought to be helping them find themselves, also seems corrupt and part of the System. Students know that something is wrong in their schooling and they agitate for university reform, but since they do not know what new world they want to make, they do not know what to demand to be taught.

| 4 |

It is not the task of 20-year-olds to devise a coherent program of social reconstruction, to rethink the uses of technology and resources, methods of management, city planning, and international relations; and they rightly accuse us of not providing them a program to work for. A small minority, I think increasing, return to Marxism, but the Marxist theorists have also not thought of anything new and relevant to over-mature societies. Most radical students, in my observation, listen to Marxist ideological speeches with polite lack of interest, and are appalled by Marxist political bullying. On the other hand, they are disgusted with official anticommunism. By an inevitable backlash, since they think all American official speech is double-talk, they disbelieve that communist states are any worse than our own.

What the American young do know, being themselves pushed around, itemized, and processed, is that they have a right to a say in what affects them; that is, they believe in democracy, which they have to call "participatory democracy," to distinguish it from double-talk democracy. Poignantly, in their ignorance of American history, they do not recognize that they are Congregationalists, town-meeting democrats, Jeffersonians, populists. But they know they want the opportunity to be responsible, to initiate and decide, instead of being mere personnel. Returning from their term overseas, the first thousand of the Peace Corps unanimously agreed that exercising responsibility and initiative had been the most worthwhile part of their experience, and they complained that back home they would not have the opportunity. (Last year at Harvard more seniors opted for the Peace Corps than for business!)

The primary area for seeking democracy would be, one would imagine, the universities, for that is where the students are and are coerced. And the radical students, who we have seen are among the best academically, have worked for *Lernfreiheit*—freedom from grading, excessive examination, compulsory attendance at lectures, and prescribed subjects—and also for the ancient privilege of a say in designing the curriculum and evaluating the teaching. But unfortunately, as we have also seen, the majority of students do not care about higher education as such; they are in college for a variety of extrinsic reasons, from earning the degree necessary for getting a salary, to evading the draft. There is no mass base for university reform in the universities.

Mainly, instead of working in their own bailiwick, the radical students have sought participatory democracy for poor people, organizing rent strikes, marching for Negro suffrage, opposing the welfare bureaucrats, and so forth. But again there is an inherent dilemma. Negroes claim, perhaps correctly, that middle-class whites cannot understand their problems, and if Negroes are going to run their own show they have to dispense with white helpers. The present policy of the Student Non-Violent Coordinating Committee is that Negroes must solve their own peculiar problems which are the only ones they care about and know anything about, and let their young white friends attend to changing the majority society. There is something in this. Certainly one would have expected northern radical students to get their heads broken in the cafeteria at the University of Mississippi, where they could talk with their peers face to face, as well as on the streets of country towns. And white southern liberals have desperately needed more support than they have gotten.

But pushed too far, separation consigns poor people to a second-class humanity. Some pressing problems are universal; the poor *must* care about them, e.g. the atom bombs. Many problems are grossly misconceived if looked at from a poor man's point of view; only a broad human point of view can save Negroes from agitating for exactly the wrong things, for example the Educational Parks, when what is needed in schooling is small human scale. Also, there is something spurious in the separation, for a poor minority in a highly technological and middle-class society will not engineer the housing and manufacture the cars, etc., that they intend to use. Finally, in fact the Negroes are, perhaps unfortunately, much more American than Negro. Especially in the North, they aspire to the same American package, though it makes even less sense for them than for anybody else. The Negro sub-culture that is talked up has about the same value as the adolescent sub-culture, with which it shares many traits in common; it has vitality and it does not add up to humanity.

As in other periods of moral change, only the young aristocrats and the intellectuals can *afford* to be disillusioned and profoundly radical.

In their own action organizations, the young are almost fanatically opposed to top-down direction. In several remarkable cases, gifted and charismatic student leaders have stepped down because their influence had become too strong. By disposition, without benefit of history, they have reinvented anarchist federation and a kind of Luxemburgian belief in spontaneous insurrection from below. They tend to the kind of non-violent resistance in which each one makes his own moral decision about getting his head broken, rather than submitting to rigid discipline. If there is violence, they will surely be guerillas rather than an organized army.

All this, in my opinion, probably makes them immune to takeover by centralists like the Marxists. When Trotskyists, for instance, infiltrate an organization and try to control it, the rest go home and activity ceases. When left to their own improvisation, however, the students seem surprisingly able to mount quite massive efforts, using elaborate techniques of communication and expert sociology. By such means they will never get power. But indeed, they do not want power, they want meaning.

The operative idea in participatory democracy is decentralizing, to multiply the number who are responsible, initiate and decide. Is this idea viable? (I have discussed the question at length in *People or Personnel*, arguing for a mixed system of central and decentral management by state, corporations, co-operatives, and independents.)

In principle, there are two opposite ways of decentralizing: either by dividing over-centralized organizations where it can be shown that decentral organization is more efficient in economic, social, and human costs—or at least not too inefficient; or by creating new small enterprises to fulfill needs that big organizations neglect or only pretend to fulfill. Obviously the first of these, to cut the present structures down to human size, is not in the power of students; but it happens that it does require a vast amount of empirical research and academic analysis, to find if, where, and how it is feasible. In the current American style, there is no such research and analysis, and on 150 campuses I have urged students to work on such problems, in business and engineering, education and communications, science and municipal administration. The students seem fascinated, but I do not know if they are coming across. (To say it wryly, there is an excellent organization called Students for a Democratic Society, but it is not enough evident that they are *students* for a democratic society.)

The opposite way of decentralizing, by creating new enterprises, better suits the student zeal for direct action, and they have applied it with a lot of energy and some inventiveness. It has been called "parallel development." Typically, students have set up a dozen little "free universities" in or next to established institutions, to teach in a more personal way and to deal with contemporary subjects that are not yet standard (e.g. "Castro's Cuba," "The Psychedelic Experience," "Sensitivity Training," "Theater of Participation"). Some of these courses are "action sociology," like organizing labor or community development. Students have established a couple of neighborhood radio stations, to broadcast local news and propaganda, and to give poor people a chance to talk into a microphone. They have set up parallel community projects to combat the welfare bureaucracy and channelize real needs and grievances. In the South they have helped form "freedom" political machines since the established machines are lily-white. They have offered to organize international service projects as an alternative to serving in the army. (As yet I have not heard of any feasible attempts at productive co-operatives or urban "intentional communities," and students do not seem to be interested in rural reconstruction.)

Looked at coldly, such parallel projects are pitifully insignificant and doomed to pass away like little magazines. Yet they are a thrilling revival of the seemingly dead spirit of American populism: get out from under the thumb of the barons and do it yourself. In my opinion the important step is the first one, to prove that such things are possible at all; then there is no telling how far they will go. There is a good hope for bringing to life many of our institutions by surrounding them with human enterprises, like a cambium or growing layer. The most telling criticism of an overgrown institution is a simpler one that works better.

This was the educational vision of John Dewey sixty years ago, of an industrial society continually democratically renewed by its young, freely educated and learning by doing. Progressive education, free-spirited but practical, was a typical populist conception. And the student movement can be regarded as progressive education at the college and graduate school level, where it begins to be indistinguishable from vocation and politics. It is the antithesis of a mandarin establishment and the social engineering that we now call education. Maybe this time around it will work.

So, describing American radical youth, and to a degree many other American youth, we have noticed their solidarity based on community rather than ideology, their style of direct and frank confrontation and personal contact, their democratic inclusiveness and aristocratic confidence careless of status, caste, or getting ahead, their selectivity and somewhat defiance of the affluent standard of living, their striving to be authentic and committed to their causes rather than merely belonging, their determination to have a say and their refusal to be pushed around or processed as standard items, their extreme distrust of top-down direction, their disposition to anarchist organization and direct action, their disillusion with the system of institutions and their belief that they can carry on major social functions in improvised parallel enterprises. Some of these traits, in my opinion, are natural to all unspoiled young people, but all of them are certainly in contradiction to the dominant organization of American society.

By and large this is as yet the disposition of a minority of the young, but it is the only articulate disposition that has emerged, and it has continuously emerged for the past ten years. It is a response not merely to "issues," like Civil Rights or Vietnam, but to deeply rooted defects in our present system and it will have an influence in the future. Those who think it is the usual "generational revolt," that will be absorbed as the students get "older and wiser," are whistling in the dark. If it is not taken seriously and compounded with, the result will be ever deepening alienation and, ultimately, worse disruption.

III

THE MORALITY OF
SCIENTIFIC TECHNOLOGY

| *1* |

The empty style of our society pervades most functions and institutions. In recent books I have described it in education and in our manner of social organization. In the next two lectures let me single out how we think about scientific technology and urbanization.

It is becoming common among social philosophers to treat the progress of science and technology as if it now goes on by itself and determines, like the Marxist "relations of production" everything else, but it is even less dependent on human choice. Whatever men wish, the independent development of scientific technology will shape the future. In more drastic versions of the theory, technology has already changed man into a product of itself, or man has become one special function in the technical system.

To Jacques Ellul, for instance, the American "empty society" can be more simply defined as an inevitable result of our high technology where, in his words, "work implies an absence of man, whereas previously it implied a presence." He means that a few motions of human labor and brains are selected and used mechanically and the rest must be deleted as an interference. (I have laid stress, rather, on the fact that large groups of people are excluded altogether, rather than exploited.) The controlling social organization, to which I have attributed independent influence, is to Ellul nothing but a function of technology itself, which in its essence standardizes, swallows up every case, and controls. And the populist and libertarian counter-forces that I described in my last lecture are to him whistling in the dark; he would say they are like his own complaints, "the work of some miserable intellectual who balks at technical progress. What good is it to pose questions of motive? Technique exists because it is technique."

Your own Marshall McLuhan of the University of Toronto pursues the same theme less pessimistically. He holds that the technical style of communications alters the nature of human perception and thought. It makes little difference, he says, what message or entertainment is broadcast on television, or whether the airways are a free forum or are regimented by monopolies, for the effect on human nature has already occurred because of the electronics medium itself. There is no point in making value judgments, and Professor McLuhan claims, at least in his delightful lectures, that he is morally neutral. (I think he is privately more disturbed.)

For Pierre Teilhard de Chardin, however, the new knowledge and technique constitute no less than a leap forward in organic evolution, transcending humanity as we have known it. Essentially, we now inhabit the Noösphere, the world-wide network of exchange of scientific information. Behavior no longer springs from animal humors, the personal conflict of passion and reason, or the politics of groups, but from the decision of the giant intellectual spirit. As a pious Christian, Teilhard de Chardin is enthusiastic about our new state of being, which is imbued with divine love. I am bemused at the nature of the love given or received, as either eros or agape, by what seem to be information-retrieval computers, but no doubt I fail to understand.

Here, then, are three strong minds who see essentially the same phenomenon, the system of scientific technology brooding free and determining the future, though they evaluate it differently as horrible, neutral, or blessed.

Yet the gross history of the past hundred years does not reveal this free floating technology. Scientific technology has certainly affected with its products, processes, and method most human beings and nearly every human function; in large areas it has created an artificial landscape and altered the balance of species; it has gotten off the planet and may destroy a good part of life on the planet. But invariably, in its quantity and in its direction of development, scientific technology has been in the employ of familiar human motives: either convenience, health, and excitement, or profits, power, and the aggrandizement of persons or groups. It has not been independent. On the contrary, it can be shown that the organization of recent scientific technology has, by and large, moved *away* from the traditional research autonomy of science and the principle of efficiency of technology, and under political, military, and economic control. If they were organized in their own terms, science and technology would be very differently organized. At present there is a waste of scientists' time and brains, and engineers are not allowed to decide like real professionals. And the increasing moral and ritual drives to standardization, rationalization, control, and self-control—what Max Weber called the Protestant Ethic—have not, in my opinion, been mainly due to technical routine but to new psychological obsessions to ward off insecurity, and compulsions to identify with power. People submit to inhuman routine out of fear and helplessness. And such routine is *not* of the essence of scientific technology. In the past both science and technology progressed better without such rituals, and they would do so now.

The present submissive state of scientific technology is a sad betrayal of the promise of independent scientific technology dreamed of by Thomas Huxley, Kropotkin, Veblen, John Dewey, Buckminster Fuller. They thought of science as humble, brave, and austere, and of technology as circumspect, neat, and serviceable. Working by its own morale, scientific technology should by now have simplified life rather than complicated it, emptied the environment rather than cluttered it, and educated an inventive and skillful generation rather than a conformist and inept one. It is the same with the effect of the technological development of communications, which Marshall McLuhan makes much of. Norbert Wiener used to point out that repetition of communication just increases the noise; in general, he said, there is more new information in a good poem than in a scientific report. Then, if our electronics media, and printing media, were doing their job, there would be less brainwashing and less gabble altogether; and Americans would not be spending six hours a day watching television and learning new habits of perception.

Jacques Ellul is mistaken about us miserable intellectuals. We complain not because we balk at technical progress but because we are disappointed in it.

| 2 |

Since I intend to complain about the present morale of scientific technology, let me first make clear what I do not complain of. Science *is* autonomous, because knowledge must be pursued for its own sake as part of the human adventure. Despite the risks involved, for instance in nuclear physics, most people honor this claim. I do. Also, technology is grounded in the human principle that you must give a workman the best tool, otherwise he is degraded. Despite the disruption sometimes involved, for instance in automation, most people are not Luddite and do not oppose technological advance. I do not.

Apart from these basic principles, however, the meaning of both science and technology has changed radically in the past fifty years. The often repeated statement that there are more scientists now alive than existed in all previous time ought to put us on the alert. How do these new multitudes of scientists take themselves? How are they in the world?

The present orthodox philosophy of scientific technology is that there is something called pure science or basic research which is morally neutral (except for the drive toward knowledge). Its inquiries may or may not lead to anything useful. Useful findings are "applied" and become part of the system of technology.

This is a peculiar position, and quite untraditional. What is neutral science? What is "applied" science? There *is* a difference between science and technology. It is reasonable to make the Aristotelian distinction between science as an act of wonder, disinterested curiosity, and esthetic construction, and technique as empirical rules of thumb for efficient practice; but, especially since the Renaissance, natural philosophers would not have made a big deal of such a distinction. Every theory has operations and apparatus; and a *reasoned* machine, like a steam engine or a storage battery, is a model of its theory, it is not an "application." It is the machine, not the theory, that is "applied" or put to use; this is a matter of choice and capitalization, not of technology as such. In fact, of course, science and technology have rarely gone separate ways anyway. It would be odd if they had. Agriculture, domestication of animals, measurement, building, machinery, navigation, transportation, communication, politics, war, pedagogy, medicine, all abound in controlled experiments that invite observation and testing; their difficulties and errors lead to new questions; new apparatus makes new theory. Contrariwise, any natural discovery is bound to be tried out; a model is built if only as a toy; and natural philosophers have always put their wits to work for industry, war, and medicine.

What is striking is that the doctrine of pure science and its moral neutrality always comes to the fore when scientists are assigned an official status and become salaried or subsidized, as in the German universities in the 19th century or in America today. It looks like an attempt, on the part of the scientists, to affirm their identity and protect themselves against officious interference by managers; but it is also, I am afraid, a self-deception and a hoax on the public. In America at present the great bulk of the billions of dollars for science is for research on extrinsically chosen problems, or even on particular products. A large part of the training of scientists in the universities is toward rather narrow technological expertness. Of nearly $20 billion marked for Research and Development, more than 90% is actually devoted to last-stage designing of hardware for production. Corporations mark up prices 1,000% in order, they say, to pay for basic research, but much of the research is to bypass other firms' patents. It is hard to credit that this kind of science is disinterested, and that promoters are not using the prestige of science as a talking-point.

It is taken for granted that amazing new developments will, if possible, at once be sequestered for military use and sometimes be made secret. Lasers will be death rays. The adventure of space will end in orbiting missile sites. The chief use of drugs that influence behavior will be to paralyze an enemy's will to resist. Anthropology is for counter-insurgency in primitive countries. And even the benevolent dolphins are to be trained as kamikaze submarines. Unfortunately this is not a caricature. Then it is dismaying to hear dedicated scientists explain that they are allowed perfect freedom to do restricted-publication research, and that any theoretical problem is indifferently good for the progress of science. The simplest explanation of the proposition that "there are more scientists alive today than existed up to now" is that business-as-usual has co-opted science. It is not that our society has become scientific, but that to be a "scientist" has become one of the acceptable roles.

Make an historical contrast. During the heroic age of modern science, say from the 16th through the 18th centuries, natural philosophers believed, uncritically and perhaps naively, that they directly confronted the nature of things and were in a kind of dialogue with Nature with a capital N. Each man was solitarily engaged in this open dialogue which might lead in any direction and hopefully surprisingly. But since all were engaged in a common enterprise on the frontier of knowledge, they eagerly communicated with one another, by publication, academies, depositing theses in university libraries, and enormous correspondence by letter. (Theorists of anarchism point to the sublime progress of modern science as a triumph of almost perfect co-ordination without top-down management.) The duty of publication to allow others to replicate the experiment became part of the definition of science; by it one became honored as the first. One is puzzled as to what restricted "scientific" information can mean. Does "replicable" mean "replicable by those cleared by the FBI"?

During the heroic period, science was not the social orthodoxy. Indeed, a disproportionate number of the natural philosophers were exploring forbidden territory and publishing defiantly. They were not getting any grants. Their image was rough and morose or moonstruck and bumbling. Their claim to freedom of inquiry was grounded not in a formal distinction about role but in a civil conflict about content; this confirmed their solidarity as a rebellious band. They were not morally neutral, nor was Nature morally neutral. Nature was wonderful or horrible or fascinating; she was surely beyond ordinary human uses, but abounding in moral as well as practical lessons for human betterment.

In their hearts, I am sure, many scientists still belong to the ancient band—just as many academics still vote with Abelard. Sometimes a great scientist talks the old language. Old-fashioned moralists hanker after a "natural ethics" or a "scientific way of life." But the official position is quite otherwise. Science is no longer a dialogue with Nature but a system of expanding knowledge that is self-contained and self-correcting, something like Hegel's progressive Absolute Idea. It is to this system that scientists are dedicated and which they serve with a special method practiced with considerable formal scrupulosity, so that it sometimes seems to be the correct method rather than the content that constitutes scientific truth. Rather than banded individuals, scientists have become an organized priesthood, and their system has become the major orthodoxy of modern society; it is the system of ideas that everybody—including myself—believes, whether or not one knows anything about it. The popular feeling about it contains both superstitious reverence and superstitious fear, and the current mass-education in science, we shall see, does not allay these. By and large, however, laymen are convinced that the progress of science will increase human happiness.

The shift of emphasis from an open dialogue of morose or

bumbling men with surprising Nature to an élite service to a progressive self-correcting system of knowledge has been accompanied by immense changes in the social organization of science, the role of the scientist, and the personal engagement of the man in the role. There is now less use for individual genius and hunch, and less opportunity for a personal ethical choice of a field of search as peculiarly fascinating, congenial, or "good." The issue is not, let me make it clear, whether the field is benevolent or useful, for it has often been the hallmark of scientific genius to research the senseless, the apparently trivial, the pathological. But I doubt that an older-style scientist paid attention to what *he* considered indifferent. His work was suffused with himself—and it is my Wordsworthian bias that scientists and artists, formed by their disinterested conversation with meaning, are usually good people. When a study is pursued as indifferently scientific, however, it is likely that extrinsic purposes will dictate the direction that is taken. Inevitably there is pressure for pay-off results rather than the wandering dialogue with surprise. A scientist becomes personnel, pursuing the goals of the organization.

More fatefully, as a great successful institution, the system of knowledge has become interlocked with the other great institutions of society, and the dominant style takes over. But this style was not devised for open dialogue with surprise; it was devised for cash-accounting, tax collection, military discipline, logistics, and mass-manufacture. Yet bureaucratic methods, it is believed, must somehow be appropriate to science too. Committees *must* be able to evaluate "projects." There *must* be profiles of gifted persons to support, and there *must* be university courses relevant to training others. Scientific thinking must be able to be parcelled out for efficient division of labor, and discoveries must occur on schedule: basic research, application, development, shaping up for production. With enough capital, one can mount a crash program and break through. To be serviceable, excellent scientists become administrators. Grant-getters, who are clever about the forms, become scientists. Corporations become impresarios for scientists. Scientific brains from other countries are bought up to work in the American style on American problems, seriously depoverishing their own peoples and precluding the development of various schools of thought. In the end, unless an hypothesis involves big cash, its author cannot afford to pursue it, though he used to love it.

The rationalization is ready to hand. Modern science *requires* big capital and big organization: take cyclotrons, moon shots, statistical surveys, universal information-retrieval. These are now science *par excellence*. There has been a re-definition. By-passing the experience of nearly four hundred years, the method of observation, analysis, deduction, and crucial experiment, we have amazingly come back full circle to the bureaucratic system of Bacon's *Novum Organum*, a dragnet of facts, stored, retrieved, and computed.

It is hard to know whether the corporate style of research is really the best one, for it tends to be self-proving. If brainy people agree to operate in this manner, they are not operating in some other manner and we do not know what they would be producing. Yet there is a curious body of evidence compiled by the Anti-Trust Committee of the United States Senate that shows rather overwhelmingly that in recent decades, even in practical Research and Development, the majority of significant advances have *not* come from big corporations and big universities, and have not been sponsored by foundations and government; they have still come from lonely (and often rejected) individuals, random amateur inventors, partnerships, tiny firms where the scientists, technicians, and craftsmen have a chance to talk to one another. One would expect this to be still more so in pure science.

Let me make myself clear once again. I am not opposed to heavy subsidies for science. It is one of the few things that make it worthwhile to be human; no price can be set on it. But, like art, perhaps science is hard to buy directly. Perhaps the best we can do is provide a decent society in which people can be themselves and children can grow up with their lively curiosity not too stultified. By definition, anything radically new must seem far-fetched except to its innovator. Certainly, as public policy—if only to increase the general cultivation—I would decentralize subsidies for science as widely as possible rather than, as we do, letting the money go to a few managers.

| 3 |

The morality of technology has also suffered a sea-change. Historically, the main origin of technology, in the work of craftsmen, miners, navigators, etc., provided a ready check on utility, efficiency, costs, and unforeseen effects. A secondary but important origin, in the natural experiments of Medieval and Renaissance alchemists and magicians, and perhaps physicians, provided no such check; the archetypal story is *The Sorcerer's Apprentice*. But therefore these groups had a strong ethical code, to permit only white magic, and prescribing Christian virtue as the priceless ingredient of the Philosopher's Stone. The Black Magician, like our Mad Scientist, was a villain for popular tragedy.

But even with the Industrial Revolution and the capitalization of machinery finally for cash profits rather than any other purpose, the market itself provided a check on the cheapness of the process and the utility of the products, although of course the whole system was notoriously careless of social costs and remote effects like enclosure, slums, air pollution, slag heaps, and the exhaustion of resources.

In principle, the discipline of Political Economy was, and is, supposed to regulate costs and benefits so as to guarantee the general good. In this discipline, the use and extent of a technology are subject to prudence, including safety, caution because of the possibility of unforeseen disadvantages, forethought to prevent over-commitment, and concern for the shape and function of the whole.

The history has been different. Political Economy did not devote itself to these matters but to the Gross National Product measured in cash; its advice was, and is, how to maximize technological growth to increase the abstract number of goods and services, whatever their quality or mutual contradictions. The check of the market has been weakened by subsidies, cost-plus contracts, monopolies, price-fixing, advertising, and the ignorance of consumers. And the various technologies increasingly interlock and depend on one another in a vast and recondite system, so that it has become fantastically difficult even for experts to decide what is by and large useful, cheap, or even safe. No one at all can trace the remote effects. And the control of the systems of technology, and of the systems of systems, is lodged in managers who finally are not interested in efficiency, not to speak of prudence. They are not in business for technical or citizenly reasons.

There ceases to be a morality of technique at all. A technician is hired to execute a detail of a program handed down to him. Apart from honestly trying to make his detail work, he is not entitled to criticize the program itself, in terms of its efficiency, common sense, beauty, effect on the community, or human scale. If management is not concerned with these either, a technician must often lend his wits to ludicrous contradictions. Cars are designed to go faster than it is safe to drive; food is processed to take out the nourishment; housing is expertly engineered to destroy neighborhoods; weapons are stockpiled that only a maniac would use. The ultimate of irresponsibility is that the engineer is not allowed to know what he is making, and we have had this too.

The interlocking of systems of technology without the direct check of personal acquaintance and use and political prudence creates a series of booby traps. Human scale may be quite disregarded, the time and energy that people actually have, the space they need to move in, and the rhythm or randomness with which they best operate. As the engineers design, we move, or sometimes can't move. Facilities are improved, but during the transition everybody is inconvenienced, and by the time the facility is completed it may be obsolescent. Fast trips are made possible by jet, but they prove to chop up our lives, to involve longer trips to airports and more waiting in terminals, so we have less free time. Business machines are installed and there is no longer any person from whom to get information or service for one's particular case. Cities spread so far that one can't get out of them; the country is deserted, so it is inefficient to provide means to get to it. Immense printing presses and other means of communication are devised, but to warrant such an investment of capital requires a mass audience, and it becomes hard to publish a serious book or transmit a serious message.

This sounds like chaos and modern life pretty nearly is. Apart from the cure of infectious diseases, some public services, and some household and farm equipment, there have been few recent advances in technique that have not proved to be a mixed bag in actual convenience. The great advantages, on balance, that came from universalizing basic conveniences or necessities, like electricity or water-supply, do not necessarily occur when massifying comforts and luxuries. The moral advantages, of enriched opportunity, are largely delusory. New opportunities do not make time available to enjoy them, and the chance for choice works out as superficial acquaintance and confusion. The marvels of fable, like flying through the air and seeing at a distance, have not proved so beautiful in reality. It is not hard to fantasize a use of our high technology that would be neat, uncomplicated, rich, and educative; but it is significant that utopian writers have stopped fantasizing in this direction. The fact remains that countries with a fifth or a tenth of our available technology have a way of life that is as good or better. I do not mean by this argument that we ought to cut back our technology, for human beings are bound to try out everything; but there is a problem here that we have no right to disregard as we do.

There is a new technological instrument of Political Economy that, ideally, could follow up some of the bewildering remote effects of innovation and detect the contradictions before they occur. This is computing costs and benefits. But it would have to be used authentically, focussing on what happens to people rather than on the convenience of the programmer or the aggrandizement of his system. Actual examples, in city planning, welfare, education, and foreign policy, have not been promising. They tend to omit from the equations factors that are unknown or stubbornly existing but excessively complicated, like individual differences, history, anomie, esthetics, the changeableness of policy. Then, though wise and impartial, the computer cannot give its best advice, which might often be: Not safe! Do not over-commit! Take it easy! Make it human! Instead, on the basis of puerile theories the programmers compute hard-nosed facts—"hard" facts are those with numbers attached—and bull through solutions to which human beings with the flexibility and fortitude that, God bless them, they have, adjust as best they can. The theories are thus confirmed.

| *4* |

Let me suggest two kinds of remedies to restore morale to scientific technology.

The first is to judge technology directly in terms of the moral criteria appropriate to it as a branch of practical philosophy. (How odd it is that today this obvious proposal has an odd ring!) Consider a possible list of criteria: Utility, Efficiency, Comprehensibility, Repairability, Flexibility, Amenity, Relevance, Modesty. By utility I mean, for instance, not pushing brand-name variety that makes no practical difference, whether in cars or drugs; not building obsolescence into expensive machines as if they were children's toys. By efficiency, I mean especially not over-riding the competence of technicians for the demands of the system; not disregarding thrift merely for convenience of administration—for instance, radical decentralization would often save on costs, as well as giving more control to those who do the work. By comprehensibility of design and concern for repairability we might alleviate the growing ineptitude of users and their bondage to repair-men and corporation service-stations. By flexibility we might stave off the increasingly frequent disasters that occur when interlocking systems of technology break down as a whole because of stoppage in a part; we might ease the entry of small enterprises and new regions into the economy. By amenity I mean concern for the whole range of feelings, not trivia like getting rid of billboards but the frayed nerves of traffic congestion, the destruction of cities by freeways, the chewing up of landscape for quick profits and transient convenience; not breeding out the taste and maturity of food for the convenience of processors and packagers. By relevance I mean concern for human scale, the time, size, energy, need for space of actual people, rather than calculating efficiency in abstract units of time, space, and energy. By modesty I mean not looming larger than a function warrants; caution about hasty commitment and over-commitment which by now have given us several generations of slums of engineering and piles of junk.

Another valuable consideration is to check competition in technology when an enterprise reaches a size and expense that makes it a natural monopoly that should be regulated in the public interest or nationalized. At present, I think, this applies especially to automating, where it is absurd to duplicate immense concentrations of tools—though it might be wise radically to decentralize the programming. It certainly applies to the crazy competition in exploring space.

Such a moral program is, I say, obvious; yet it is revolutionary and beyond our present political means. We can legislate, and exact penalties for, hazard, dishonest claims, and malpractice, but not for slovenliness, childish gluttony, callousness about the community, and indecency. Then the public becomes resigned. Nevertheless, in my opinion, a lot would be accomplished if technicians would take the lead and insist on acting like professionals. Common people would follow their lead and find political means. It is endlessly amazing how people spring back to life and good instincts if they see a glimmer of hope; there is a dramatic reversal in the opinion polls.

| 5 |

Much could be accomplished also by a different kind of mass education in science. I agree with the current wisdom that in a world pervaded with scientific technology, a great part of the curriculum must be scientific. The question is for what purpose and how. At present, there is some effort to teach the excitement and beauty of science and natural truth, and to get great men to give the TV lessons; this is laudable. But the chief purpose of most recent curriculum reform seems to me to be wrongheaded: it is to process Ph.D.'s or even to educate creative scientists; and the method is to teach the latest findings. The time of the vast majority who are not going on to scientific careers is wasted. Yet it is likely that most of those who are scientifically gifted will follow their bent anyway, quicker than they can in standard courses. We really do not know how to educate for creative genius. And it is not the case, as is claimed, that in a high technology average workmen need extensive scientific schooling; on the contrary, a few weeks to a year on the job, rather than years of lessons, is still the best way to train adequate low-level technicians.

Entirely neglected in the present curriculum, however, is what science *is*, as a way of being in the world. For instance, its austerity and honesty. For this, it is worse than useless for the average student to learn answers for the College Board examinations. This turns the whole thing into an abstraction or a hoax. The student ought instead to be scrupulously reporting what happened in his laboratory, why his experiment did *not* "work out"—of course, it has worked out some way or other.

There should be heavy emphasis on becoming at home in the actual technology, making model machines and learning to repair intelligently the usual standard machines. This was the scientific program of classical progressive education fifty years ago, to make critical and self-reliant users in an industrial society, to restore the sense of causal control of things rather than feeling powerless among things.

As part of social studies, a major subject should be the economics, politics, and organization of science and technology. I do not see any way for the average citizen to be able to judge the substantive issues relevant to the vast sums for research and development, medicine, space exploration, and technical training; but it would be helpful if he understood the interests and politics involved.

With regard to one area of science, however, it is essential that citizens do learn to judge the substantive issues. This is human ecology, combining physical science, physical and mental hygiene, sociology, and political economy, to analyze problems of urbanism, transportation, pollution, degenerative disease, mental disease, pesticides, indiscriminate use of antibiotics and other powerful drugs, and so forth. These matters are too important to be delegated to experts.

| 6 |

A few years ago, C. P. Snow created a stir by speaking of the chasm between "two cultures," that of the scientists and that of the humanists. Since we live in times dominated by scientific technology, he castigated the humanists especially for not knowing the other language. The point of this lecture has been that Sir Charles posed the issue wrongly. There is only one culture; and probably the scientific technologists have betrayed it most. Science, the dialogue with the unknown, is itself one of the humanities; and technology, practical efficiency, is a part of moral philosophy. Scientific technology has become isolated by becoming subject to the empty system of power: excluding, expanding, controlling. The remedy is for scientists and technicians to reassert their own proper principles and for ordinary people to stop being superstitious and to reassert their own control over their environment. Then there will be communication again.

IV

URBANIZATION AND
RURAL RECONSTRUCTION

| *1* |

I started the last lecture by pointing out how the present style of technology is regarded as an autonomous cause of history. It is even more so with urbanization. It is as if by a law of Nature—the favored metaphor is that the City is a Magnet—that by 1990 75% of the Americans will live in dense metropolitan areas. At present only about 6% are listed as rural.

Yet, first of all, the urbanization is not a necessity of technology. On the contrary, the thrust of modern technology, e.g. electricity, power tools, automobiles, distant communication, and automation, would seem to be disurbanization, dispersal of population and industry: this was the thinking of Marx and Engels, Kropotkin, Patrick Geddes, Frank Lloyd Wright, and other enthusiasts of scientific technology.

The urbanization is not a necessity of population growth. In fact, with the bankruptcy of small farming, vast beautiful regions have been depopulating and sometimes returning to swamp. American growth is supposed to level off, in fifty years, at 300 million, not a crowded number for such a big area. Yet the cities already show signs of overpopulation. They do not provide adequate city services and probably cannot provide them; they are vulnerable to urban catastrophes that might destroy thousands; it is prohibitively costly to live decently in them; and, in my opinion, though this is hard to prove, the crowding is already more than is permissible for mental health and normal growing up.

But it is as with the misuse of technology: the urbanization is mainly due not to natural or social-psychological causes, but to political policy and an economic style careless of social costs and even money costs. Certainly cities are magnets, of excitement and high culture, markets, centers of administration, and arenas to make careers; but these classical functions of cities of 100,000, capitals of their regions or nations, do not explain our sprawling agglomerations of many millions with no environment at all— Metropolitan New York City has 15 million, and most people cannot get out of it. In general, magnet or no magnet, average people have been content to remain in the provinces and poor people never leave the land, unless they are driven out by some kind of enclosure system that makes it impossible to earn a living. Especially today, when the great American cities are morally and physically less and less attractive, while the towns and farms, equipped with TV, cars, and small machines that really pay off in the country, are potentially more and more attractive.

Like the rest of our interlocking system, the American system of enclosure has been an intricate complex. National farm subsidies have favored big plantations which work in various combinations with national chain grocers who now sell 70% of the food—100 companies more than 50%. Chains and processors

rural depopulation = political

merge. The chains and processors have used the usual tactics to undercut independents and co-operatives. In the cities, Federally financed urban renewal has bulldozed out of existence small vegetable stores and grocers, who are replaced by the chains. Shopping centers on new subsidized highways bypass villages and neighborhoods. Guaranteed by Federal mortgages, real estate promoters transform farmland into suburbs. Farmers' markets disappear from the cities. As rural regions depopulate, railroads discontinue service, with the approval of the Interstate Commerce Commission. Rural schools are encouraged to degenerate, and land-grant colleges change their curricula toward urban occupations. The Army and Navy recruit apace among displaced farmboys (as they do also among city Negroes and Spanish-Americans).

All this, which sounds like Oliver Goldsmith and Wordsworth, is rationalized by saying, as usual, that it is efficient. One farmer can now feed thirty people. Yet strangely, though most of the farmers are gone and the take of the remaining farmers indeed tends to diminish every year, the price of food is *not* cheaper, it is about the same. The difference goes to the processors, packagers, transporters, and middle-men. (Of course, with the present war-time inflation, food prices have risen spectacularly; but again, a disproportionate amount of the rise is due to processing and distribution.) These operate in the established style. That is, the urbanization and rural depopulation is not technical nor economic but political. The remarkable increase in technical efficiency could just as well produce rural affluence or a co-operative society of farmers and consumers.

It has certainly not been technically efficient to bulldoze the garden land of the missions of Southern California into freeways, aircraft factories, and suburbs choked by smog, and then to spend billions of public money to irrigate deserts, robbing water from neighboring regions. The destruction of California is probably our worst example of bad ecology, but it is all of a piece with the destruction of the fish and trees, the excessive use of pesticides, the pollution of the streams, the strip-mining of the land.

Of course, the galloping urbanization has been worldwide and it is most devastating in the so-called underdeveloped countries which cannot afford such blunders. Here the method of enclosure is more brutal. Typically, my country or some other advanced nation introduces a wildly inflationary standard, e.g. a few jobs at $70 a week when the average cash income of a peon is $70 a year. If only to maintain their self-respect, peasants flock to the city where there are no jobs for them; they settle around it in shanty-towns, and die of cholera. They used to be poor but dignified and fed, now they are urbanized, degraded, and dead. Indeed, a striking contrast between the 18th-century enclosures and our own is that the dark Satanic mills needed the displaced hands, whereas we do not need unskilled labor. So along with our other foreign aid, we will have to bring literacy and other parts of the Great Society.

In the United States, though we collect the refugees in slums, we do not permit them to die of starvation or cholera. But I am again bemused at the economics of the welfare procedure. For instance, first, for 60 years, by a mercantilism worthy of George III, we destroyed Puerto Rican agriculture and prevented an industrialism solidly based at the bottom; then recently we allowed 800,000 Puerto Ricans—a majority with some rural back-ground—to settle in New York City, the most expensive and morally strange possible environment, rather than bribing them to disperse. When share-cropping failed in the South, rather than subsidizing subsistence farming and making a try at community development, we give relief-money and social-work in Chicago and Los Angeles. Take it at its crudest level: if the cheapest urban public housing costs $20,000 a unit to build, and every city has a housing shortage, would it not be better to give farmers $1,000 a year for twenty years, just for rent, to stay home and drink their own water?

| 2 |

Partly our urban troubles spring from no planning, partly from just the planning that there is. When concrete observation and sympathy for human convenience are called for, there is no fore-thought and we drift aimlessly; when there is planning, it is abstract and aimed at keeping things under control. For instance, in the last sentence of my previous paragraph, I contrast "$20,000 a unit" with "staying home," but no such equation could occur in urban planning, for the word "home" has ceased to exist; the term is "dwelling unit" or D.U. The D.U. is analyzed to meet certain biological and sociological criteria, and it is also restricted by certain rules, e.g. in public housing one cannot nail a picture on the wall, climb a tree in the landscaping, keep pets, engage in immoral sex, or get a raise in salary. There is a theory, as yet unproved, that planning can dispense with the concept "home"; it is a debased version of Le Corbusier's formula that a house is a machine for living, equal for any tenant and therefore controlled to be interchangeable. But is it the case that people thrive without an own place, unanalyzable because it is the matrix in which other functions occur and is idiosyncratic? Maybe they can, maybe they can't. My point is not that the D.U. is not so good as the shack in a white supremacist county down South; it is better. But that home in a shack plus $1,000 a year to improve it is much better even down South, where money talks as loud as elsewhere.

Another term that has vanished from planning vocabulary is "city." Instead there are urban areas. There is no longer an art of city-planning but a science of urbanism, which analyzes and relates the various urban functions, taking into account priorities and allocating available finances. There is no architectonic principle of civic identification or community spirit which the planner shares as a citizen and in terms of which he makes crucial decisions, including uneconomic choices. Such a principle is perhaps unrealistic in a natural culture, economy, and technology; we are citizens of the United States, not of New York City. In planning, the interstate and national highway plan will surely be laid down first and local amenity or existing situations must conform to it; and Washington's ideas about the type of financing, and administration of housing will surely determine what is built. (Oddly, just in such urban functions as highways and housing, local patriotism and neighborhood feeling suddenly assert themselves and exert a veto, though rarely providing a plan of their own.)

But is it the case that urban areas, rather than cities, are governable? Every municipality deplores the lack of civic pride, for instance in littering and vandalism, but it is a premise of its own planning. Anomie is primarily giving up on the immediate public environment: the children are bitten by rats, so why bother? The river stinks, so why bother? This kind of depression can go as far as tuberculosis, not to speak of mental disease. In my opinion it is particularly impossible for the young to grow up without a community or local patriotism, for the locality is their only real environment. In any case, when the going gets rough, which happens more and more frequently in American cities, poor people retreat into their neighborhoods and cry "It's ours!" or they burn them because they are not citizens in their own place. The middle class, as usual, makes a more rational choice: since the center offers neither home nor city nor an acceptable environment for their children, they leave it, avoiding its jurisdiction, taxes, and responsibilities, but staying near enough to exploit its jobs and services.

It is painfully reminiscent of imperial Rome, the return of the farmland to swamp and the flight of the *optimati* from the city center. The central city is occupied by a stinking mob who can hardly be called citizens, and the periphery by the knights and senators who are no longer interested in being citizens. This is an urban area.

| 3 |

Moral defects are disastrous in the long run; but American cities are also vulnerable to more immediate dangers, to life and limb. In my own city of New York, during the past year we have been visited by ten critical plagues, some of them temporary emergencies that could recur at any time, some abiding sores that are getting worse. It is interesting to list these and notice the responses of New Yorkers to them.

There was a power failure that for a few hours blacked out everything and brought most activity to a stop. There was a subway and bus strike that for a couple of weeks slowed down everything and disrupted everybody's business. There was a threatened water shortage persisting for four years and which, if the supply had really failed, would probably have made the city unlivable. In these "objective" emergencies, the New Yorkers responded with fine citizenship, good humor, and mutual aid. By and large, they remember the emergencies as better than business as usual. Everybody was in the same boat.

(By contrast, during the long heat wave of last summer—no joke in the asphalt oven of a giant city—there was less enthusiasm. In Chicago it was the occasion for a bad race riot, when a fire hydrant was shut off in a Negro neighborhood but, it was said, not in a white neighborhood. In New York it came out that the poor in public housing could not use air-conditioners because of inadequate wiring. Evidently, everybody was not in the same boat.)

The rivers and bays are polluted and often stink; in a huge city with no open space and few facilities for recreation, this is a calamity. The air is bad but not critical, so I will not include it. The congestion is critical. Traffic often hardly moves, and new highways will only make the situation worse; there is no solution but to ban private cars, but no politician has the nerve to do it. As for human crowding, it is hard to know at what density people can no longer adapt, but there must be a point at which there are too many signals and the circuits become clogged, and where people do not have enough social space to feel self-possessed. In some areas, in my opinion, we have passed that point. In Harlem, there are 67,000 to the square mile; people live two and three to a room; and the average child of 12 will not have been half a mile from home.

Toward these abiding ills, the attitude of New Yorkers is characteristically confused. They overwhelmingly, and surprisingly, vote a billion dollars to clean up the pollution; they co-operate without grumbling with every gimmick to speed up traffic (though taxi-drivers tell me most of them are a lot of nonsense); they are willing to pay bigger bills than anywhere else for public housing and schools. As people they are decent. But they are entirely lacking in determination to prevent the causes and to solve the conditions; they do not believe that anything will be done, and they accept this state of things. As citizens they are washouts.

Finally, there are the plagues that indicate breakdown, psychopathology and sociopathology. There are estimated 70,000 dope-addicts, with the attendant desperate petty burglary. The juvenile delinquency starts like urban juvenile delinquency of the past, but it persists into addiction or other social withdrawal because there is less neighborhood support and less economic opportunity. Families have now grown up for several generations dependent on relief, reformatories, public hospitals, and asylums as the normal course of life. A psychiatric survey of midtown Manhattan has shown that 75% have marked neurotic symptoms and 25% need psychiatric treatment, which is of course unavailable.

Given the stress of such actual physical and psychological dangers, we can no longer speak, in urban sociology, merely of urban loneliness, alienation, mechanization, delinquency, class and racial tensions, and so forth. Anomie is one thing; fearing for one's life and sanity is another. On the present scale, urbanization is an unique phenomenon and we must expect new consequences. To put it another way, it becomes increasingly difficult for candid observers to distinguish between populist protest, youth alienation, delinquency, mental disease, civil disobedience, and outright riot. All sometimes seem to be equally political; at other times, all seem to be merely symptomatic.

| 4 |

Inevitably, the cities are in financial straits. (At a recent Senate hearing, Mayor Lindsay of New York explained that to make the city "livable" would require $50 billion more in the next ten years, over and above the normal revenue.) Since they are not ecologically viable, the costs for services, transportation, housing, schooling, welfare, and policing steadily mount with diminishing benefits. Meantime, the blighted central city provides less revenue; the new middle class, as we have seen, pays its taxes in suburban counties; and in the state legislatures the rural counties, which are over-represented because of the drastic shift in population, are stingy about paying for specifically urban needs, which are indeed out of line in cost. Radical liberals believe, of course, that all troubles can be immensely helped if urban areas get much more money from national and state governments, and they set store by the re-apportionment of the state legislatures as ordered by the Supreme Court. In my opinion, if the money is spent for the usual liberal social-engineering, for more freeways, bureaucratic welfare and schooling, bulldozing Urban Renewal, subsidized suburbanization, and police, it will not only fail to solve the problems but will aggravate them, it will increase the anomie, the crowding.

The basic error is to take the present urbanization for granted, both in style and extent, rather than to rethink it: (1) To alleviate anomie, we must, however "inefficient" and hard to administer it may be, avoid the present massification and social engineering; we must experiment with new forms of democracy, so that the urban areas can become cities again and the people citizens. I shall return to this subject in the following lectures. But (2) to relieve the absolute over-crowding that has already occurred or is imminent, nothing else will do but a certain amount of dispersal, which is unlikely in this generation in the United States. It involves rural reconstruction and the building up of the country towns that are their regional capitals. (I do not mean New Towns, Satellite Towns, or Dormitory Towns.) In Scheme II of *Communitas*, my brother and I have fancifully sketched such a small regional city, on anarcho-syndicalist principles, as a symbiosis of farm and city activities and values. (Incidentally, Scheme II would make a lot of sense in Canada.) But this is utopian. In this lecture let me rather outline some principles of rural reconstruction for the United States at present, during a period of excessive urbanization.

Liberals, when they think about urbanization, either disregard the country or treat it as an enemy in the legislature. A result of such a policy is to aggravate still another American headache, depressed rural areas. The few quixotic friends of rural reconstruction, on the other hand, like Ralph Borsodi and the people of the Green Revolution, cut loose from urban problems altogether as from a sinking ship. But this is morally unrealistic, since in fact serious people cannot dissociate themselves from the main problems of society; they would regard themselves as deeply useless—just as small farmers do consider themselves. A possible basis of rural reconstruction, however, is for the country to help with urban problems, where it can more cheaply and far more effectively, and thus to become socially important again. (An heroic example is how the Israeli kibbutzim helped with the influx of the hundreds of thousands of Oriental Jews who came destitute and alien.)

Radicals, what I have called the wave of urban populists, the students, Negroes, radical professors, and just irate citizens, are on this subject no better than the liberals. They are busy and inventive about new forms of urban democracy, but they are sure to call the use of the country and rural reconstruction reactionary. Typically, if I suggest to a Harlem leader that some of the children might do better boarding with a farmer and going to a village school, somewhat like children of the upper middle class, I am told that I am downgrading Negroes by consigning them to the sticks. It is a curious reversal of the narrowness of the agrarian populism of eighty years ago. At that time the farmers lost out by failing to ally themselves with city industrial workers, who were regarded as immoral foreigners and coolie labor. Now farmers are regarded as backward fools, like one's sharecropper father. Although the urban areas are patently unlivable, they have narrowed their inhabitants' experience so that no other choice seems available.

In Canada, a more rational judgment is possible. You have a rural ratio—15-20%, including independent fishermen, lumbers, etc.—that we ought to envy. Your cities, though in need of improvement, are manageable in size. There is still a nodding acquaintance between city and country. I urge you not to proceed down our primrose path, but to keep the ratio you have and, as your technology and population grow, to work out a better urban-rural symbiosis.

| 5 |

Traditionally in the United States, farming as a way of life and the maintenance of a high rural ratio have been regarded as the source of all moral virtue and political independence; but by and large public policy has tended to destroy them. The last important attempt to increase small farming was during the Great Depression when subsistence farms were subsidized as a social stabilizer, preferable to shanties in the park and breadlines. The program lapsed with the war-production prosperity that we still enjoy, and for twenty years, as we have seen, public policy has conspired to liquidate rural life completely. There were no Jeffersonian protests when President Johnson declared two years ago that it is his intention to get two-million more families off the land. (Lo and behold, *this* year LBJ has made a speech for massive migration *to* the land!) Nevertheless, in the present emergency of excessive urbanization, let me offer five ideas for rural reconstruction:

(1) At once re-assign to the country urban services that can be better performed there. Especially to depopulating areas, to preserve what there is. And do not do this by setting up new urban-run institutions in the country, but using local families, facilities and institutions, administered by the new underemployed county agents, Farmers Union, 4-H Clubs, and town governments. Consider a few examples:

For a slum child who has never been half a mile from home, a couple of years boarding with a farm family and attending a country school is what anthropologists call a culture-shock, opening wide the mind. The cost per child in a New York grade school is $850 a year. Let us divide this sum equally between farmer and local school. Then, the farmer gets $30 a week for three boarders (whom he must merely feed well and not beat), and add on some of the children's welfare money, leaving some for the mothers in the city. With a dozen children, $5,000, the under-used school can buy a new teacher or splendid new equipment. Add on the school lunch subsidy.

In New York City or Chicago, $2,500 a year of welfare money buys a family destitution and undernourishment. In beautiful depopulating areas of Vermont, Maine, or upper New York State, or southern Iowa and northern Wisconsin, it is sufficient for a decent life and even owning a house and land. (Indeed, if we had a reasonable world, the same sum would make a family quite well-to-do in parts of Mexico, Greece, or even Ireland.)

The same reasoning applies to the aged. Given the chance, many old people would certainly choose to while away the years in a small village or on a farm, where they would be more part of life and might be useful, instead of in an institution with occupational therapy.

Vacations are an expensive function in which the city uses the country and the country the city. In simpler times, when the rural ratio was high, people exchanged visits with their country cousins or sent the children "to the farm." At present, vacations from the city are largely spent at commercial resorts that tend rather to destroy the country communities than to support them. There are many ways to revive the substance of the older custom, and it is imperative to do so in order to have some social space and escape, which, needless to say, the urbanized resorts do not provide.

Here is a more touchy example: the great majority of inmates in our vast public mental institutions are harmless themselves but in danger on the city streets. Many, perhaps most, rot away without treatment. A certain number would be better off—and there would be more remissions—if they roamed remote villages and the countryside as the local eccentrics or loonies, and if they lived in small nursing homes or with farm families paid well to fetch them home. (I understand that this system worked pretty well in Holland.)

(2) Most proposals like these, however, require changes in jurisdiction and administrative purpose. A metropolitan school board will not give up a slum child, though the cost is the same and the classrooms are crowded. No municipality will pay welfare money to a non-resident to spend elsewhere. (I do not know the attitude in this respect of frantically overworked mental hospitals, which do try to get the patients out.) Besides, often in the American federal system, one cannot cross state lines: a New York child would not get state education aid in Vermont.

So, in conditions of excessive urbanization, let us define a "region" symbiotically rather than economically or technologically. It is the urban area and the surrounding country *with a contrasting way of life and different conditions* that can therefore help solve urban human problems. This classical conception of the capital and its province is the opposite of usual planning. In terms of transportation and business, planners regard the continuous conurbation from north of Boston to Washington as one region and ask for authority to override state and municipal boundaries; for tax purposes, New York would like authority to treat the suburban counties as part of the New York region. These things are, I think, necessary; but their effect must certainly be to increase the monstrous conurbation and make it even more homogeneous. If I regard Vermont, northern New Hampshire and New York, and central Pennsylvania as part of the urban area, however, the purpose of the regional authority is precisely to prevent conurbation and strengthen locality, to make the depopulating areas socially important by their very difference.

(3) The chief use of small farming, at present, cannot be for cash but for its independence, simplicity, and abundance of subsistence; and to make the countryside beautiful. Rural reconstruction must mainly depend on other sources of income, providing urban social services and, as is common, part-time factory work. Nevertheless, we ought carefully to re-examine the economics of agriculture, the real costs and the quality of the product. With some crops, certainly with specialty and gourmet foods, the system of intensive cultivation and hothouses serving farmers' markets in the city and contracting with restaurants and hotels, is quite efficient; it omits processing and packaging, cuts down on the cost of transportation, and is indispensable for quality. The development of technology in agriculture has no doubt been as with technology in general, largely determined by economic policy and administration. If there were a premium on small intensive cultivation, as in Holland, technology would develop to make it the "most efficient."

In our big cities, suburban development has irrevocably displaced nearby truck gardening. But perhaps in the next surrounding ring, now often devastated, small farming can revive even for cash.

(4) National TV, movies, news services, etc., have offset provincial narrowness and rural idiocy, but they have also had a more serious effect of brainwashing than in, at least, the big cities which have more intellectual resistance. Country culture has quite vanished. Typical are the county papers which now contain absolutely nothing but conventional gossip notes and ads.

Yet every region has seventeen TV channels available, of which only three or four are used by the national networks. (I think the Americans would be wise to have also a public national channel like CBC.) Small broadcasting stations would be cheap to run if local people would provide the programs. That is, there is an available community voice if there were anything to say. The same holds for little theaters and local newspapers. I have suggested elsewhere that such enterprises, and small design offices and laboratories, could provide ideal apprenticeships for bright high school and college youth who are not academic and who now waste their time and the public money in formal schools. These could be adolescents either from the country or the city. (In New York, it costs up to $1,400 a year to keep an adolescent in a blackboard jungle.) Perhaps if communities got used to being participants and creators rather than spectators and consumers of canned information, entertainment, and design, they might recall what they are about.

All such cultural and planning activities, including the sociology of the urban services, ought to be the concern of the landgrant college. At present in the United States we have pathetically perverted this beautiful institution. The land-grant college, for "mechanics and agriculture," was subsidized to provide cultural leadership for its region, just as the academic university was supposed to be international and to teach humanities and humane professions. But now our land-grant and other regional colleges have lost their community function and become imitations of the academic schools, usually routine and inadequate, while the academic universities have alarmingly been corrupted to the interests of the nation and the national corporations. Naturally, the more its best young are trained to be personnel of the urban system, the more the country is depleted of brains and spirit.

(5) The fruition of rural reconstruction would consist of two things: a strong co-operative movement and a town-meeting democracy that makes sense, in its own terms, on big regional and national issues. A century ago Tocqueville spoke with admiration of how the Americans formed voluntary associations to run society; they were engaged citizens. This would seem to be the natural

tendency of independent spirits conscious of themselves as socially important; they can morally afford to pool their resources for their own purposes. At present it is dismaying to see individual farmers, almost on the margin, each buying expensive machinery to use a few days a year, and all totally unable to co-operate in processing or distribution. They are remarkably skillful men in a dozen crafts and sciences, but they are like children. They feel that they do not count for anything. And unable to co-operate with one another, they cannot compete and they do not count for anything. Correspondingly, their political opinions, which used to be stubbornly sensible though narrow, are frightened, and parrot the national rhetoric as if they never engaged in dialogue and had no stake of their own.

| 6 |

To sum up, in the United States the excessive urbanization certainly cannot be thinned out in this generation and we are certainly in for more trouble. In some urban functions, perhaps, like schooling, housing, and the care of mental disease, thinning out by even a few percent would be useful; and the country could help in this and regain some importance in the big society, which is urban. Nevertheless, the chief advantage of rural reconstruction is for its own sake, as an alternative way of life. It could develop a real countervailing power because it is relatively independent; it is not like the orthodox pluralism of the sociologists that consists of differences that make no difference because the groups depend on one another so tightly that they form a consensus willy-nilly.

The Scandinavian countries are a good model for us. By public policy over a century and a half, they have maintained a high rural ratio; for a century they have supported a strong co-operative movement; and they have devised a remarkably various and thoughtful system of education. These things are not unrelated, and they have paid off in the most decent advanced society that there is, with a countervailing mixed economy, a responsible bureaucracy, and vigilant citizens.

V

THE PSYCHOLOGY OF
BEING POWERLESS

| *1* |

Americans believe that the great background conditions of modern life are beyond our power to influence. The abuse of technology is autonomous and cannot be checked. The galloping urbanization is going to gallop on. Our over-centralized administration, both of things and men, is impossibly cumbersome and costly, but we cannot cut it down to size. These are inevitable tendencies of history. More dramatic inevitabilities, in the popular belief, are the explosions, the scientific explosion and the population explosion. And there are more literal explosions, the dynamite accumulating in the slums of a thousand cities and the accumulating stockpiles of nuclear bombs in nations great and small. Our psychology, in brief, is that history is out of control. It is no longer something that we make but something that happens to us. Politics is not prudent steering in difficult terrain, but it is—and this is the subject of current political science—how to get power and keep power, even though the sphere of effective power is extremely limited and it makes little difference who is in power. The psychology of historical powerlessness is evident in the reporting and the reading of newspapers: there is little analysis of how events are building up, but we read—with excitement, spite, or fatalism, depending on our characters—the headlines of crises for which we are unprepared. Statesmen cope with emergencies, and the climate of emergency is chronic.

I have been trying to show that some of these historical conditions are not inevitable at all but are the working out of willful policies that aggrandize certain interests and exclude others, that subsidize certain styles and prohibit others. But of course, *historically*, if almost everybody believes the conditions are inevitable, including the policy makers who produce them, then they are inevitable. For to cope with emergencies does not mean, then, to support alternative conditions, but further to support and institutionalize the same conditions. Thus, if there are too many cars, we build new highways; if administration is too cumbersome, we build in new levels of administration; if there is a nuclear threat, we develop anti-missile missiles; if there is urban crowding and anomie, we step up urban renewal and social work; if there are ecological disasters because of imprudent use of technology, we subsidize Research and Development by the same scientific corporations working for the same ecologically irrelevant motives; if there is youth alienation, we extend and intensify schooling; if the nation-state is outmoded as a political form, we make ourselves into a mightier nation-state.

In this self-proving round, the otherwise innocent style of input-output economics, games-theory strategy, and computerized social science becomes a trap. For the style dumbly accepts the self-proving program and cannot compute what is not mentioned.

Then the solutions that emerge ride even more roughshod over what has been left out. Indeed, at least in the social sciences, the more variables one can technically compute, the less likely it is that there will be prior thinking about their import, rather than interpretation of their combination. Our classic example—assuming that there will be a future period to which we provide classic examples—is Herman Kahn on Thermonuclear War.

In this lecture, therefore, I will no longer talk about the error of believing that our evils are necessary, but stick to the more interesting historical fact of that belief. What is the psychology of feeling that one is powerless to alter basic conditions? What is it as a way of being in the world? Let me list half a dozen kinds of responses to being in a chronic emergency; unfortunately, in America they are exhibited in rather pure form. I say unfortunately, because a pure response to a chronic emergency is a neurotic one; healthy human beings are more experimental or at least muddling. Instead of politics, we now have to talk psychotherapy.

| 2 |

By definition, governors cannot forfeit the symbol that everything is under control, though they may not think so. During President Kennedy's administration, Arthur Schlesinger expressed the problem poignantly by saying, "One simply *must* govern." The theme of that administration was to be "pragmatic"; but by this they did not mean a philosophical pragmatism, going toward an end in view from where one in fact is and with the means one has; they meant turning busily to each crisis as it arose, so that it was clear that one was not inactive. The criticism of Eisenhower's administration was that it was stagnant. The new slogan was "get America moving."

This was rather pathetic; but as the crises have become deeper, the response of the present administration is not pathetic but, frankly, delusional and dangerous. It is to *will* to be in control, without adjusting to the realities. They seem to imagine that they will in fact buy up every economy, police the world, social-engineer the cities, school the young. In this fantasy they employ a rhetoric of astonishing dissociation between idea and reality, far beyond customary campaign oratory. For example, they proclaim that they are depolluting streams, but they allot no money; forty "demonstration cities" are to be made livable and show the way, but the total sum available is $1.5 billion (we saw that Mayor Lindsay asked for $50 billion for New York alone); the depressed area of Appalachia has been reclaimed, but the method is an old highway bill under another name; poor people will run their own programs, but any administrator is fired if he tries to let them; they are suing for peace, but they despatch more troops and bombers. This seems to be just lying but, to my ear, it is nearer to magic thinking. The magic buoys up the self-image; the activity is either nothing at all or brute force to make the problem vanish.

In between the ideality and the brutality there occurs a lot of obsessional warding off of confusion by methodical calculations that solve problems in the abstract, in high modern style. A precise decimal is set beyond which the economy will be inflationary, but nobody pays any mind to it. We know at what average annual income how many peoples cause what percentage of disturbances. A precise kill-ratio is established beyond which the Viet Cong will fold up, but they don't. Polls are consulted for the consensus, like the liver of sheep, without noticing signs of unrest and even though the administration keeps committing itself to an irreversible course that allows for no choice. And they are everlastingly righteous.

In more insane moments, however, they manufacture history

out of the whole cloth, so there is no way of checking up at all. They create incidents in order to exact reprisals; they invent (and legislate about) agitators for demonstrations and riots that are spontaneous; they project bogey-men in order to arm to the teeth. Some of this, to be sure, is cynical, but that does not make it less mad; for, clever at it or not, they still avoid the glaring realities of world poverty, American isolation, mounting urban costs, mounting anomie, and so forth. I do not think the slogan, "The Great Society," is cynical; it is delusional.

Perhaps the epitome of will operating in panic—like a case from a textbook in abnormal psychology—has been the government's handling of the assassination of John Kennedy. The Warren Commission attempted to "close" the case, to make it not exist in the public mind. Thus it hastily drew firm conclusions from dubious evidence, disregarded counter-evidence, defied physical probabilities, and even may have accepted manufactured evidence. For a temporary lull it has run the risk of total collapse of public trust that may end up in a Dreyfus case.

| *3* |

Common people, who do not have to govern, can let themselves feel powerless and resign themselves. They respond with the familiar combination of not caring and, as a substitute, identifying with those whom they fancy to be powerful. This occurs differently, however, among the poor and the middle class.

The poor simply stop trying, become dependent, drop out of school, drop out of sight, become addicts, become lawless. It seems to be a matter of temperature or a small incident whether or not they riot. As I have said before, in anomic circumstances it is hard to tell when riot or other lawlessness is a political act toward a new set-up and when it is a social pathology. Being powerless as citizens, poor people have little meaningful structure in which to express, or know, what they are after. The concrete objects of their anger make no political sense: they are angry at themselves or their own neighborhoods, at white people passing by, at Jewish landlords and shopkeepers. More symbolic scapegoats like either "the capitalist system" or "communism" do not evoke much interest. One has to feel part of a system to share its bogey-men or have a counter-ideology, and by and large the present-day poor are not so much exploited as excluded.

But to fill the void, they admire, and identify with, what is strong and successful, even if—perhaps especially if—it is strong and successful at their own expense. Poor Spanish youth are enthusiastic about our mighty bombs and bombers, though of course they have no interest in the foreign policy that uses them. (If anything, poor people tend to be for de-escalation and peace rather than war.) Readers of the *Daily News* are excited by the dramatic confrontation of statesmen wagging fingers at each other. Negroes in Harlem admire the Cadillacs of their own corrupt politicians and racketeers. Currently there is excitement about the words "Black Power," but the confusion about the meaning is telling: in the South, where there is little Negro anomie, Black Power has considerable political meaning; in the northern cities it is a frantic abstraction. Similarly, the contrary word "Integration" makes economic and pedagogic sense if interpreted by people who have some feeling of freedom and power, but if interpreted by resentment and hopelessness it turns into a fight for petty victories or spite, which are not political propositions, though they may be good for the soul.

The anomie of middle-class people, on the other hand, appears rather as their privatism; they retreat to their families and consumer goods where they still have some power and choice. It is always necessary to explain to non-Americans that middle-class Americans are not so foolish and piggish about their Standard of Living as it seems; it is that the Standard of Living has to provide all the achievement and value that are open to them. But it is a strange thing for a society to be proud of its Standard of Living, rather than taking it for granted as a background for worthwhile action.

Privacy is purchased at a terrible price of anxiety, excluding, and pettiness, the need to delete anything different from oneself and to protect things that are not worth protecting. Nor can they be protected; few of the suburban homes down the road, that look so trim, do not have cases of alcoholism, insanity, youngsters on drugs, or in jail for good or bad reasons, ulcers, and so forth. In my opinion, middle-class squeamishness and anxiety, a kind of obsessional neurosis, are a much more important cause of segregation than classical race-prejudice which is a kind of paranoia that shows up most among failing classes, bankrupt small property owners, and proletarians under competitive pressure. The squeamishness is worse, for it takes people out of humanity, whereas prejudice is at least passionate. Squeamishness finally undercuts even the fairness and decency that we expect from the middle class.

The identification with power of the powerless middle class is also characteristic. They do not identify with brutality, big men, or wealth, but with the efficient system itself, which is what renders *them* powerless. And here again we can see the sharp polarity between those who are not politically resigned and those who are. Take the different effects of what is called education. On the one hand, the universities, excellent students and distinguished professors, are the nucleus of opposition to our war policy. On the other hand, in general polls there is always a dismaying correlation between years of schooling and the "hard line" of bombing China during the Korean War or bombing

Hanoi now. But this is not because the educated middle class is rabidly anti-communist, and certainly it is not ferocious; rather, it is precisely because it is rational, it approves the technically efficient solution that does not notice flesh and blood suffering. In this style the middle class feels it has status, though no more power than anybody else. No doubt these middle-class people are influenced by the magazines they read, which explain what *is* efficient; but they are influenced because they are "thinking" types, for whom reality is what they read.

The bathos of the irresponsible middle class is the nightly TV newscast on our national networks. This combines commercials for the High Standard of Living, scenes of war and riot, and judicious pro-and-con commentary on what it all means. The scenes arouse feeling, the commentary provokes thought, the commercials lead to action. It is a total experience.

| 4 |

Let me illustrate the anomic psychology with another example, for it has come to be accepted as the normal state of feeling rather than as pathological. (I apologize to the Canadian audience for choosing my example again from the Vietnam War. But my country is bombing and burning those people, and my friends and I are unable to prevent it.)

During the hearings on Vietnam before the Senate Foreign Relations Committee, Senator Dodd of Connecticut was asked what he thought of the sharp criticism of the government. "It is the price we pay," he said, "for living in a free country." This answer was routine and nobody questioned it. Yet what an astonishing evaluation of the democratic process it is, that free discussion is a weakness we must put up with in order to avoid the evils of another system! To Milton, Spinoza, or Jefferson free discussion was the strength of a society. Their theory was that truth had power, often weak at first but steady and cumulative, and in free debate the right course would emerge and prevail. Nor was there any other method to arrive at truth, since there was no other authority to pronounce it than all the people. Thus, to arrive at wise policy, it was essential for everybody to say his say, and the more disparate the views and searching the criticism the better.

Instead, Senator Dodd seems to have the following epistemology of democracy: We elect an administration and it, through the intelligence service, secret diplomacy, briefings by the Department of Defense and other agencies, comes into inside information that enables it alone to understand the situation. In principle we can repudiate its decisions at the next election, but usually they have led to commitments and actions that are hard to repudiate. Implicit is that there is a permanent group of selfless and wise public servants, experts and impartial reporters, who understand the technology, strategy, and diplomacy that we cannot understand, and therefore we must perforce do what they advise. To be sure, they continually make bad predictions and, on the evidence, they are not selfish but partial or at least narrow in their commercial interests and political outlook. Yet this does not alter the picture, for if the President goes along with them, outside criticism is irrelevant anyway and no doubt misses the point, which, it happens, cannot be disclosed for reasons of national security. And surely irrelevant discussion is harmful because it is divisive. But it is the price we pay for living in a free country.

What can be the attraction of such a diluted faith in democracy? It is what is appropriate in a chronic low-grade emergency. In an emergency it is rational, and indeed natural, to concentrate temporary power in a small center, as the ancient Romans appointed dictators, to decide and act, and for the rest of us to support the *faits accomplis* for better or worse. But since we face a low-grade emergency—nobody is about to invade San Francisco —we like to go on as usual, including sounding off and criticizing, so long as it does not effect policy.

Unfortunately, this psychology keeps the low-grade emergency chronic. There is no way to get back to normal, no check on *faits accomplis*, no accountability of the decision-makers till so much damage has been done that there is a public revulsion (as after a few years of Korea), or, as seems inevitable, one day a catastrophe. Worst of all there is no way for a philosophic view to emerge that might become effectual. Who would present such a view? In the classical theory of democracy, the electorate is educated by the clashing debate and the best men come forward and gain a following. But in Senator Dodd's free country, acute men are likely to fall silent, for what is the use of talk that is irrelevant and divisive?

The discussion in the Foreign Relations Committee, excellent as it was, was itself typical of a timid democracy. Not a single Senator was able to insist on basic realities that could put the Vietnam War in a philosophic light and perhaps work out of its dilemmas. (Since then, Senator Fulbright has become more outspoken.) In this context, here are some of the basic realities: In a period of world-wide communications and spread of technology, and therefore of "rising aspirations," nevertheless a majority of mankind is fast becoming poorer. For our own country, is it really in our national interest to come on as a Great Power, touchy about saving face and telling other peoples how to act or else? In the era of One World and the atom bomb, is there not something baroque in the sovereignty of nation-states and legalisms about who aggressed on whom?

It will be objected that such anti-national issues can hardly be raised by Senators, even in a free debate. But the same limitation exists outside of government. In the scores of pretentious TV debates and panel discussions on Vietnam during the past two years, I doubt that there have been half a dozen—and these not on national networks—in which a speaker was invited who might conceivably go outside the official parameters and raise the real questions. Almost always the extreme opposition is himself a proponent of power politics, like Hans Morgenthau. (It usually *is* Hans Morgenthau.) Why not A. J. Muste, for instance? Naturally the big networks would say that there is no use in presenting quixotic opinions that are irrelevant. (The word "quixotic" was used by General Sarnoff of the National Broadcasting Company in his successful bid to Congress to deny to third party candidates equal free time.) By this response, the broadcasters guarantee that the opinions will remain irrelevant, until history, "out of control," makes them relevant because they were true.

| 5 |

This brings me back to my subject, how people are in the world when history is "out of control." So far I have noticed those who unhistorically will to be in control and those who accept their powerlessness and withdraw. But there is another possibility, apocalypse, not only to accept being powerless but to expect, or perhaps wish and hasten, the inevitable historical explosion. Again there are two variants, for it is usually a different psychology, entailing different behavior, to expect a catastrophe and beat around for what to do for oneself, or to wish for the catastrophe and identify with it.

To expect disaster and desert the sinking ship is not a political act, but it is often a profoundly creative one, both personally and socially. To do it, one must have vitality of one's own that is not entirely structured and warped by the suicidal system. Going it alone may allow for new development. For instance, when the youth of the Beat movement cut loose from the organized system, opted for voluntary poverty, and invented a morals and culture out of their own guts and some confused literary memories, they exerted a big, and on the whole good, influence. Also, the disposition of the powers-that-be to treat gross realities as irrelevant has driven many intellectual and spirited persons into deviant paths just to make sense of their own experience; thus, at present, perhaps most of the best artists and writers in America are unusually far out of line, even for creative people. They hardly seem to share the common culture, yet they are what culture we have. (According to himself, Dr. Timothy Leary, the psychedelics man, espouses the extreme of this philosophy, "Turn on, tune in, and drop out"; but I doubt that relying on chemicals is really a way of dropping out of our drug-ridden and technological Society.)

We must remember that with the atom bombs there is a literal meaning to deserting the ship. This factor is always present in the background of the young. For instance, during the Cuban missile crisis I kept getting phone calls from college students asking if they should at once fly to New Zealand. I tried to calm their anxiety by opining that the crisis was only diplomatic maneuvering, but I now think that I was wrong, for eyewitnesses of behavior in Washington at the time tell me that there *was* a danger of nuclear war.

More generally, the psychology of apocalypse and the decision to go it alone are characteristic of waves of populism such as we are now surprisingly witnessing in the United States. The rhetoric of the agrarian populism of the Eighties and Nineties was vividly apocalyptic, and that movement brought forth remarkable feats of co-operation and social invention. The current urban and student populism, as I have pointed out in these lectures, has begun to produce its own para-institutional enterprises, some of which are viable.

The practice of civil disobedience also must often be interpreted in terms of the psychology of apocalypse, but even sympathetic legal analysts of civil disobedience fail to take this into account. It is one thing to disobey a law because the authorities are in moral error on some point, in order to force a test case and to rally opposition and change the law. It is another thing to disobey authorities who are the Whore of Babylon and the Devil's thrones and dominions. In such a case the conscientious attitude may be not respect but disregard and disgust, and it may be more moral for God's creatures to go underground rather than to confront, especially if their theology does not include an article on paradise for martyrs. As a citizen of the uncorrupted polity in exile, it might be one's civil duty to be apparently lawless. There is a fairly clearcut distinction between civil disobedience in a legitimate order and revolution that may or may not prove its own legitimacy; but the politics and morality of apocalypse fall in between and are ambiguous.

| 6 |

Quite different, finally, is the psychology of those who unconsciously or consciously wish for catastrophe and work to bring it about. (Of course, for the best youth to desert the sinking ship also brings about disaster, by default.) The wish for a blow-up occurs in people who are so enmeshed in a frustrating system that they have no vitality apart from it; and their vitality in it is explosive rage.

Very poor people, who have "the culture of poverty," as Oscar Lewis calls it, are rarely so psychologically committed to a dominant social system that they need its total destruction. They have dreams of heaven but not of hellfire. A few exemplary burnings and beheadings mollify their vengeance. Their intellectual leaders, however, who are verbal and willy-nilly psychologically enmeshed in the hated system, might be more apocalyptic. For instance, Malcolm X once told me—it was before his last period which was more rational and political—that he would welcome the atom bombing of New York to vindicate Allah, even though it destroyed his own community. James Baldwin is full of hellfire, but I have never heard much of it in popular religion.

On the whole, at present in the United States the psychology of explosive apocalypse is not to be found among rioting Negroes crying "Burn, baby, burn," nor among utopian beatniks on hallucinogens; it is to be found among people who believe in the system but cannot tolerate the anxiety of its not working out for them. Unfortunately, it is a pretty empty system and anxiety is widespread.

Most obviously there is a large group of people who have been demoted or are threatened with demotion, business-men and small property owners who feel they have been pushed around; victims of inflation; displaced farmers; dissatisfied ex-soldiers; proletarians who have become petty bourgeois but are now threatened by automation or by Negroes invading their neighborhoods. Consciously these people do not want a blow-up but power to restore the good old days; but when they keep losing out, they manifest an astounding violence and vigilantism and could become the usual mass base for fascism. In foreign policy, where immigration has freer rein, they are for pre-emptive first strikes, bombing China, and so forth. I do not think this group is dangerous in itself—I do not think there is an important Radical Right in the United States—but it is a sounding board to propagate catastrophic ideas to more important groups.

My guess is that, under our bad urban conditions, a more dangerous group is the uncountable number of the mentally ill and psychopathic hoodlums from all kinds of backgrounds. Given the rate of mental disease and the arming and training in violence of hundreds of thousands of young men, there is sure to be an increase of berserk acts that might sometimes amount to a reign of terror, and could create a climate for political enormities. Not to speak of organized Storm Trooping.

The most dangerous group of all, however, is the established but anomic middle class that I described previously. Exclusive, conformist, squeamish, and methodical, it is terribly vulnerable to anxiety. When none of its rational solutions work out, at home or abroad, its patience will wear thin, and then it could coldly support a policy of doom, just to have the problems over with, the way a man counts to three and blows his brains out. But this cold conscious acceptance of a "rational solution" would not be possible if unconsciously there were not a lust for destruction of the constraining system, as sober citizens excitedly watch a house burn down.

The conditions of middle-class life are exquisitely calculated to increase tension and heighten anxiety. It is not so much that the pace is fast—often it consists of waiting around and is slow and boring—but that it is somebody else's pace or schedule. One is continually interrupted. And the tension cannot be normally discharged by decisive action and doing things one's own way. There is competitive pressure to act a role, yet paradoxically one is rarely allowed to do one's best or use one's best judgment. Proofs of success or failure are not tangibly given in the task, but always in some superior's judgment. Spontaneity and instinct are likely to be gravely penalized, yet one is supposed to be creative and sexual on demand. All this is what Freud called civilization and its discontents. Wilhelm Reich showed that this kind of anxiety led to dreams of destruction, self-destruction, and explosion, in order to release tension, feel something, and feel free.

A chronic low-grade emergency is not psychologically static. It builds up to and invites a critical emergency.

But just as we are able to overlook glaring economic and ecological realities, so in our social engineering and system of education glaring psychological realities like anomie and anxiety are regarded almost as if they did not exist.

The psychological climate explains, I think, the peculiar attitude of the Americans toward the escalation of the Vietnam War. (At the time I am writing this, more bombs are being rained on that little country than on Germany at the peak of World War II, and there is talk of sending half a million men.) The government's statements of purpose are inconsistent week by week and are belied by its actions. Its predictions are ludicrously falsified by what happens. Field commanders lie and are contradicted by the next day's news. Yet a good majority continues to acquiesce with a paralyzed fascination. This paralysis is not indifference, for finally people talk about nothing else—as I in these lectures. One has the impression that it is an exciting attraction of a policy that it is doomed.

VI

Is American Democracy Viable?

| *1* |

I have been giving you a gloomy picture of my country. Our policies range from dishonest to delusional. Our system of interlocking institutions finally mechanically goes its own way and runs over human beings. Our people have become stupid and uncitizenly and are lusting for an explosion.

Nevertheless, let me praise us for a moment. We are headed for trouble but we have moral strengths. We have a healthy good humor, that is neither cynical nor resigned. We are seasoned—we got there first—in the high technology, high standard of living, and other conditions of modern times. I think we have fewer illusions about them than other advanced peoples; we are not so foolish and piggish about them as we seem. Morally, despite what seems, Americans are classless and democratic and cannot think in other terms; and if a case *really* comes to public notice, we will not tolerate an individual's being pushed around—though it certainly takes a lot to get some cases to public notice. We are not cowed by authority. And we are energetic and experimental, though not very intelligent about it.

Perhaps our greatest strength is an historical one. Quixotic as it seems, we have an abiding loyalty to the spirit, and sometimes unfortunately the letter, of the American political system. Unlike in many other countries, our extreme groups—Birchites, students of the New Left, Negroes who want Black Power—are sincerely loyal to this history and spirit, more loyal indeed than the center is, which is lulled by its self-satisfied belief in social engineering. In a crisis, the great majority will continue to be historically loyal and we will not have fascism or 1984, though we may well have disaster. Thus, to repeat what I said at the beginning of this series of lectures, the question is whether our beautiful libertarian, pluralist, and populist experiment is indeed viable in modern conditions. We *can* make it so, both institutionally and because we have the will; the present trends are not inevitable. However, I am not sure that we will make it so, because of pressure of time and panicking.

| 2 |

A few weeks ago I had to give a talk at the dedication of the new law school at Rutgers University. What an exciting period it is for a law student, I said, if the study of law is regarded not as a technique for winning cases but as jurisprudence, the relation of law to justice and politics and the historical changes of law to meet new conditions. In the American tradition, the constitution-makers have been lawyers; and since we have so many new conditions, it is the task of young lawyers to come up with constitutional innovations to keep the American polity alive. Consider some of our unique domestic problems, passing by the whole field of world law, that must be developed almost from scratch. When the media of mass communications require immense capital or, like the broadcasting channels, are scarce and licensed, how to safeguard against *de facto* censorship and the brainwashing that is now evident? When mass compulsory education stretches for longer years, how to give rights to the young so that they are not regimented like conscripts and processed as things? When nearly half the young adults are obliged to go to college, what are their social, political, and academic rights; what do *Lehrfreiheit* and *Lernfreiheit* now mean? In a hardening mandarin establishment of mutually accrediting universities, state boards, and corporate employers, how to change the licensing of professionals and indeed of ordinary employment, so that competent people are not stymied because they do not have irrelevant diplomas? When corporations have grown to the size of feudal baronies and the lines of communication within them become tenuous, the traditional concepts of responsibility of principal and agent are inadequate; how to protect subordinates as moral beings? what are their rights in the decisions they must execute? As technologies expand and their remote effects cannot be avoided by anybody, how to give citizens an effective voice in the shape of the environment, not to speak of a remedy against abuses? As the technical and staff power of the police and other bureaucracies increases, how to bolster the resources of citizens so that there is a fair contest in court and agency? As the complexity, delays, and distance of ordinary political processes become greater, while often the tension of problems becomes worse, it is inevitable that spirited people will resort to various degrees of protest and civil disobedience; how to encourage this rather than render it destructive by disregarding the need for it or even exacting draconian penalties to stamp it out? Finally, in a national corporate economy most taxes must be channeled through the national government, yet municipal and community functions must still be locally controlled to be humanly relevant; then how to organize jurisdiction and budgeting so that people do not dodge their community responsibilities and yet central authorities do not take over?

Here, I said, are some of the crashingly important legal problems that must be solved in order to make American democracy work. And the behavior of the guild of lawyers is itself a case in point. If they simply accept the present formulations and try to win cases under them, they are avoiding their professional responsibility and giving authority by default to incompetent and unbridled powers, or to the drift of things. The same holds, of course, in other professions: in engineering, when the engineer merely executes a program handed down to him, rather than criticizing the program in terms of its community meaning and remote effects; in education, when a teacher serves as personnel in a school system, rather than contributing to the growing up of the young; in journalism, when a reporter follows an official line or caters to a mass market, rather than reporting the events and trying to tell their meaning. But there is no higher principle or authority (excepting the holy spirit and the nature of things) to which professional authority can be delegated, whether in Washington or the president of a university or the board of directors of a corporation or the electorate. It is only each profession, in touch with its own raw materials, daily practice, the judgment of peers, and its professional tradition that can initiate and decide on professional matters.

| 3 |

I chose this list, of course, to invent new rights, duties, and safeguards in our increasingly monolithic system of institutions, to make an effective pluralism. They are nothing but an extension to modern technological and social functions of the checks and balances discussions in the *Federalist Papers* that dealt mainly with territorial and commercial functions.

Now we have a school of sociology in the United States, that is the liberal orthodoxy, that holds that democratic rights are effectively secured by our present pluralism of institutions and interest groups, labor, capital, the professions, the universities, religious sects, ethnic groups, sectional interests, government, and the general public. According to this theory, these struggle for advantage and countervail one another, and through them each man can exert influence. Admittedly the institutions and interest groups are centralized and bureaucratized, but this is an advantage; for an individual can compete to rise in his own interest group, and the decision-makers of the various bureaucracies, each backed by massive power, can treat with one another in a rational way according to the rules of the game, for example by collective bargaining, and so avoid unseemly strikes, cut-throat competition, riot, and other disorder. This, in turn, makes possible a general harmony and diminishes everybody's anxiety. It is a sociologist's dream.

I am afraid that there is nothing in this theory. For the genius of our centralized bureaucracies has been, as they interlock, to form a mutually accrediting establishment of decision-makers, with common interests and a common style that nullify the diversity of pluralism. Conflict becomes coalition, harmony becomes consensus, and the social machine runs with no check at all. For instance, our regulatory agencies are wonderfully in agreement with the corporations they regulate. It is almost unheard of for the universities or scientists to say Veto, whether to the pesticides, or the causes of smog, the TV programming, the military strategy, or the moon-shot. (An exception was the fallout from the bomb-testing.) When labor leaders become labor statesmen, somehow the labor movement dies. The farm bloc enters the harmony precisely by getting rid of farming and ceasing to have special interests. Press and broadcasting seem never to have to mount a determined campaign against either official handouts or their advertisers. And as for the classical countervalence of parliamentary democracy, the two-party system, after all the fury of campaigning, it almost never makes any difference which party has won. It seems to me impossible that there should be so much happiness.

But perhaps it is a pre-established harmony. I don't know if there is one power Elite, and I am sure that the conspiratorial System is a paranoia of the radical students; nevertheless, it is said that the President has a file of 25,000 names from which appointments are made, after a computer has brought forth the sub-group that fits the profile for the particular role. These are the good guys who count and who can be counted on to initiate and decide in style. Perhaps these sub-groups are what is left of the Plural Interests, and the file is what we mean by the Establishment. (I don't know if there is actually such a file, but there *is* a police-file of bad guys who use the wrong style.)

There is a metaphysical defect in our pluralism. The competing groups are all after the same values, the same money, the same standard of living and fringe benefits. There can then be fierce competition between groups for a bigger cut in the budget, but there is no moral or constitutional countervalence of interests. Let me put this another way: the bother with the profit system has turned out to be not, as the socialists predicted, that it doesn't work, but that it works splendidly; and so long as a person's activity pays off in the common coin, he doesn't much care about his special vocation, profession, functional independence, way of life, way of being in the community, or corporate responsibility for public good.

In the major decisions that are made by the interlocking decision-makers, the democratic representation of the ordinary person is "virtual" rather than actual, as with the American colonists in the British Parliament. If this is so, there is no pluralism. Interest groups become nothing but means of social engineering, to cushion protest and expedite communication from top down. (In my opinion, by the way, the transmission belt doesn't work. When a group does not have real power, the members simply stop attending meetings. In the New York City school system, it doesn't pay to be an active member of the Parents-Teachers Association.)

| 4 |

For a pluralism to work democratically—like a guild socialism, a syndicalist system, or a medieval commune—it must proceed in just the opposite direction than that envisaged by our orthodox sociologists. It must try to increase class consciousness, craft pride, professional autonomy, faculty power in the universities, co-operative enterprise, local patriotism, and rural reconstruction. When members of a group stubbornly stand for something, the association will throw its weight around in the community; when the association insists on its special role in the community that must be accommodated to in its own terms (though not, of course on its terms), the members will be active in the association. What would such a medieval pluralism entail?

In the first place, there would be conflict and not harmony. At present, labor and capital can come to an agreement on wages, hours, and benefits, and pass on the costs; but the situation is much more electric if workmen ask, as they should, for a say in the work-process and the quality and utility of the product on which they spend their lives. In an authentic pluralism, a teachers' union will want to determine curriculum, method, and class-size in the public schools; but neither the administrators, the Mayor, nor the parents will agree to this. If the Medical Association comes on as a professional group, it will support rather than oppose community payment of fees, which is good for the health of the poor, but it will also intervene on slum conditions and the narcotic laws. The radio and television people will want some control over how they are edited and programmed. We are currently witnessing the conflicts that arise when ethnic groups are organized in their neighborhoods in an authentically pluralistic fashion.

The peaceful settlement of a dispute by rational means in due process is certainly better than agitated conflict; but it must be my dispute in my terms, and my representative must be my agent; if, as usual, the issue has suffered a sea-change by being taken out of my hands, and I find that once again I have not been taken seriously, the apparent harmony only increases my anxiety rather than diminishes it. If, on the other hand, a conflict is about what we really mean, it will rouse excitement and anger and may cause suffering, but it will diminish anxiety and be safer in the long run.

Next, let us look at the other side of the medal, the specific community responsibility of corporate groups which they now disregard. At present we make a thing of corporations policing themselves—probably wisely, since external regulation does not work anyway—but of course this can help only to prevent abuses, not to guarantee positive performance. Also, if the spirit is lacking, the flesh tends to default. To give a ludicrous example: when our Congress passed a law requiring fair TV coverage on both sides of controversial questions, the broadcasters responded simply by cutting back on controversial programs altogether. (Alas! the bland is also a point of view and sometimes very controversial, but I cannot get the Federal Communications Commission to see it this way.)

But consider the following as a better model. Since our vastly expanding armaments industries create in whole sections and in millions of workmen a vested economic interest in war, a bill was introduced in Congress—I think by Kastenmeier of Wisconsin—to require armaments manufacturers to prepare plans for alternative peaceful use of the expanded plant as a condition for getting an armaments contract. On this model I have suggested a proposal, that might be applicable in Canada: to countervail the brain-washing inevitable with the vast audiences of mass-media controlled by a few centers, impose a small progressive tax on audience size—a tax for revenue, not to prohibit—to underwrite independent media with rival views. By the same reasoning, corporations that greatly improve their position by technological advances, e.g. automation, have a responsibility to provide relevant education of the young, whose entry into society is made more difficult. At present, of course, these corporations do just the opposite: they urge the public and parents to spend money to train A algebrists whom they will use, after national examinations have weeded out the B's and C's. And they have even managed to get the public to pay for training their semi-skilled workmen, by taking over the job camps of the poverty program.

The advantage of proposals like these is that they constitutionally guarantee countervalence whenever a group begins to have a great influence: the danger generates its own antidote, without punitive machinery which has no positive result and without adding new levels of regulation and administration.

A major means of creating an effective pluralism is decentralization, to increase the amount of mind and the number of wills initiating and deciding. Very many functions of modern society must, of course, be centralized, and in my opinion there are many other functions which should be more centralized than they are now. (I have discussed this question in a book called *People or Personnel.*) On the whole, however, we would be wise at present to decentralize wherever it is feasible without too great loss of efficiency. Indeed, in a wide range of enterprises, decentralization means a gain in efficiency.

The current style is the opposite: big corporations invade new fields in which they have no competence, just to get contracts, and they will not easily be persuaded to change. Yet a lot could be done by public policy, e.g. to give out public money preferably to small independent firms in Research and Development, urban planning and renewal, and communications. At present, farm subsidies favor big plantations and chain-grocers; they could often as well or better favor smaller farmers and co-operatives. In schooling, a case can be made for the consolidation of rural schools, but there is no doubt that urban systems should be radically decentralized. Many giant universities would have more vitality, and be cheaper to run, if they were allowed to fall apart into their natural faculties and schools. It is indispensable for social work to be administered locally and democratically in order to combat anomie. Neighborhood treatment of mental diseases seems to make sense in most cases. The experience of the Peckham Health Centre in London suggests that it is better for many other parts of medicine. And, as I argued in a previous lecture, many urban problems that are prohibitively expensive and intractable in the city could be better handled in the depopulating countryside and be a grounds for rural reconstruction.

A chief reason to encourage decentralism is just to have a countervailing style of enterprise, one that does not require big capital, grandiose overhead, and all kinds of connections and credentials. The liberal sociologists of pluralism don't understand the matter of style, but many conservatives understand it very well and therefore have much in common with the new radicals. The older "planning" radicalism of the Thirties, however, played right into the present liberal social engineering.

To conclude this series of lectures on the crisis of the American political experiment, populist, pluralist, libertarian, let me say something about our peculiar American libertarianism, which is, I guess—along with our energy and enterprise—what most impresses Europeans about us. As a theme of history, the American kind of freedom has been traced to many things: the Americans were Englishmen, they were yeomen, they were Protestant refugees, they were other refugees, they had an open frontier—all these are relevant. But I am struck also by a constitutional aspect which I like, perhaps, to exaggerate.

Of all politically advanced peoples, the Americans are the only ones who started in an historical golden age of Anarchy. Having gotten rid of the King—and he was always far away, as well as being only an English king—they were in no hurry to reconstruct another sovereign, or even a concept of sovereignty. For more than thirty years after the outbreak of the Revolution, almost nobody bothered to vote in formal elections (often less than 2%), and the national Constitution was the concern of a few merchants and lawyers. Yet the Americans were not a primitive or unpolitical people; on the contrary they had many kinds of civilized democratic and hierarchical structures: town meetings, congregational parishes, masters with apprentices and indentured servants, gentry with slaves, professionals and clients, provincial assemblies. The pluralism goes way back. But where was the sovereignty?

Theoretically, the sovereignty resided in the People. But except for sporadic waves of protest, like the riots, Tea Parties, and the Revolutionary War itself—the populism also goes way back—who were the People? One does not at all have the impression, in this congeries of families, face to face communities, and pluralist social relations, that there was anything like a General Will, except maybe to be let alone.

Nevertheless, there *is*—it is clear from American behavior—a characteristic kind of sovereignty. It is what is made up by political people as they go along, a continuous series of existential constitutional acts, just as they invented the Declaration, the Articles, and the Constitution, and obviously expected to keep re-writing the Constitution. The founding fathers were saddled with a Roman language, so they spoke of "inalienable rights"; but the American theory is idiomatically expressed by pragmatists like William James: I have certain rights and will act accordingly, including finally punching you in the nose if you don't concede them.

I was recently vividly reminded of the American idea of sovereignty when there were some sit-ins at the City Hall in Detroit and the Governor of Michigan said, in a voice that could only be called plaintive, "There is no Black Power, there is no White Power, there is no Mixed Power; the only power belongs to the government"—I presume that his textbook had said, "The only power belongs to the State." But there was no mystique in the Governor's textbook proposition; I doubt if anybody, but anybody, took it seriously as an assertion of moral authority, or as anything but a threat to call the cops. On the question of sovereignty, the unmistakable undertone in these incidents is, "Well, that remains to be seen."

| 6 |

In the context of this pragmatic American attitude toward sovereignty, what is the meaning of the present wave of civil disobedience? Against direct actions like the civil rights sit-ins, the student occupation of Sproul Hall at Berkeley, the draft-card burnings, it is always said that they foment disrespect for law and order and lead to a general breakdown of civil society. Although judicious people are willing to grant that due process and ordinary administration are not working well, because of prejudice, unconcern, doubletalk, arrogance, or perhaps just the cumbersomeness of overcentralized bureaucracy, nevertheless, they say, the recourse to civil disobedience entails even worse evils.

This is an apparently powerful argument. Even those who engage in civil disobedience tend to concede it, but, they say, in a crisis they cannot act otherwise; they are swept by indignation, or they are morally compelled to resist evil. Or, as I mentioned in my last lecture, they have an apocalyptic theory in which they are acting for a "higher" justice, and the present order is no longer legitimate.

In my opinion, all these views are exaggerations because they assign a status and finality to the sovereign which in America it does not have. If the State is not quite so determinate, then the insult to it does not necessarily have such global consequences. Certainly the American genius, whether we cite Jefferson or James and Dewey more than a century later, is that the State is in process, in a kind of regulated permanent revolution.

Empirically, is it the case that direct actions which are aimed at specific abuses lead to general lawlessness? Where is the evidence to prove the connection, e.g. statistics of correlative disorder in the community, or an increase of unspecific lawless acts among the direct activists? The flimsy evidence that there is tends to weigh in the opposite direction. Crime and delinquency seem to diminish where there has been political direct action by Negroes. The community and academic spirit at Berkeley has been better this year than it used to be. In 1944 the warden of Danbury prison assured me that the war-objectors penned up there were, in general, "the finest type of citizens!"

On sociological grounds, indeed the probability is that a

specific direct action, that cuts through frustrating due process, and especially if it is successful or partially successful, will tend to increase civil order rather than to destroy it, for it revives the belief that the community is one's own, that one has influence; whereas the inhibition of direct action against an intolerable abuse inevitably increases anomie and therefore *general* lawlessness. The enforcement of law and order at all costs aggravates the tensions that lead to explosions. But if place is allowed for "creative disorder," as Arthur Waskow calls it, there is less tension, less resignation, and more likelihood of finding social, economic, and political expedients to continue with.

Of course, this raises a nice legal question: how to distinguish between a rioting mob and citizens engaging in creative disorder? Theoretically, it is a rioting mob, according to the wisdom of LeBon and Freud, if it is in the grip of unconscious ideas of Father or the need to destroy Father, if it is after senseless power or to destroy senseless power. Perhaps it is a group of confused Americans if it is demanding to be paid attention to, and included, as the first step of political thinking. Perhaps it is petitioning for a redress of grievances, even if it has no writ of grievances to present, and even if there is no sovereign to petition. In any case, the part of wisdom is to take people seriously and come up with a new idea that might make a difference to their problems. If the governors won't, or can't, do this, then we must do it. I am often asked by radical students what I am trying to do with all my utopian thinking and inventing of alternatives; perhaps the use of intellect is to help turn riot into creative disorder.

In brief, contrary to the conventional argument, anarchic incidents like civil disobedience are often essential parts of the democratic process as Americans understand it. So it was understood by Jefferson when, after Shays's rebellion was disarmed, he urged that nobody be punished, for that might discourage mutiny in the future, and then what check would there be on government? So, in milder terms, it has been recently understood by the pragmatic Court, where many cases of apparently obvious trespass and violation have turned out to be legal after all, and only subsequently made legal by statute. This is not, I believe, because the Court has been terrorized or has blinked in order to avoid worse evils, but because in rapidly changing circumstances, there is often no other way to know what the Constitution is.

| 7 |

Finally, I need hardly point out that in American rhetoric, American freedom—in an anarchic sense—has been held to be the philosopher's stone of our famous energy and enterprise. Mossback conservatives have always spoken for laissez-faire as the right climate for economic progress (though, to be sure, they then connive for tariffs and subsidies, hire strikebreakers, and form monopolies in restraint of trade). Radical liberals have cleaved to the Bill of Rights, for to be cowed by authority makes it impossible to think and experiment. Immigrants used to flock to the United States to avoid conscription, as some of our best youth now go to Canada. They came because there were no class barriers, and because there was open opportunity to make good in one's own way. And every American kid soon learns to say, "It's a free country—you can't make me!"

By and large, let me say, this rhetoric has been true. Anarchism is grounded in a rather definite social-psychological hypothesis: that forceful, graceful, and intelligent behavior occurs only when there is an uncoerced and direct response to the environment; that in most human affairs, more harm than good results from compulsion, top-down direction, bureaucratic planning, preordained curricula, jails, conscription, States. Sometimes it is necessary to limit freedom, as we keep a child from running across the highway, but this is usually at the expense of force, grace, and learning; and in the long run it is usually wiser to remove the danger and simplify the rules than to hamper the activity. I think, I say, that this hypothesis is true, but whether or not it is, it would certainly be un-American to deny it. Everybody knows that America is great because America is free; and by freedom is not finally meant the juridical freedom of the European tradition, freedom under law, having the legal rights and duties of citizens; what is meant is the spontaneous freedom of anarchy, opportunity to do what you can, although hampered by necessary conventions, as few as possible.

Then, how profoundly alien our present establishment is!—that has in one generation crept up on us and occupied all the positions of power. It has been largely the product of war, of the dislocations after World War I, the crash programs of World War II, and going on for twenty years the chronic low-grade emergency of the Cold War. It is fanning again into war.

The term "establishment" itself is borrowed from the British—for snobbish and literary reasons, and usually with an edge of satire. But we have had no sovereign to establish such a thing, and there is no public psychology to accept it as legitimate. It operates like an establishment: it is the consensus of politics, the universities and science, big business, organized labor, public schooling, the media of communications, the official language; it determines the right style and accredits its own members; it hires and excludes, subsidizes and neglects. But it has no warrant of legitimacy, it has no tradition, it cannot talk straight English, it neither has produced nor could produce any art, it does not lead by moral means but by a kind of social engineering, and it is held in contempt and detestation by the young. The American tradition—I think the *abiding* American tradition—is pluralist, populist, and libertarian, while the establishment is monolithic, mandarin, and managed. Its only claim, that it is efficient, is false. It is fantastically wasteful of brains, money, the environment, and people. It is channeling our energy and enterprise to its own aggrandizement and power, and it will exhaust us.

I would almost say that my country is like a conquered province with foreign rulers, except that they are not foreigners and we are responsible for what they do.

| 8 |

Let me assess our situation as soberly as I can. The system at present dominant in America will not do, it is too empty. On the other hand, it is possible that classical American democracy is necessarily a thing of the past; it may be too wild, too woolly, too mixed—too anarchic, too populist, too pluralist—for the conditions of big population and high technology in a world that has become small. I hope not, for I love the American experiment, but I don't know.

We Americans have not suffered as most other peoples have, at least not since the Civil War a century ago. We have not been bombed, we have not been occupied. We have not cringed under a real tyranny. Perhaps we would not ride so high today if we knew what it felt like to be badly hurt.

The American faces that used to be so beautiful, so resolute and yet poignantly open and innocent, are looking ugly these days, hard, thin-lipped, and like innocence spoilt without having become experienced. For our sake, as well as your own, be wary of us.

CONSCIENCE FOR CHANGE

by
MARTIN LUTHER KING, JR.

I

Impasse in Race Relations

It is a deep personal privilege to address a nation-wide Canadian audience. Over and above any kinship of U.S. citizens and Canadians as North Americans there is a singular historical relationship between American Negroes and Canadians.

Canada is not merely a neighbor to Negroes. Deep in our history of struggle for freedom Canada was the north star. The Negro slave, denied education, de-humanized, imprisoned on cruel plantations, knew that far to the north a land existed where a fugitive slave if he survived the horrors of the journey could find freedom. The legendary underground railroad started in the south and ended in Canada. The freedom road links us together. Our spirituals, now so widely admired around the world, were often codes. We sang of "heaven" that awaited us and the slave masters listened in innocence, not realizing that we were not speaking of the hereafter. Heaven was the word for Canada and the Negro sang of the hope that his escape on the underground railroad would carry him there. One of our spirituals, "Follow the Drinking Gourd," in its disguised lyrics contained directions for escape. The gourd was the big dipper, and the north star to which its handle pointed gave the celestial map that directed the flight to the Canadian border.

So standing to-day in Canada I am linked with the history of my people and its unity with your past.

The underground railroad could not bring freedom to many Negroes. Heroic though it was, even the most careful research cannot reveal how many thousands it liberated. Yet it did something far greater. It symbolized hope when freedom was almost an impossible dream. Our spirit never died even though the weight of centuries was a crushing burden.

To-day when progress has abruptly stalled and hope withers under bitter backlashing, Negroes can remember days that were incomparably worse. By ones and twos more than a century ago Negroes groped to freedom, and its attainment by a pitiful few sustained hundreds of thousands as the word spread through the plantations that someone had been reborn far to the north.

Our freedom was not won a century ago—it is not won to-day but some small part of it is in our hands and we are marching no longer by ones and twos but in legions of thousands convinced now it cannot be denied by any human force.

To-day the question is not whether we shall be free but by what course we will win. In the recent past our struggle has had two phases. The first phase began in the early 'fifties when Negroes slammed the door shut on submission and subservience. Adapting non-violent resistance to conditions in the United States we swept into southern streets to demand our citizenship and manhood. For the south with its complex system of brutal segregation we were inaugurating a rebellion. Merely to march in public streets was to rock the *status quo* to its roots. Boycotting busses in Montgomery, demonstrating in Birmingham, the citadel of segregation, and defying guns, dogs, and clubs in Selma, while maintaining disciplined non-violence, totally confused the rulers of the south. If they let us march they admitted their lie that the black man was content. If they shot us down they told the world they were inhuman brutes. They tried to stop us by threats and fear, the tactic that had long worked so effectively. But non-violence had muzzled their guns and Negro defiance had shaken their confidence. When they finally reached for clubs, dogs, and guns they found the world was watching, and then the power of non-violent protest became manifest. It dramatized the essential meaning of the conflict and in magnified strokes made clear who was the evil-doer and who was the undeserving victim. The nation and the world were sickened and through national legislation wiped out a thousand southern laws, ripping gaping holes in the edifice of segregation.

These were days of luminous victories. Negroes and whites collaborated for human dignity. But there was a limitation to our achievements.

Negroes were outraged by inequality; their ultimate goal was freedom. Most of the white majority were outraged by brutality; their goal was improvement, not freedom nor equality. When Negroes could use public facilities, register and vote in some areas of the south, find token educational advancement, again in token form find new areas of employment, it brought to the Negro a sense of achievement but it brought to the whites a sense of completion. When Negroes assertively moved on to ascend the second rung of the ladder a firm resistance from the white community developed. This resistance characterized the second phase which we are now experiencing. In some quarters it was a courteous rejection, in others it was a stinging white backlash. In all quarters unmistakably it was outright resistance.

The arresting of the limited forward progress by white resistance revealed the latent racism which was deeply rooted in U.S. society. The short era of widespread good will evaporated rapidly. As elation and expectations died, Negroes became more sharply aware that the goal of freedom was still distant and our immediate plight was substantially still an agony of deprivation. In the past decade little had been done for northern ghettos. All the legislation was designed to remedy southern conditions—and even these were only partially improved. A sense of futility and frustration spread and choked against the hardened white attitudes.

Non-violence as a protest form came under attack as a tactical theory and northern Negroes expressed their dismay and hostility in a succession of riots.

The decade of 1955 to 1965 with its constructive elements misled us. Everyone underestimated the amount of violence and rage Negroes were suppressing and the amount of bigotry the white majority was disguising.

The riots are now in the center of the stage, and are being offered as basis for contradictory positions by whites and Negroes. Some Negroes argue they are the incipient forms for rebellion and guerrilla tactics that will be the feature of the Negro revolt. They are represented as the new stage of Negro struggle replacing the old and allegedly outworn tactic of non-violent resistance. At the same time some white forces are using riots as evidence that Negroes have no capacity for constructive change and in their lawless behavior forfeit all rights and justify any form of repressive measures. A corollary of this theory is the position that the outbursts are unforgivable, ungrateful, and menace the social order.

I would like to examine both questions: Is the guilt for riots exclusively that of Negroes and are they a natural development to a new stage of struggle.

A million words will be written and spoken to dissect the ghetto outbreaks, but for a perceptive and vivid expression of culpability I would submit two sentences written a century ago by Victor Hugo:

If the soul is left in darkness, sins will be committed. The guilty one is not he who commits the sin, but he who causes the darkness.

The policy makers of the white society have caused the darkness; they created discrimination; they created slums; they perpetuate unemployment, ignorance, and poverty. It is incontestable and deplorable that Negroes have committed crimes; but they are derivative crimes. They are born of the greater crimes of the white society. When we ask Negroes to abide by the law, let us also declare that the white man does not abide by law in the ghettos. Day in and day out he violates welfare laws to deprive the poor of their meager allotments; he flagrantly violates building codes and regulations; his police make a mockery of law; he violates laws on equal employment and education and the provisions for civic services. The slums are the handiwork of a vicious system of the white society; Negroes live in them but they do not make them, any more than a prisoner makes a prison.

Let us say it boldly that if the total slum violations of law by the white man over the years were calculated and were compared with the law-breaking of a few days of riots, the hardened criminal would be the white man.

In using the term white man I am seeking to describe in general terms the Negro's adversary. It is not meant to encompass all white people. There are millions who have morally risen above prevailing prejudices. They are willing to share power and to accept structural alterations of society even at the cost of traditional privilege. To deny their existence as some ultra-nationalists do is to deny an evident truth. More than that it drives away allies who can strengthen our struggle. Their support serves not only to enhance our power but in breaking from the attitudes of the larger society it splits and weakens our opposition. To develop a sense of black consciousness and peoplehood does not require that we scorn the white race as a whole. It is not the race *per se* that we fight but the policies and ideology that leaders of that race have formulated to perpetuate oppression.

To sum up the general causes of riots we would have to say that the white-power structure is still seeking to keep the walls of segregation and inequality substantially intact while Negro determination to break through them has intensified. The white society unprepared and unwilling to accept radical structural change is resisting firmly and thus producing chaos because the force for change is vital and aggressive. The irony is that the white society ruefully complains that if there were no chaos great changes would come, yet it creates the circumstances breeding the chaos.

Within the general cause of riots it is possible to identify five specific elements: (1) *The white backlash* (2) *Pervasive discriminatory practices* (3) *Unemployment* (4) *War in Vietnam* (5) *Urban problems and extensive migration.*

The white backlash is a primary cause because it explains the ferocity of the emotional content of the outbursts and their spontaneity. Negroes have endured insults and humiliation for decades and centuries but in the past ten years a growing sensitivity in the white community was a gratifying indication of progress. The depravity of the white backlash shattered the hope that new attitudes were in the making. The reversion to savage white conduct marked by a succession of murders in the south, the recrudescence of white hoodlumism in northern streets and coldly systematic withdrawal of support by some erstwhile white allies constituted a grim statement to Negroes. They were told there were firm limits to their progress; that they must expect to remain permanently unequal and permanently poor; they were warned not to confuse cautiously measured improvements with expectation of full equality. The white backlash declared true equality could never be a reality in the United States.

The pervasiveness of discriminatory practices is so taken for granted that its provocative effect is readily forgotten. There are generational differences in character among Negroes. The older generation has substantially inured itself to daily insults but a younger generation has a lower threshold of tolerance. The thousands of fences, visible and invisible, that confine Negroes to restricted neighborhoods, schools, jobs, and social activity incite an intensely hostile reaction in the young. They have rejected the old way and cannot be soothed and tranquilized by promises of a new way in some distant future. Discrimination cuts off too large a part of their life to be endured in silence and apathy.

Even when a Negro manages to grasp a foothold on the economic ladder, discrimination remains to push him off after he has ascended a few rungs. It hounds him at every level to stultify his initiative and insult his being. For the pitiful few who climb into economic security it persists and closes different doors to them.

Intimately related to discrimination is one of its worst consequences—unemployment. The United States teetered on the edge of revolution in the 1930s when unemployment ranged up to 25%. To-day in the midst of historic prosperity unemployment for Negro youth, according to government figures, runs as high as 30 to 40% in many cities. With most of their lives yet to live, the slamming of doors in their faces can be expected to induce rage and rebellion.

The fourth cause is the war in Vietnam. Negroes are conscripted in double measure for combat. They constitute more than 20% of the front line troops in a war of unprecedented savagery although their proportion in the population is 10%. They are marching under slogans of democracy, to defend a Saigon government that scorns democracy. At home they know there is no genuine democracy for their people and on their return they will be restored to a grim life as second-class citizens even if they are bedecked with heroes' medals.

Finally, a complex of causes are found in the degenerating conditions of urban life. The cities are gasping in polluted air and enduring contaminated water; public facilities are outworn and inadequate; financial disaster is an annual crisis. Within this chaos of neglect Negroes are stifled at the very bottom in slums so squalid their equal is not to be found in any other industrial nation of the world.

Most of the largest cities are victims of the large migration of Negroes. Although it was well known that millions of Negroes would be forced off the land in the south by the contraction of agricultural employment during the past two decades, no national planning was done to provide remedies. When white immigrants arrived in the United States in the late 19th century a beneficent government gave them free land and credit to build a useful independent life.

In contrast, when the Negro migrated he was left to his own resources. He crowded the cities and was herded into ghettos, left in unemployment, or subjected to gross exploitation within a context of searing discrimination. Though other minorities had encountered obstacles, none was so brutally scorned or so consistently denied opportunity and hope as was the Negro.

All of these conditions were the fuel for violence and riots. As the social psychologist Kenneth Clark has said, it is a surprise only that outbreaks were not experienced earlier. There are many thoughtful social scientists who are now acknowledging that the elements of social catastrophe have accumulated in such vast array that no remedies may be available.

I am not sanguine but I am not ready to accept defeat. I believe there are several programs that can reverse the tide of social disintegration and beyond that I believe that destructive as the riots may be they have been analyzed substantially in a one-sided fashion.

There is a striking aspect to the violence of riots that has stimulated little comment and even less analysis. In all of the riots, taken together, the property damage reached colossal proportions (exceeding a billion dollars). Yet the physical injury inflicted by Negroes upon white people was inconsequential by comparison. The bruising edge of the weapon of violence in Negro hands was employed almost exclusively against property—not persons.

It is noteworthy that many distinguished periodicals and leaders of the white community, even while the conflict raged, in clear terms accepted the responsibility for neglect, evasion, and centuries of injustice. They did not quibble nor did they seek to fasten exclusive culpability on the Negro. They asked for action and a facing-up to the need for drastic social reformation. It is true that not all were motivated by morality. The crisis of Negro aspirations intersects with the urban crisis. Some white leaders may not be moved by humanity to save Negroes but they are moved by self interest to save their cities. But even their moral and selfish motives which merge toward a constructive end have not yet made government act. It is preoccupied with war and is determined to husband every resource for military adventures rather than for social reconstruction.

Negroes must therefore not only formulate a program but they must fashion new tactics which do not count on government good will but instead serve to compel unwilling authorities to yield to the mandates of justice.

We are demanding an emergency program to provide employment for everyone in need of a job or, if a work program is impracticable, a guaranteed annual income at levels that sustain life in decent circumstances. It is now incontestable that the wealth and resources of the United States make the elimination of poverty perfectly practicable.

A second feature of our program is the demolition of slums and rebuilding by the population that live in them.

There is scarcely any division among Negroes for these measures. Divisions arise only around methods for their achievement.

I am still convinced that a solution of non-violence remains possible. However, non-violence must be adapted to urban conditions and urban moods. The effectiveness of street marches in cities is limited because the normal turbulence of city life absorbs them as mere transitory drama quite common in the ordinary movement of masses. In the south, a march was a social earthquake; in the north, it is a faint, brief exclamation of protest.

Non-violent protest must now mature to a new level to correspond to heightened black impatience and stiffened white resistance. This higher level is mass civil disobedience. There must be more than a statement to the larger society; there must be a force that interrupts its functioning at some key point. That interruption must however not be clandestine or surreptitious. It is not necessary to invest it with guerrilla romanticism. It must be open and, above all, conducted by large masses without violence. If the jails are filled to thwart it the meaning will become even clearer.

The Negro will be saying: I am not avoiding penalties for breaking the law—I am willing to endure all your punishment because your society will not be able to endure the stigma of violently and publicly oppressing its minority to preserve injustice.

Mass civil disobedience as a new stage of struggle can transmute the deep rage of the ghetto into a constructive and creative force.

To dislocate the functioning of a city without destroying it can be more effective than a riot because it can be longer lasting, costly to the larger society but not wantonly destructive. Finally it is a device of social action that is more difficult for the government to quell by superior force.

The limitation of riots, moral questions aside, is that they cannot win and their participants know it. Hence, rioting is not revolutionary but reactionary because it invites defeat. It involves an emotional catharsis but it must be followed by a sense of futility.

Where does the future point? The character of the next period is being determined by the response of white decision-makers to this crisis. It is a harsh indictment, but it is an inescapable conclusion, that Congress is not horrified with the conditions of Negro life but with the product of these conditions—the Negro himself. It could, by a single massive act of concern expressed in a multi-billion-dollar program to modernize and humanize Negro communities, do more to obviate violence than could be done by all the armies at its command. Whether it will summon the wisdom to do it is the question of the hour.

It is a shattering historical irony that the American Revolution of 1776 was the consequence of many of the same conditions that prevail today. King George adamantly refused to share power even in modest degree with the colonies. He provoked violence by scorning and spurning the appeals embodied in non-violent protests such as boycotts, peaceful demonstrations, and petitions. In their resort to violence the colonists were pressed ideologically beyond their original demands and put into question the system of absolute monarchical rule. When they took up arms and searched for the rationale for independence they broke with all traditions of imperial domination and established a unique and unprecedented form of government—the democratic republic.

The Negro revolt is evolving into more than a quest for desegregation and equality. It is a challenge to a system that has created miracles of production and technology to create justice. If humanism is locked outside of the system, Negroes will have revealed its inner core of despotism and a far greater struggle for liberation will unfold. The United States is substantially challenged to demonstrate that it can abolish not only the evils of racism but the scourge of poverty of whites as well as of Negroes and the horrors of war that transcend national borders and involve all of mankind.

The first man to die in the American Revolution was a Negro seaman, Crispus Attucks. Before that fateful struggle ended the institution of absolute monarchy was put on its death bed.

We may now only be in the initial period of an era of change as far-reaching in its consequences as the American Revolution. The developed industrial nations of the world, which include Canada, as much as the United States, cannot remain secure islands of prosperity in a seething sea of poverty. The storm is rising against the privileged minority of the earth, from which there is no shelter in isolation and armament. The storm will not abate until a just distribution of the fruits of the earth enables man everywhere to live in dignity and human decency. The American Negro of 1967, like Crispus Attucks, may be the vanguard in a prolonged struggle that may change the shape of the world, as billions of deprived shake and transform the earth in their quest for life, freedom, and justice.

II

Conscience and the Vietnam War

It is many months now since I found myself obliged by conscience to end my silence and to take a public stand against my country's war in Vietnam. The considerations which led me to that painful decision have not disappeared; indeed they have been magnified by the course of events since then. The war itself is intensified; the impact on my country is even more destructive.

I cannot speak about the great themes of violence and nonviolence, of social change and of hope for the future, without reflecting on the tremendous violence of Vietnam, not even when I am speaking to an audience of Canadians, who are not directly involved in the war.

Since the spring of 1967, when I first made public my opposition to my Government's policy, many persons have questioned me about the wisdom of my decision. Why *you*, they have said. Peace and civil rights don't mix. Aren't you hurting the cause of your people? And when I hear such questions I have been greatly saddened, for they mean that the inquirers have never really known me, my commitment or my calling. Indeed, that question suggests that they do not know the world in which they live.

In explaining my position, I have tried to make it clear that I remain perplexed—as I think everyone must be perplexed—by the complexities and ambiguities of Vietnam. I would not wish to underrate the need for a collective solution to this tragic war. I would wish neither to present North Vietnam or the National Liberation Front as paragons of virtue, nor to overlook the role they can play and the successful resolution of the problem. While they both may have justifiable reasons to be suspicious of the good faith of the United States, life and history give eloquent testimony to the fact that conflicts are never resolved without trustful give-and-take on both sides.

Since I am a preacher by calling, I suppose it is not surprising that I had several reasons for bringing Vietnam into the field of my moral vision. There is at the outset a very obvious and almost facile connection between the war in Vietnam and the struggle I and others have been waging in America. A few years ago there was a shining moment in that struggle. It seemed as if there was a real promise of hope for the poor, both black and white, through the Poverty Program. There were experiments, hopes, new beginnings. Then came the buildup in Vietnam, and I watched the program broken and eviscerated as if it were some idle political plaything of a society gone mad on war, and I knew that America would never invest the necessary funds or energies in rehabilitation of its poor, so long as adventures like Vietnam continued to draw men and skills and money like some demoniacal destructive suction tube. And so I was increasingly compelled to see the war not only as a moral outrage but also as an enemy of the poor, and to attack it as such.

Perhaps a more tragic recognition of reality took place when it became clear to me that the war was doing far more than devastating the hopes of the poor at home. It was sending their sons and their brothers and their husbands to fight and to die and in extraordinarily higher proportions relative to the rest of the population. We were taking the black young men who had been crippled by our society and sending them 8,000 miles away to guarantee liberties in Southeast Asia which they had not found in Southwest Georgia and East Harlem. And so we have been repeatedly faced with the cruel irony of watching Negro and white boys on TV screens as they kill and die together for a nation that has been unable to seat them together in the same schools. We watch them in brutal solidarity burning the huts of a poor village but we realize that they would never live on the same block in Detroit. I could not be silent in the face of such cruel manipulation of the poor.

My third reason moves to an even deeper level of awareness, but it grows out of my experience in the ghettos of the north over the last three years—especially the last three summers. As I have walked among the desperate, rejected, angry young men, I have told them that Molotov cocktails and rifles would not solve their problems. I have tried to offer them my deepest compassion, while maintaining my conviction that social change comes most meaningfully through non-violent action. But, they asked, and rightly so, what about Vietnam? They asked if our own nation wasn't using massive doses of violence to solve its problems, to bring about the changes it wanted. Their questions hit home, and I knew that I could never again raise my voice against the violence of the oppressed in the ghettos without having first spoken clearly to the greatest purveyor of violence in the world today: my own Government. For the sake of those boys, for the sake of this Government, for the sake of the hundreds of thousands trembling under our violence, I cannot be silent.

For those who ask the question "Aren't you a civil-rights leader?" and thereby mean to exclude me from the movement for peace, I answer by saying that I have worked too long and hard now against segregated public accommodations to end up segregating my moral concern. Justice is indivisible. It must also be said that it would be rather absurd to work passionately and unrelentingly for integrated schools and not be concerned about the survival of a world in which to be integrated. I must say further that something in the very nature of our organizational structure in the Southern Christian Leadership Conference led me to this decision. In 1957, when a group of us formed that organization, we chose as our motto: "To save the soul of America." Now it should be incandescently clear that no one who has any concern for the integrity and life of America to-day can ignore the present war.

As if the weight of such a commitment were not enough, another burden of responsibility was placed upon me in 1964: I cannot forget that the Nobel Prize for Peace was also a commission—a commission to work harder than I had ever worked before for "the brotherhood of man". This is a calling which takes me beyond national allegiances, but even if it were not present, I would yet have to live with the meaning of my commitment to the ministry of Jesus Christ. To me the relationship of this ministry to the making of peace is so obvious that I sometimes marvel at those who ask me why I am speaking against the war. We are called to speak for the weak, for the voiceless, for the victims of our nation, and for those it calls enemy, for no document from human hands can make these humans any less our brothers.

And as I ponder the madness of Vietnam and search within myself for ways to understand and respond in compassion, my mind goes constantly to the people of that peninsula. I speak now not of the soldiers of each side, not of the junta in Saigon, but simply of the people who have been living under the curse of war for almost three continuous decades now. I think of them, too, because it is clear to me that there will be no meaningful solution until some attempt is made to know them and to hear their broken cries.

They must see the Americans as strange liberators. The Vietnamese people proclaimed their own independence in 1945 after a combined French and Japanese occupation and before the communist revolution in China. They were led by Ho Chi Minh. Even though they quoted the American Declaration of Independence in their own document of freedom, we refused to recognize them. Our Government felt then that the Vietnamese people weren't ready for independence and we again fell victim to the deadly Western arrogance that has poisoned the international atmosphere for so long.

For nine years following 1945 we vigorously supported the French in their abortive effort to re-colonize Vietnam. After the French were defeated, it looked as if independence and land reform would come through the Geneva Agreements. But instead there came the United States, determined that Ho should not unify the temporarily divided nation, and the peasants watched again as we supported one of the most vicious modern dictators, our chosen man, Premier Diem. The peasants watched and cringed as Diem ruthlessly rooted out all opposition, supported their extortionist landlords and refused even to discuss re-unification with the North. The peasants watched as all this was presided over by U.S. influence and then by increasing numbers of U.S. troops, who came to help quell the insurgency that Diem's methods had aroused. When Diem was overthrown, they may have been happy, but the long line of military dictatorships seemed to offer no real change, especially in terms of their need for land and peace.

The only change came from America, as we increased our

troop commitments in support of governments which were singularly corrupt, inept, and without popular support. All the while, the people read our leaflets and received regular promises of peace and democracy—and land reform. Now they languish under our bombs and consider us—not their fellow Vietnamese—the real enemy. They move sadly and apathetically as we herd them off the land of their fathers into concentration camps where minimal social needs are rarely met. They know that they must move or be destroyed by our bombs and they go, primarily women and children and the aged. They watch as we poison their water, as we kill a million acres of their crops, and they wander into the hospitals with at least 20 casualties from American fire power for one Viet Cong inflicted injury. They wander into the towns and see thousands of children homeless, without clothes, running in packs on the streets like animals. They see the children selling their sisters to our soldiers, soliciting for their mothers.

What do the peasants think, as we ally ourselves with the landlords, and as we refuse to put any action into our many words concerning land reform? Where are the roots of the independent Vietnam we claim to be building? Is it among these voiceless ones?

We have destroyed their two most cherished institutions: the family and the village. We have destroyed their land and their crops. We have co-operated in crushing one of the nation's only non-communist revolutionary political forces, the United Buddhist Church. We have supported the enemies of the peasants of Saigon. We have corrupted their women and children and killed their men. What liberators!

Now there is little left to build on—save bitterness. And soon the only solid physical foundations remaining will be found at our military bases and in the concrete of the concentration camps we call fortified hamlets. The peasants may well wonder if we plan to build our new Vietnam on such grounds as these; could we blame them for such thoughts? We must speak for them, and raise the questions they cannot raise. These too are our brothers.

Perhaps the more difficult but no less necessary task is to speak for those who have been designated as our enemies. What of the National Liberation Front? How can they believe in our integrity when now we speak of "aggression from the North" as if there were nothing more essential to the war? How can they trust us when now we charge them with violence after the murderous reign of Diem? And charge them with violence when we pour every new weapon of death into their land? Surely we must understand their feelings, even if we do not condone their actions. How do they judge us, when our officials know that their membership is less than 25% communist, and yet insist on giving them the blanket name. They ask how we can speak of free elections, when the Saigon press is censored and controlled by the military junta. Their questions are frighteningly relevant. Is our nation planning to build on political myth again and then shore it up with the power of new violence?

Here is the true meaning and value of compassion and non-violence, when it helps us to see the enemy's point of view, to hear his questions, to know his assessment of ourselves. For from his view we may indeed see the basic weaknesses of our own condition, and if we are mature, we may learn and grow and profit from the wisdom of the brothers who are called the opposition.

So, too, with Hanoi. In the North where our bombs now pummel the land, and our mines endanger the waterways, we are met by a deep but understandable mistrust. In Hanoi are the men who led the nation to independence against the Japanese and the French. It was they who led a second struggle against French domination, and then were persuaded to give up the land they controlled between the 13th and 17th parallels as a temporary measure at Geneva. After 1954 they watched us conspire with

Diem to prevent elections which would surely have brought Ho Chi Minh to power over a united Vietnam, and they realized they had been betrayed again.

When we ask why they do not leap to negotiate, these things must be remembered. Also, it must be clear that the leaders of Hanoi consider the presence of American troops in support of the Diem regime to have been the initial military breach of the Geneva Agreements concerning foreign troops. They remind us that they did not begin to send in any large number of supplies or men until American forces had moved in to the tens of thousands. Hanoi remembers how our leaders refused to tell us the truth about the earlier North Vietnamese overtures for peace, how we claimed that none existed when they had clearly been made. Ho Chi Minh has watched as America has spoken of peace and built up its forces, and now he has surely heard the increasing international rumors of American plans for an invasion of the North.

At this point, I should make it clear that while I have tried in these last few minutes to give a voice to the voiceless on Vietnam and to understand the arguments of those who are called enemy, I am as deeply concerned about our own troops there as anything else. For it occurs to me that what we are submitting them to in Vietnam is not simply the brutalizing process that goes on in any war, where armies face each other and seek to destroy. We are adding cynicism to the process of death, for they must know after a short period there that none of the things we claim to be fighting for are really involved, and the more sophisticated surely realize that we are on the side of the wealthy and the secure while we create a hell for the poor.

If we continue, there will be no doubt in my mind and in the mind of the world that we have no honorable intentions in Vietnam. It will become clear that our minimal expectation is to occupy it as an American colony and men will not refrain from thinking that our maximum hope is to goad China into a war so that we may bomb her nuclear installations.

Somehow this madness must cease. We must stop now. I speak as a child of God and brother to the suffering poor of Vietnam. I speak for those whose land is being laid waste, whose homes are being destroyed, whose culture is being subverted. I speak for the poor of America who are paying the double price of smashed hopes at home and death and corruption in Vietnam. I speak as a citizen of the world, for the world as it stands aghast at the path we have taken. I speak as an American to the leaders of my own nation, the great initiative in this war is ours. The initiative to stop it must be ours.

In the spring of 1967, I made public the steps I consider necessary for this to happen. I should add now only that while many Americans have supported the proposals, the Government has so far not recognized one of them. These are the times for real choices and not false ones. We are at the moment when our lives must be placed on the line if our nation is to survive its own folly. Every man of humane convictions must decide on the protest that best suits his convictions, but we must all protest.

There is something seductively tempting about stopping there and sending us all off on what in some circles has become a popular crusade against the war in Vietnam. I say we must enter that struggle, but I wish to go on now to say something even more disturbing. The war in Vietnam is but a symptom of a far deeper malady within the American spirit.

In 1957, a sensitive American official overseas said that it seemed to him that our nation was on the wrong side of a world revolution. I am convinced that if we are to get on the right side of the world revolution we as a nation must undergo a radical revolution of values. A true revolution of values will soon cause us to question the fairness and justice of many of our past and present policies. A true revolution of values will soon look uneasily on the glaring contrast of poverty and wealth. With righteous indignation, it will look across the seas and see individual capitalists of the West investing huge sums of money in Asia, Africa, and South America only to take the profits out with no concern for the social betterment of the countries, and say: "This is not just." It will look at our alliance with the landed gentry of Latin America and say: "This is not just." The Western arrogance of feeling that it has everything to teach others and nothing to learn from them is not just. A true revolution of values will lay hands on the world order and say of war: "This way of settling differences is not just." This business of burning human beings with napalm, of filling our nation's homes with orphans and widows, of injecting poisonous drugs of hate into the veins of peoples normally humane, of sending men home from dark and bloody battlefields physically handicapped and psychologically deranged, cannot be reconciled with wisdom, justice, and love. A nation that continues year after year to spend more money on military defense than on programs of social uplift is approaching spiritual doom.

This kind of positive revolution of values is our best defense against communism. War is not the answer. Communism will never be defeated by the use of atomic bombs or nuclear weapons.

These are revolutionary times, all over the globe men are revolting against old systems of exploitation and oppression. The shirtless and barefoot people of the land are rising up as never before. "The people who sat in darkness have seen a great light." We in the West must support these revolutions. It is a sad fact that because of comfort, complacency, a morbid fear of communism, and our proneness to adjust to injustice, the Western nations that initiated so much of the revolutionary spirit of the modern world have now become the arch anti-revolutionaries. This has driven many to feel that only Marxism has the revolutionary spirit.

Therefore, communism is a judgment against our failure to make democracy real and follow through on the revolutions that we initiated. We must move past indecision to action. We must find new ways to speak for peace in Vietnam and for justice throughout the developing world, a world that borders on our doors. If we do not act, we shall surely be dragged down the long, dark, and shameful corridors of time reserved for those who possess power without compassion, might without morality, and strength without sight.

III

YOUTH AND SOCIAL ACTION

When Paul Goodman wrote *Growing Up Absurd*, in 1959, he electrified the public with his description of the shattering impact on the young generation of the spiritual emptiness of contemporary society. Now, years later, it is not spiritual emptiness that is terrifying, but spiritual evil.

Today, young men of America are fighting, dying, and killing in Asian jungles in a war whose purposes are so ambiguous the whole nation seethes with dissent. They are told they are sacrificing for democracy, but the Saigon regime, their ally, is a mockery of democracy, and the black American soldier has himself never experienced democracy.

While the war devours the young abroad, at home urban outbreaks pit black youth against young soldiers and guardsmen, as racial and economic injustice exhaust human endurance. Prosperity gluts the middle and upper class, while poverty imprisons more than 30-million Americans and, literally, starvation stalks rural areas of the south.

Crime rises in every segment of society. As diseases are conquered and health improved, mass drug consumption and alcoholism assume epidemic proportions.

The alienation of young people from society rises to unprecedented levels, and masses of voluntary exiles emerge as modern gypsies, aimless and empty.

This generation is engaged in a cold war, not only with the earlier generation, but with the values of its society. It is not the familiar and normal hostility of the young groping for independence. It has a new quality of bitter antagonism and confused anger, which suggests basic issues are being contested.

These are unprecedented attitudes because this generation was born and matured in unprecedented conditions.

The generation of the past 25 years cannot be understood without remembering that it has lived during that period through the effects of four wars: World War II, the "cold war," the Korean War, and Vietnam. No other generation of young Americans was ever exposed to a remotely similar traumatic experience. Yet as spiritually and physically abrasive as this may be, it is not the worst aspect of contemporary experience. This is the first generation to grow up in the era of the nuclear bomb, knowing that it may be the last generation of mankind.

This is the generation not only of war, but of war in its ultimate revelation. This is the generation that truly has no place to hide, and no place to find security.

These are evils enough to send reason reeling. And of course they are not the only ones. All of them form part of the matrix in which this generation's character and experience were formed. The tempest of evils provides the answer for those adults who ask why this young generation is so unfathomable, so alienated, and frequently so freakish. For the young people of to-day, peace and social tranquility are as unreal and remote as knight errantry.

Under the impact of social forces unique to their times, young people have splintered into three principal groups, though of course there is some overlap among the three.

The largest group of young people is struggling to adapt itself to the prevailing values of our society. Without much enthusiasm, they accept the system of government, the economic relationships of the property system, and the social stratifications both engender. But even so, they are a profoundly troubled group, and are harsh critics of the *status quo*.

In this largest group, social attitudes are not congealed or determined; they are fluid and searching. Though all recent studies point to the fact that the war in Vietnam is a focus of concern, most of them are not ready to resist the Draft or to take clear-cut stands on issues of violence and non-violence. But their consciences have been touched by the feeling that is growing, all over the world, of the horror and insanity of war, of the imperative need to respect life, of the urgency of moving past war as a way to solve international problems. So while they will not glorify war, and while they feel ambiguous about America's military posture, this majority group reflects the confusion of the larger society, which is itself caught up in a kind of transitional state of conscience as it moves slowly toward the realization that war can not be justified in the human future.

There is a second group of young people, the radicals. They range from moderate to extreme in the degree to which they want to alter the social system. All of them agree that only by *structural* change can current evils be eliminated, because the roots are in the system rather than in men or in faulty operation. These are a new breed of radicals. Very few adhere to any established ideology; some borrow from old doctrines of revolution; but practically all of them suspend judgment on what the form of a new society must be. They are in serious revolt against old values and have not yet concretely formulated the new ones. They are not repeating previous revolutionary doctrines; most of them have not even read the revolutionary classics. Ironically, their rebelliousness comes from having been frustrated in seeking change within the framework of the existing society. They tried to build racial equality, and met tenacious and vicious opposition. They worked to end the Vietnam War, and experienced futility. So they seek a fresh start with new rules in a new order. It is fair to say, though, that at present they know what they don't want rather than what they do want. Their radicalism is growing because the power structure of to-day is unrelenting in defending not only its social system, but the evils it contains; so, naturally, it is intensifying the opposition.

What is the attitude of this second radical group to the problem of violence? In a word, mixed; there are young radicals to-day who are pacifists, and there are others who are armchair revolutionaries who insist on the political and psychological need for violence. These young theorists of violence elaborately scorn the process of dialogue in favor of the "tactics of confrontation"; they glorify the guerrilla movement and especially its new martyr, Che Guevara; and they equate revolutionary consciousness with the readiness to shed blood. But across the spectrum of attitudes towards violence that can be found among the radicals is there a unifying thread? I think there is. Whether they read Gandhi or Franz Fannon, all the radicals understand the need for action— direct self-transforming and structure-transforming action. This may be their most creative, collective insight.

The young people in the third group are currently called "hippies." They may be traced in a fairly direct line from yesterday's beatniks. The hippies are not only colorful, but complex; and in many respects their extreme conduct illuminates the negative effect of society's evils on sensitive young people. While there are variations, those who identify with this group have a common philosophy.

They are struggling to disengage from society as their expression of their rejection of it. They disavow responsibility to organized society. Unlike the radicals, they are not seeking change, but flight. When occasionally they merge with a peace demonstration, it is not to better the political world, but to give expression to their own world. The hard-core hippy is a remarkable contradiction. He uses drugs to turn inward, away from reality, to find peace and security. Yet he advocates love as the highest human value—love, which can exist only in communication between people, and not in the total isolation of the individual.

The importance of the hippies is not in their unconventional behavior, but in the fact that some hundreds of thousands of young people, in turning to a flight from reality, are expressing a profoundly discrediting judgment on the society they emerge from.

It seems to me that the hippies will not last long as a mass group. They cannot survive because there is no solution in escape. Some of them may persist by solidifying into a secular religious sect: their movement already has many such characteristics. We might see some of them establish utopian colonies, like the 17th and 18th century communities established by sects that profoundly opposed the existing order and its values. Those communities did not survive. But they were important to their contemporaries because their dream of social justice and human value continues as a dream of mankind.

In this context, one dream of the hippy group is very significant: and that is its dream of peace. Most of the hippies are pacifists, and a few have thought their way through to a persuasive and psychologically sophisticated "peace strategy." And society at large may be more ready now to learn from that dream than it was a century or two ago; to listen to the argument for peace, not as a dream, but as a practical possibility: something to choose and use.

From this quick tour of the three main groupings of our young people, it should be evident that this generation is in substantial ferment. Even the large group that is not disaffected from society is putting forward basic questions, and its restlessness helps us understand the radicals with their angry protest, and the hippies with their systematic withdrawal.

When the less sensitive supporters of the *status quo* try to argue against some of these condemnations and challenges, they usually cite the technological marvels our society has achieved. However, that only reveals their poverty of spirit. Mammoth productive facilities with computer minds, cities that engulf the landscape and pierce the clouds, planes that almost outrace time: these are awesome, but they cannot be spiritually inspiring. Nothing in our glittering technology can raise man to new heights, because material growth has been made an end in itself, and, in the absence of moral purpose, man himself becomes smaller as the works of man become bigger.

Another distortion in the technological revolution is that instead of strengthening democracy at home, it has helped to eviscerate it. Gargantuan industry and government, woven into an intricate computerized mechanism, leaves the person outside. The sense of participation is lost, the feeling that ordinary individuals influence important decisions vanishes, and man becomes separated and diminished.

When an individual is no longer a true participant, when he no longer feels a sense of responsibility to his society, the content of democracy is emptied. When culture is degraded and vulgarity enthroned, when the social system does not build security but induces peril, inexorably the individual is impelled to pull away from a soulless society. This process produces alienation—perhaps the most pervasive and insidious development in contemporary society.

Alienation is not confined to our young people, but it is rampant among them. Yet alienation should be foreign to the young. Growth requires connection and trust. Alienation is a form of living death. It is the acid of despair that dissolves society.

Up to now, I have been looking at the tragic factors in the quarter-century of history that to-day's youth has lived through. But is there another side? Are there forces in that quarter-century that could reverse the process of alienation? We must now go back over those 25 years to search for positive ingredients which have been there, but in relative obscurity.

Against the exaltation of technology, there has always been a force struggling to respect higher values. None of the current evils rose without resistance, nor have they persisted without opposition.

During the early 1950s the hangman operating with the cold-war troops was McCarthyism. For years it decimated social organizations, throttled free expression, and intimidated into bleak silence not only liberals and radicals but men in high and protected places. A very small band of courageous people fought back, braving ostracism, slander, and loss of livelihood. Gradually and painfully, however, the democratic instinct of Americans was awakened, and the ideological brute force was routed. By the way, Canada played a valuable role. CBC radio produced a satire of extraordinary brilliance on McCarthyism entitled *The Investigator*, which was recorded and widely circulated in the United States with devastating effect.

However, McCarthyism left a legacy of social paralysis. Fear persisted through succeeding years, and social reform remained inhibited and defensive. A blanket of conformity and intimidation conditioned young and old to exalt mediocrity and convention. Criticism of the social order was still imbued with implications of treason. The war in Korea was unpopular, but it was never subject to the searching criticisms and mass demonstrations that currently characterize opposition to the war in Vietnam.

The blanket of fear was lifted by Negro youth. When they took their struggle to the streets, a new spirit of resistance was born. Inspired by the boldness and ingenuity of Negroes, white youth stirred into action and formed an alliance that aroused the conscience of the nation.

It is difficult to exaggerate the creative contribution of young Negroes. They took non-violent resistance, first employed in Montgomery, Alabama, in mass dimensions, and developed original forms of application—sit-ins, freedom rides, and wade-ins. To accomplish these, they first transformed themselves. Young Negroes had traditionally imitated whites in dress, conduct, and thought in a rigid, middle-class pattern. Gunnar Myrdal described them as exaggerated Americans. Now they ceased imitating and began initiating. Leadership passed into the hands of Negroes, and their white allies began learning from them. This was a revolutionary and wholesome development for both. It is ironic that to-day so many educators and sociologists are seeking methods to instill middle-class values in Negro youth as the ideal in social development. It was precisely when young Negroes threw off their middle-class values that they made an historic social contribution. They abandoned those values when they put careers and wealth in a secondary role. When they cheerfully became jailbirds and trouble makers, when they took off their Brooks Brothers attire, and put on overalls to work in the isolated rural south, they challenged and inspired white youth to emulate them. Many left school, not to abandon learning, but to seek it in more direct ways. They were constructive school dropouts; a variety that strengthened the society and themselves. These Negro and white youth preceded the conception of the Peace Corps, and it is safe to say that their work was the inspiration for its organization on an international scale.

The collective effort that was born out of the civil-rights alliance was awesomely fruitful for this country in the first years of the 1960s. The repressive forces that had not been seriously challenged for almost a decade now faced an aroused adversary. A torrent of humanist thought and action swept across the land, scoring first small and then larger victories. The awakening grew in breadth, and the contested issues encompassed other social questions. A phalanx of reliable young activists took protest from hiding and revived a sense of responsible rebellion. A peace movement was born.

The Negro freedom movement would have been historic and worthy even if it had only served the cause of civil rights. But its laurels are greater because it stimulated a broader social movement that elevated the moral level of the nation. In the struggle against the preponderant evils of the society, decent values were preserved. Moreover, a significant body of young people learned that in opposing the tyrannical forces that were crushing them, they added stature and meaning to their lives. The alliance of Negro and white youth that fought bruising engagements with the *status quo* inspired each other with a sense of moral mission, and both gave the nation an example of self-sacrifice and dedication.

These years—the late '60s—are a most crucial time for the movement I have been describing. There is a sense in which it can be said that the civil rights and peace movements are over—at least in their first form, the protest form, which gave them their first victories. There is a sense in which the alliance of responsible young people which the movement represented has fallen apart under the impact of failures, discouragement, and consequent extremism and polarization. The movement for social change has entered a time of temptation to despair because it is clear now how deep and systemic are the evils it confronts. There is a strong temptation to despair of programs and action, and to dissipate energy in hysterical talk. There is a temptation to break up into mutually suspicious extremist groups, in which blacks reject the participation of whites, and whites reject the realities of their own history.

But meanwhile, as the young people face this crisis, leaders in the movement are working out programs to bring the social movements through from their early, and now inadequate, protest phase to a new stage of massive, active, non-violent resistance to the evils of the modern system. As this work and this planning proceed, we begin to glimpse tremendous vistas of what it might mean for the world if the new programs of resistance succeed in forging an even wider alliance of to-day's awakened youth.

Non-violent active resistance to social evils, including massive civil disobedience when there is need for it, can unite in a new action-synthesis the best insights of all three groups I have pointed out among our young people. From the hippies, it can accept the vision of peaceful means to a goal of peace, and also their sense of beauty, gentleness, and of the unique gifts of each man's spirit. From the radicals, it can adopt the burning sense of urgency, the recognition of the need for direct and collective action, and the need for strategy and organization. And because the emerging program is neither one of anarchy nor of despair, it can welcome the work and insights of those young people who have not rejected our present society in its totality. They can challenge the more extreme groups to integrate the new vision into history as it actually is, into society as it actually works. They can help the movement not to break the bruised reed or to quench the smoking wick of values that are already recognized in the society that we want to change. And they can help keep open the possibility of honorable compromise.

If the early civil-rights movement bore some international fruit in the formation of a peace corps, this new alliance could do far more. Already our best young workers in the United States are talking about the need to organize in international dimensions. They are beginning to form conscious connections with their opposite numbers in other countries. The conscience of an awakened activist cannot be satisfied with a focus on local problems, if only because he sees that local problems are all inter-connected with world problems. The young men who are beginning to see that they must refuse to leave their country in order to fight and kill others might decide to leave their country, at least for a while, in order to share their life with others. There is as yet not even an outline in existence of what structure this growing world-consciousness might find for itself. But a dozen years ago there was not even an outline for the Negro civil-rights movement in its first phase. The spirit is awake now: structures will follow, if we keep our ears open to the spirit. Perhaps the structural forms will emerge from other countries, propelled by another experience of the shaping of history.

But we do not have much time. The revolutionary spirit is already world wide. If the anger of the peoples of the world at the injustice of things is to be channelled into a revolution of love and creativity, we must begin now to work, urgently, with all the peoples, to shape a new world.

IV

Non-Violence and
Social Change

There is nothing wrong with a traffic law which says you have to stop for a red light. But when a fire is raging, the fire truck goes right through that red light, and normal traffic had better get out of its way. Or, when a man is bleeding to death, the ambulance goes through those red lights at top speed.

There is a fire raging now for the Negroes and the poor of this society. They are living in tragic conditions because of the terrible economic injustices that keep them locked in as an "underclass," as the sociologists are now calling it. Disinherited people all over the world are bleeding to death from deep social and economic wounds. They need brigades of ambulance drivers who will have to ignore the red lights of the present system until the emergency is solved.

Massive civil disobedience is a strategy for social change which is at least as forceful as an ambulance with its siren on full. In the past ten years, non-violent civil disobedience has made a great deal of history, especially in the southern United States. When we and the Southern Christian Leadership Conference went to Birmingham, Alabama, in 1963 we had decided to take action on the matter of integrated public accommodation. We went knowing that the Civil Rights Commission had written powerful documents calling for change, calling for the very rights we were demanding. But nobody did anything about the Commission's report. Nothing was done until we acted on these very issues, and demonstrated before the court of world opinion the urgent need for change. It was the same story with voting rights. The Civil Rights Commission, three years before we went to Selma, had recommended the changes we started marching for, but nothing was done until, in 1965, we created a crisis the nation couldn't ignore. Without violence, we totally disrupted the system, the life style of Birmingham, and then of Selma, with their unjust and unconstitutional laws. Our Birmingham struggle came to its dramatic climax when some 3,500 demonstrators virtually filled every jail in that city and surrounding communities, and some 4,000 more continued to march and demonstrate non-violently. The city knew then in terms that were crystal clear that Birmingham could no longer continue to function until the demands of the Negro community were met. The same kind of dramatic crisis was created in Selma two years later. The result on the national scene was the Civil Rights Bill and the Voting Rights Act, as President and Congress responded to the drama and the creative tension generated by the carefully planned demonstration.

Of course, by now it's obvious that new laws are not enough. The emergency we now face is economic, and it is a desperate and worsening situation. For the 35-million poor people in America—not even to mention, just yet, the poor in the other nations—there is a kind of strangulation in the air. In our society it's murder, psychologically, to deprive a man of a job or an income. You're in substance saying to that man that he has no right to exist. You're in a real way depriving him of life, liberty, and the pursuit of happiness, denying in his case the very creed of his society. Now, millions of people are being strangled that way. The problem is at least national (in fact, it's international) in scope. And it is getting worse, as the gap between the poor and the "affluent society" increases.

The question that now divides the people who want radically to change that situation is: can a program of non-violence—even if it envisions massive civil disobedience—realistically expect to meet such an enormous, entrenched evil?

First of all, will non-violence work, psychologically, after the summer of 1967? Many people feel that non-violence as a strategy for social change was cremated in the flames of the urban riots of the last two years. They tell us that Negroes have only now begun to find their true manhood in violence; that the riots prove not only that Negroes hate whites, but that, compulsively, they must destroy them.

This blood lust interpretation ignores one of the most striking features of the city riots. Violent they certainly were. But the violence, to a startling degree, was focussed against property rather than against people. There were very few cases of injury to persons, and the vast majority of the rioters were not involved at all in attacking people. The much publicized "death toll" that marked the riots, and the many injuries, were overwhelmingly inflicted on the rioters by the military. It is clear that the riots were exacerbated by police action that was designed to injure or even to kill people. As for the snipers, no accounts of the riots claim that more than one or two dozen people were involved in sniping. From the facts, an unmistakable pattern emerges: a handful of Negroes used gunfire substantially to intimidate, not to kill; and all of the other participants had a different target—property.

I am aware that there are many who wince at a distinction between property and persons—who hold both sacrosanct. My views are not so rigid. A life is sacred. Property is intended to serve life, and no matter how much we surround it with rights and respect, it has no personal being. It is part of the earth man walks on; it is not man.

The focus on property in the 1967 riots is not accidental. It has a message; it is saying something.

If hostility to whites were ever going to dominate a Negro's attitude and reach murderous proportions, surely it would be during a riot. But this rare opportunity for bloodletting was sublimated into arson, or turned into a kind of stormy carnival of free merchandise distribution. Why did the rioters avoid personal attacks? The explanation can't be fear of retribution, because the physical risks incurred in the attacks on property were no less than for personal assaults. The military forces were treating acts of petty larceny as equal to murder. Far more rioters took chances with their own lives, in their attacks on property, than threatened the life of anyone else. Why were they so violent with property, then? Because property represents the white-power structure, which they were attacking and trying to destroy. A curious proof of the symbolic aspect of the looting for some who took part in it is the fact that, after the riots, police received hundreds of calls from Negroes trying to return merchandise they had taken. Those people wanted the experience of taking, of redressing the power imbalance that property represents. Possession, afterwards, was secondary.

A deeper level of hostility came out in arson, which was far more dangerous than the looting. But it, too, was a demonstration and a warning. It was directed against symbols of exploitation, and it was designed to express the depth of anger in the community.

What does this restraint in the summer riots mean for our future strategy?

If one can find a core of non-violence towards persons, even during the riots when emotions were exploding, it means that non-violence should not be written off for the future as a force in Negro life. Many people believe that the urban Negro is too angry and too sophisticated to be non-violent. Those same people dismiss the non-violent marches in the south and try to describe them as processions of pious, elderly ladies. The fact is that in all the marches we have organized some men of very violent tendencies have been involved. It was routine for us to collect hundreds of knives from our own ranks before the demonstrations, in case of momentary weakness. And in Chicago last year we saw some of the most violent individuals accepting non-violent discipline. Day after day during those Chicago marches I walked in our lines and I never saw anyone retaliate with violence. There were lots of provocations, not only the screaming white hoodlums lining the sidewalks, but also groups of Negro militants talking about guerrilla warfare. We had some gang leaders and members marching with us. I remember walking with the Blackstone Rangers while bottles were flying from the sidelines, and I saw their noses being broken and blood flowing from their wounds; and I saw them continue and not retaliate, not one of them, with violence. I am convinced that even very violent temperaments can be channelled through non-violent discipline, if the movement is moving; if they can act constructively, and express through an effective channel their very legitimate anger.

But even if non-violence can be valid, psychologically, for the protesters who want change, is it going to be effective, strategically, against a Government and a *status quo* that has so far resisted this summer's demands on the grounds that "we must not reward the rioters"? Far from rewarding the rioters, far from even giving a hearing to their just and urgent demands, the Administration has ignored its responsibility for the causes of the riots, and instead has used the negative aspects of them to justify continued inaction on the underlying issues. The Administration's only concrete response was to initiate a study and call for a day of prayer. As a minister, I take prayer too seriously to use it as an excuse for avoiding work and responsibility. When a Government commands more wealth and power than has ever been known in the history of the world, and offers no more than this, it is worse than blind, it is provocative. It is paradoxical, but fair to say, that Negro terrorism is incited less on ghetto street corners than in the halls of Congress.

I intend to show that non-violence will be effective; but not until it has achieved the massive dimensions, the disciplined planning, and the intense commitment of a sustained, direct-action movement of civil disobedience on the national scale.

The dispossessed of this nation—the poor, both white and Negro—live in a cruelly unjust society. They must organize a revolution against that injustice, not against the lives of the persons who are their fellow citizens, but against the structures through which the society is refusing to take means which have been called for, and which are at hand to lift the load of poverty.

The only real revolutionary, people say, is a man who has nothing to lose. There are millions of poor people in this country who have very little, or even nothing, to lose. If they can be helped to take action together, they will do so with a freedom and a power that will be a new and unsettling force in our complacent national life. Beginning in the New Year, we will be recruiting 3,000 of the poorest citizens from ten different urban and rural areas to initiate and lead a sustained, massive, direct-action movement in Washington. Those who choose to join this initial 3,000, this non-violent army, this "freedom church" of the poor, will work with us for three months to develop non-violent action skills. Then we will move on Washington, determined to stay there until the legislative and executive branches of the Government are taking serious and adequate action on jobs and income. A delegation of poor people can walk into a high official's office with a carefully, collectively prepared list of demands. (If you're poor, if you're unemployed anyway, you can choose to stay in Washington as long as the struggle needs you.) And if that official says: "But Congress would have to approve this" or, "But the President would have to be consulted on that," you can say: "All right, we'll wait." And you can settle down in his office for as long a stay as necessary. If you are, let's say, from rural Mississippi, and have never had medical attention, and your children are undernourished and unhealthy, you can take those little children into the Washington hospitals and stay with them there until the medical workers cope with their needs, and in showing it your children, you will have shown this country a sight that will make it stop in its busy tracks and think hard about what it has done. The many people who will come and join this 3,000, from all groups in the country's life, will play a supportive role, deciding to be poor for a time along with the dispossessed who are asking for their right to jobs or income—jobs, income, the demolition of slums, and the rebuilding by the people who live there of new communities in their place; in fact, a new economic deal for the poor.

Why camp in Washington to demand these things? Because only the federal Congress and Administration can decide to use the billions of dollars we need for a real war on poverty. We need, not a new law, but a massive, new national program. This Congress has done nothing to help such measures, and plenty to hinder them. Why should Congress care about our dying cities? It is still dominated by senior representatives of the rural south, who still unite in an obstructive coalition with unprogressive northerners to prevent public funds from going where they are socially needed. We broke that coalition in 1963 and 1964, when the Civil Rights and Voters Rights laws were passed. We need to break it again by the size and force of our movement, and the best place to do that is before the eyes and inside the buildings of these same congressmen. The people of this country, if not the congressmen, are ready for a serious economic attack on slums and unemployment, as two recent polls by Lou Harris have revealed. So we have to make Congress ready to act on the plight of the poor. We will prod and sensitize the legislators, the administrators, and all the wielders of power until they have faced this utterly imperative need.

I have said that the problem, the crisis we face, is at least national in scope. In fact, it is inseparable from an international emergency which involves the poor, the dispossessed, and the exploited of the whole world.

Can a non-violent, direct-action movement find application on the international level, to confront economic and political problems? I believe it can. It is clear to me that the next stage of the movement is to become international. National movements within the developed countries—forces that focus on London, or Paris, or Washington, or Ottawa—must help to make it politically feasible for their governments to undertake the kind of massive aid that the developing countries need if they are to break the chains of poverty. We in the West must bear in mind that the poor countries are poor primarily because we have exploited them through political or economic colonialism. Americans in particular must help their nation repent of her modern economic imperialism.

But movements in our countries alone will not be enough. In Latin America, for example, national reform movements have almost despaired of non-violent methods; many young men, even many priests, have joined guerrilla movements in the hills. So many of Latin America's problems have roots in the United States of America that we need to form a solid, united movement, non-violently conceived and carried through, so that pressure can be brought to bear on capital and government power-structures concerned, from both sides of the problem at once. I think that may be the only hope for a non-violent solution in Latin America today; and one of the most powerful expressions of non-violence may come out of that international coalition of socially aware forces, operating outside governmental frameworks.

Even entrenched problems like the South African Government and its racial policies could be tackled on this level. If just two countries, Britain and the United States, could be persuaded to end all economic interaction with the South African regime, they could bring that Government to its knees in a relatively short time. Theoretically, the British and American governments could make that kind of decision; almost every corporation in both countries has economic ties with its government which it could not afford to do without. In practice, such a decision would represent such a major reordering of priorities that we should not expect that any movement could bring it about in one year or two. Indeed, although it is obvious that non-violent movements for social change must internationalize, because of the interlocking nature of the problems they all face, and because otherwise those problems will breed war, we have hardly begun to build the skills and the strategy, or even the commitment, to planetize our movement for social justice.

In a world facing the revolt of ragged and hungry masses of God's children; in a world torn between the tensions of East and West, white and colored, individualists and collectivists; in a world whose cultural and spiritual power lags so far behind her technological capabilities that we live each day on the verge of nuclear co-annihilation; in this world, non-violence is no longer an option for intellectual analysis, it is an imperative for action.

V

A Christmas Sermon on Peace

The text of this chapter was delivered by Dr. King as a Christmas sermon in Ebenezer Baptist Church at Atlanta, Georgia, and was broadcast by CBC as the final Massey Lecture, on Christmas Eve, 1967.

*P**eace on Earth* . . .

This Christmas season finds us a rather bewildered human race. We neither have peace within nor peace without. Everywhere, paralyzing fears harrow people by day and haunt them by night. Our world is sick with war; everywhere we turn we see its ominous possibilities. And yet, my friends, the Christmas hope for peace and good will toward all men can no longer be dismissed as a kind of pious dream of some utopian. If we don't have good will toward men in this world, we will destroy ourselves by the misuse of our own instruments and our own power. Wisdom born of experience should tell us that war is obsolete. There may have been a time when war served as a negative good by preventing the spread and growth of an evil force, but the very destructive power of modern weapons of warfare eliminates even the possibility that war may any longer serve as a negative good. And so, if we assume that life is worth living, if we assume that mankind has a right to survive, then we must find an alternative to war—and so let us this morning explore the conditions for peace. Let us this morning think anew on the meaning of that Christmas hope: Peace on Earth, Good Will toward Men. And as we explore these conditions, I would like to suggest that modern man really go all out to study the meaning of non-violence, its philosophy and its strategy.

We have experimented with the meaning of non-violence in our struggle for racial justice in the United States, but now the time has come for man to experiment with non-violence in all areas of human conflict, and that means non-violence on an international scale.

Now let me suggest first that if we are to have peace on earth, our loyalties must become ecumenical rather than sectional. Our loyalties must transcend our race, our tribe, our class, and our nation; and this means we must develop a world perspective. No individual can live alone; no nation can live alone, and as long as we try, the more we're going to have war in this world. Now the judgment of God is upon us, and we must either learn to live together as brothers, or we're all going to perish together as fools.

Yes, as nations and individuals, we are inter-dependent. I have spoken to you before of our visit to India some years ago. It was a marvellous experience; but I say to you this morning that there were those depressing moments. How can one avoid being depressed when one sees with one's own eyes evidences of millions of people going to bed hungry at night. How can one avoid being depressed when one sees with one's own eyes thousands of people sleeping on the sidewalks at night. More than a million people sleep on the sidewalks of Bombay every night; more than half a million sleep on the sidewalks of Calcutta every night. They have no houses to go in. They have no beds to sleep in. As I beheld these conditions, something within me cried out: "Can we in America stand idly by and not be concerned?" And an answer came: "Oh, no!" And I started thinking about the fact that right here in our country we spend millions of dollars every day to store surplus food; and I said to myself: "I know where we can store that food free of charge—in the wrinkled stomachs of the millions of God's children in Asia, Africa, Latin America, and even in our own nation, who go to bed hungry at night."

It really boils down to this: that all life is inter-related. We are all caught in an inescapable network of mutuality, tied in a single garment of destiny. Whatever affects one directly, affects all indirectly. We are made to live together because of the inter-related structure of reality. Did you ever stop to think you can't leave for your job in the morning without being dependent on most of the world? You get up in the morning and go to the bathroom and reach over for the sponge, and that's handed to you by a Pacific islander. You reach for a bar of soap, and that's given to you at the hands of a Frenchman. And then you go into the kitchen to drink your coffee for the morning, and that's poured in your cup by a South American. And maybe you want tea: that's poured in your cup by a Chinese. Or maybe you're desirous of having cocoa for breakfast, and that's poured in your cup by a West African. And then you reach over for your toast, and that's given to you at the hands of an English-speaking farmer, not to mention the baker. And before you finish eating breakfast in the morning, you've depended on more than half of the world. This is the way our universe is structured, it is its inter-related quality. We aren't going to have peace on earth until we recognize this basic fact of the inter-related structure of all reality.

Now let me say, secondly, that if we are to have peace in the world, men and nations must embrace the non-violent affirmation that ends and means must cohere. One of the great philosophical debates of history has been over the whole question of means and ends. And there have always been those who argued that the end justifies the means, that the means really aren't important. The important thing is to get to the end, you see.

So, if you're seeking to develop a just society, they say, the important thing is to get there, and the means are really unimportant; any means that will get you there—they may be violent, they may be untruthful means, they may even be unjust means to a just end. There have been those who have argued this throughout history. But we will never have peace in the world until men everywhere recognize that ends are not cut off from means, because the means represent the ideal in the making, and the end in process, and ultimately you can't reach good ends through evil means, because the means represent the seed and the end represents the tree.

It's one of the strangest things that all of the great military geniuses of the world have talked about peace. The conquerors of old who came killing in pursuit of peace, Alexander, Julius Caesar, Charlemagne, and Napoleon, were akin in seeking a peaceful world order. If you will read *Mein Kampf* close enough, Hitler contended that everything he did in Germany was for peace. And the leaders of the world to-day talk eloquently about peace. Every time we drop our bombs in North Vietnam, President Johnson is talking eloquently about peace. What is the problem? They are talking about peace as a distant goal, as an end we seek, but one day we must come to see that peace is not merely a distant goal that we seek, that it is a means by which we arrive at that goal. We must pursue peaceful ends through peaceful means. All of this is saying that, in the final analysis, means and ends must cohere because the end is pre-existent in the means, and ultimately destructive means cannot bring about constructive ends.

Now let me say the next thing we must be concerned about if we're to have peace on earth and good will toward men must be the non-violent affirmation of the sacredness of all human life. Every man is somebody because he is a child of God. And so when we say "thou shalt not kill" we're really saying that human life is too sacred to be killed on the battlefields of the world. Man is more than a tiny vagary of whirling electrons or a wisp of smoke from a limitless smoldering. Man is a child of God, made in His image, and therefore must be respected as such. Until men see this everywhere, until nations see this everywhere, we will be fighting wars. One day somebody should remind us that even though there may be political and ideological differences, the Vietnamese are our brothers; the Russians are our brothers; the Chinese are our brothers; and one day we've got to sit down together at the table of brotherhood. But in Christ there is neither Jew nor Gentile. In Christ, there is neither male nor female. In Christ, there is neither communist nor capitalist. In Christ, somehow, there is neither bond nor free. We are all one in Christ Jesus. And when we truly believe in the sacredness of human personality, we won't exploit people, we won't trample over people with the iron feet of oppression, we won't kill anybody.

There are three words for "love" in the Greek New Testament; one is the word "eros." Eros is a sort of aesthetic, romantic love. Plato used to talk about it a great deal in his dialogues, the yearning of the soul for the realm of the divine. And there is and can always be something beautiful about eros, even in its expressions of romance. Some of the most beautiful love in all of the world has been expressed this way.

Then the Greek language talks about "philos," which is another word for love, and philos is a kind of intimate love between personal friends. This is the kind of love you have for those people that you get along with well, and those that you like on this level you love because you are loved.

Then the Greek language had another word for love, and that is the word "agape." Agape is more than romantic love, it is more than friendship. Agape is understanding, creative, redemptive good will for all men. Agape is an overflowing love which seeks nothing in return. Theologians would say that it is the love of God operating in the human heart. When you rise to love on this level, you love all men not because you like them, not because their ways appeal to you, but you love every man because God loves them. This is what Jesus meant when He said "love your enemies." And I'm happy that He didn't say "like your enemies" because there are some people that I find it pretty difficult to like. Like is an affectionate emotion and I can't like anybody bombing my home. I can't like anybody who would exploit me. I can't like anybody who would trample over me with injustices; I can't like them. I can't like anybody who threatens to kill me day in and day out. But Jesus reminds us that love is greater than like. Love is understanding, creative, redemptive good will for all men. And I think this is where we are as a people, in our struggle for racial justice. We can't ever give up. We must work passionately and unrelentingly for first-class citizenship. We must never let up in our determination to remove every vestige of segregation and discrimination from our nation, but we shall not in the process relinquish our privilege to love.

I've seen too much hate to want to hate myself, and I've seen hate on the faces of too many sheriffs, too many white citizens' councillors, and too many Klansmen of the South to want to hate myself; and every time I see it, I say to myself, hate is too great a burden to bear. Somehow we must be able to stand up before our most bitter opponents and say: "We shall match your capacity to inflict suffering by our capacity to endure suffering. We will meet your physical force with soul force. Do to us what you will and we will still love you. We cannot in all good conscience obey your unjust laws and abide by the unjust system, because non-co-operation with evil is as much a moral obligation as is co-operation with good, and so throw us in jail and we will still love you. Bomb our homes and threaten our children, and as difficult as it is, we will still love you. Send your hooded perpetrators of violence into our communities at the midnight hour and drag us out on some wayside road and leave us half-dead as you beat us, and we will still love you. Send your propaganda agents around the country, and make it appear that we're not fit culturally and otherwise for integration, but we'll still love you. But be assured that we'll wear you down by our capacity to suffer, and one day we will win our freedom. We will not only win freedom for ourselves, we will so appeal to your heart and conscience that we will win you in the process, and our victory will be a double victory."

If there is to be peace on earth and good will toward men, we must finally believe in the ultimate morality of the universe, and believe that all reality hinges on moral foundations. Something must remind us of this as we once again stand in the Christmas season and think of the Easter season, simultaneously, for the two somehow go together. Christ came to show us the way. Men love darkness rather than the light, and they crucified Him, and there on Good Friday on the Cross it was still dark, but then Easter came and Easter is an eternal reminder of the fact that truth-crushed earth will rise again. Easter justifies Carlyle in saying "No lie can live for ever." And so this is our faith, as we continue to hope for peace on earth and good will toward men, let us know that in the process, we have cosmic companionship.

In 1963, on a sweltering August afternoon, we stood in Washington, D.C., and talked to the nation about many things. Toward the end of that afternoon, I tried to talk to the nation about a dream that I had had, and I must confess to you to-day that not long after talking about that dream I started seeing it turn into a nightmare. I remember the first time I saw that dream turn into a nightmare, just a few weeks after I had talked about it. It was when four beautiful, unoffending, innocent Negro girls were murdered in a church in Birmingham, Alabama. I watched that dream turn into a nightmare as I moved through the ghettos of the nation and saw my black brothers and sisters perishing on a lonely island of poverty in the midst of a vast ocean of material prosperity, and saw the nation doing nothing to grapple with the Negroes' problem of poverty. I saw that dream turn into a nightmare as I watched my black brothers and sisters in the midst of anger and understandable outrage, in the midst of their hurt, in the midst of their disappointment, turn to misguided riots to try to solve that problem. I saw that dream turn to a nightmare as I watched the war in Vietnam escalating, and as I saw so-called military advisers, 16,000 strong, turn into fighting soldiers while to-day over 500,000 American boys are fighting on Asian soil. Yes, I am personally the victim of deferred dreams, of blasted hopes, but in spite of that I close to-day by saying I still have a dream, because, you know, you can't give up in life. If you lose hope, somehow you lose that vitality that keeps life moving, you lose that courage to be, that quality that helps you to go on in spite of all. And so to-day I still have a dream.

I have a dream that one day men will rise up and come to see that they are made to live together as brothers. I still have a dream this morning that one day every Negro in this country, every colored person in the world, will be judged on the basis of the content of his character, rather than the color of his skin, and every man will respect the dignity and worth of human personality. I still have a dream to-day, that one day the idle industries of Appalachia will be revitalized, and empty stomachs of Mississippi will be filled, and brotherhood will be more than a few words at the end of a prayer but rather the first order of business on every legislative agenda. I still have a dream to-day, that one day justice will roll down like water, and righteousness like a mighty stream. I still have a dream to-day, that in all of our state houses and city halls, men will be elected to go there who will do justly and love mercy and walk humbly with their God. I still have a dream to-day, that one day war will come to an end, that men will beat their swords into plow shares and their spears into pruning hooks, that nations will no longer rise up against nations, neither will they study war any more. I still have a dream to-day, that one day the lamb and the lion will lie down together and every man will sit under his own vine and fig tree and none shall be afraid. I still have a dream to-day, that one day every valley shall be exalted and every mountain and hill will be made low, the rough places will be made plain and the crooked places straight, and the glory of the Lord shall be revealed, and all flesh shall see it together. I still have a dream, that with this faith we will be able to adjourn the councils of despair and bring new light into the dark chambers of pessimism. With this faith we will be able to speed up the day when there will be peace on earth, and good will toward men. It will be a glorious day, the morning stars will sing together, and the sons of God will shout for joy.

CANADIAN CITIES AND SOVEREIGNTY ASSOCIATION

by

JANE JACOBS

I

EMOTIONS AND A TALE OF
TWO CITIES

The other day I asked a bright young electronics engineer from the west—born and now living in British Columbia, brought up in Alberta—what he thought would happen in the forthcoming Quebec referendum. It's a question I often ask. In reply what I usually get is a statement, either indifferent or impassioned, of how the person I am addressing feels about Quebec separatism.

But this time I got a flat, forthright prediction. "They'll vote No," he said. "Why are you so sure?" I asked. "Because," he answered, "nothing really interesting ever happens in Canada."

Now, I myself have no idea how the referendum will turn out so I am not going to speculate about that. But I agree with my young friend that sovereignty-association is an interesting possibility. As an idea, it can mean two very different things. It can mean new arrangements among already existing nations as in the case of the European Economic Community or the younger five-member Andean community in South America. On the other hand it might also mean new arrangements among parts of already existing nations, as has been tentatively suggested by some European separatists and as René Lévesque is proposing. That second version of the idea forces us not only to think about sovereignty-association itself, but also to confront the idea of separation or secession.

It's hard even to think about separations because the subject is so charged with emotion. Sometimes people literally acknowledge this when they say "It's unthinkable."

Nationalistic emotions are dangerous of course. They've helped fuel many a war, many an act of terrorism, many a tyranny. But they are valuable emotions too. One thing they mean is that we are profoundly attached to the communities of which we are part, and this attachment includes for most of us our nations. We care that we have communities. We care how our nations fare, care on a level deeper by far than concern with what is happening to the gross national product. Our sheer feelings of who we are twine with feelings about our nations, so that when we feel proud of our nations we somehow feel personally proud; when we feel ashamed of our nations, or sorrow for them, the shame or the sorrow hits home.

These emotions are felt deeply by separatists and they are felt deeply by those who ardently oppose separatists. The conflicts are not between different kinds of emotions. They are conflicts, rather, between different ways of identifying the nation, different choices as to what the nation is. For Quebec separatists, the nation is Quebec. For their opponents, either inside the province or outside it, the nation is Canada defined as including Quebec. Canadians who are indifferent to the question of Quebec separatism, or who can be as cool about it as my friend who rated it on a scale marked from "dull" to "interesting," are likely either to identify emotionally chiefly with some other province of Canada or else to identify emotionally with a Canada that they define to themselves as not-necessarily-including-Quebec.

That last is my own emotional identification. I can't justify it as rational because the fact is that on some level of sheer feeling, not of reason, Quebec seems to me to be already separate and different from what I understand as my own community. Not that Quebec seems to me to be inferior, or threateningly strange or the wrong way for a place to be, or anything of that sort. Just not my community. When I asked my engineer friend whether he identified emotionally with all of Canada or a part he said, "That's such a personal question I feel it's my own business." But then he relented enough to say, "My place is out west."

Trying to argue about these feelings is as fruitless as trying to argue that people in love ought not to be in love, or that if they must be then they should be cold and hard-headed about choosing their attachments. It doesn't work that way. We feel. The feelings are their own argument.

The irrationality of all this shows up in universal patterns of inconsistency. DeGaulle, who said "Vive le Québec Libre!" never said "Vive le Provence Libre!" nor "Long live a free Brittany!" He could feel for separatists abroad but not for separatists at home.

This pattern is perfectly ordinary, perhaps always has been. The same Englishmen who ardently favoured Greek independence from Turkish rule in the 19th century did not therefore also campaign for Irish independence from English rule. Rationally the one would certainly follow from the other; emotionally, no. British support of Pakistani separatists at the time when India became independent did not imply any comfort or support for Scottish nationalists. Just so, many a Canadian who opposes Quebec separatism was sympathetic to the unsuccessful Biafran secession movement in Nigeria. I know some of those people. The same Canadians who can argue eloquently that justice and good sense, both, are on the side of Esthonian, Latvian, Lithuanian, Walloon, Kurdish, or Palestinian separatists can maintain that Quebec separatists must be out of their minds to want something so impractical and destructive.

Separatists are quite as rationally inconsistent themselves. If and when they win their way they always promptly forget their championship of self-determination and oppose any further separation at home. The colonies that became the United States declared their independence on the grounds that their grievances made it "necessary for one people to dissolve the political bands which have connected them with another, and to assume among the Powers of the Earth the separate and equal Station to which the Laws of Nature and of Nature's God entitle them." It has often been remarked how inconsistent this is with the war waged by the Union forces against the secessionist Confederate States some four score and seven years later.

Today's newly independent nations are one and all against their own separatists or potential separatists. As one student of government has put it, "Leaders of these new regimes are desperately concerned to argue that self-determination can be employed once in the process of securing independence . . . but that it cannot be resorted to subsequently."[1] Finland, after having achieved independence from Russia, promptly refused the right of self-determination to the population of the Aaland Islands; they were ethnically Swedish and sought to break away from finland with the object of joining Sweden. Pakistan, having won its own separation, then went on to fight the separation of East Pakistan, now Bangladesh. And so on. We can be sure that if Quebec ever negotiates a separation it will oppose adamantly, whether then or thereafter, any separations from Quebec. That is the way all nations behave, no matter how old or young, how powerful or weak, how developed or undeveloped, or how they themselves came into being. But this inconsistency is inconsistent only in the light of reason. The behavior and attitudes are really quite remarkably consistent. The consistency is emotional and unreasonable.

These emotions of course are always being presented as reasoned and reasonable but that does not always stand up to inspection. Take, for instance, the word "Balkanization." Spoken with the ring of authority, "Balkanization" can be made to sound like a compressed history lesson proving the folly of small sovereignties. But what about the Balkans, really?

Before they became small and separate sovereignties after the first World War they had been portions of very large sovereignties indeed, the Turkish and Austro-Hungarian Empires. As portions of large sovereignties they had lain poor, backward and stagnant for centuries. That's how they happened to be poor and backward when at last they became independent. If a fate called Balkanization means anything reasoned at all, it has to mean that the Balkans were somehow made to be poor, backward and generally unfortunate by having been cut up small, but that's simply untrue. Or else it has to mean that if Rumania, Bulgaria, Yugoslavia and Albania had been joined together in one sovereignty after the Great War, or perhaps had been united with Greece to form a still larger sovereignty, they would be better off now. Who knows? In the nature of the thing there is no shred of evidence either to support such a conclusion or to contradict it.

Consider a scholarly and rational sounding prediction like this one for Canada if Quebec should separate. "Deprived of real authority or purpose, the federal state would simply disintegrate, like the Austro-Hungarian Empire in 1918."[2] That appears in a new book by a professor of political science at the University of Alberta. The trouble with his analogy is that the Austro-Hungarian Empire did not disintegrate because a successful separatist movement occurred there. It had its separatists, especially in the

Balkans, some of whom were violent, but the movements were kept in check. The empire was defeated in a great war and as it lay in chaos it was deliberately dismembered by the conquerors. The analogy to Canada is so far-fetched historically and so specious factually that we can only understand it as an emotional cry of anguish—not a true account of how things are in this country.

To understand why sovereignty-association has been raised as a serious issue in Canada at this time, we must look at two cities, Montreal and Toronto. They are responsible for what has been happening in Quebec. Between them, they have converted a province into something more nearly resembling a new nation. Nobody planned this outcome. Nobody even recognized what was happening at the time it happened. The events that worked this transformation don't go back very far; we can date them statistically as having begun in 1941, but that is simply because '41 was a census year. I suspect they actually began in 1939 with the war economy.

Let us begin with the part played by Montreal. Between 1941 and 1971, Montreal grew enormously. In those thirty years, the city more than doubled its population, increasing from a little more than a million persons to more than two million.[3]

These were the years that led up to and included "the quiet revolution," the turning point in modern Quebec history, when French Quebec culture came out of its shell, welcomed change instead of resisting it, and moved into the modern world. The 1960's were the decade of the quiet revolution.

Immigrants from other countries contributed to Montreal's growth between 1941 and 1971; so did people from other parts of Canada, and of course some were born there. But the major influx of population was from rural and small town Quebec itself.[4] Previously, rural Quebecois had migrated into Montreal, Quebec City and to New England. But nothing in the past resembled this migration. It dwarfed previous rural-to-city movements within the province. Furthermore, the rapidity with which the movement happened, as well as the absolute numbers of people involved, was unprecedented.

These French-speaking migrants into Montreal spent the 1940's and 1950's finding each other. The quiet revolution of the 1960's was then built on their networks of new interests and relationships: in the arts, in politics, working life, and education. French culture in Montreal was in a quiet ferment, as people built these relationships and put together ambitions and ideas they could not have developed even in a smaller city like the capital, Quebec City.

In the 1960's the evidence of this ferment burst forth in French theatre, music, films and television. Talent and audiences had now found each other. There was a new and rapidly growing readership for Quebec books and periodicals; writers and readers had found each other. At about the same time, for a combination of reasons, new kinds of opportunities finally began opening up to Quebecois in city professions and commerce. The most important of those reasons was the economic growth of Montreal.

Until the early 1960's, Montreal still seemed to be what it had been: an English city with many French-speaking workers and inhabitants. But now, because of the growth and the accompanying cultural processes just described, Montreal had become a French Canadian city with many English-speaking inhabitants. By the time people in Montreal, let alone the rest of Canada, recognized what had been happening, it had already happened.

Out in rural Quebec, the old stronghold of French culture, another kind of quiet revolution was taking place. From farming villages, fishing villages, market towns and mill towns, hundreds of thousands of people, especially young people, were trickling and then pouring into Montreal. As the stream swelled, it had its effects on education and aspirations.

But life also changed for many of the people who stayed put in rural Quebec. A million extra city people eat a lot. And even though many of these extra city people had previously been eating on farms right there in Quebec, feeding them now involved city trade and city money. With this growing city market, and so many young people leaving the farms too, equipment was needed to improve rural productivity. Tractors, trucks, piped water, electrical appliances began showing up in places where, in the past, there would have been neither money to buy them nor much reason to need them.

These changes had a profound effect on religious life in Quebec. Contrary to what most people believe, the Quebec religious revolution, meaning loss of authority by the Catholic Church, was not a cause of the city and rural changes I've mentioned, but a result of them. The local priest's word about the world and its ways was no longer the last word in settlements where almost everyone was now at least distantly acquainted with somebody who had been off to a Montreal university for a secular education; in settlements where people now listened to radio, watched television, went to the movies when they got into town; in settlements where changes in the everyday economy and everyday working methods had burst out of the bounds of traditional ways of life. One and the same force, the great growth surge of Montreal, was simultaneously undermining an old culture in the countryside and developing it into something new in the metropolis, and sending this new city-shaped culture back into the countryside.

Now we need to bring Toronto into the story. Montreal used to be the chief metropolis, the national economic centre of all of Canada. It is an older city than Toronto, and until only a few years ago was larger. At the beginning of this century Toronto was only two-thirds the size of Montreal, and Montreal was much the more important centre of finance, publishing, wholesaling, retailing, manufacturing, entertainment—everything that goes into making a city economy.

The first small and tentative shifts of finance from Montreal to Toronto began in the 1920's when Montreal banks overlooked the financing of new mining opportunities which were then opening up in Ontario. That neglect created an opportunity for Toronto banks. The stock exchange set up in Toronto for trading mining shares then merged, in 1934, with the older, generalized Toronto stock exchange and by the 1940's the volume of stocks traded in Toronto had exceeded that in Montreal.[5]

During the great growth surge of Montreal, from 1941 to 1971, Toronto grew at a rate that was even faster. In the first of those decades, when Montreal was growing by about 20%, Toronto was growing by a rate closer to 25%. In the next decade, from 1951 to 1961, when Montreal was adding a bit over 35% its population, Toronto was adding about 45%. And from 1961 to 1971, while Montreal was growing by less than 20%, Toronto was growing by 30%. The result was that Toronto finally overtook Montreal in the late 1970's.[6]

However, even these measurements are deceptive as measurements of what was happening economically. Thought of as an economic unit or economic force, Toronto has in fact been a great deal larger than Montreal for many years. This is because Toronto forms the centre of a collection of satellite cities and towns, in addition to its suburbs. Those satellites contain a great range of economic activities, from steel mills to art galleries. Like many of the world's large metropolises, Toronto has been spilling out enterprises into its nearby region, causing many old and formerly small towns and little cities to grow. In addition to that, many enterprises that needed a metropolitan market and a reservoir of metropolitan skills and other producers to draw upon have established themselves in Toronto's orbit, but in places where costs are lower or space more easily available.

The English call a collection of cities and towns with this kind of economic integration a conurbation, a term now widely adopted. Toronto's conurbation, curving around the western end of Lake Ontario, has been nicknamed the Golden Horseshoe. Hamilton, which is in the horseshoe, is larger than Calgary.[7] Georgetown, north of Toronto, qualifies as only a small Ontario town, one of many in the conurbation. In New Brunswick it would be a major economic settlement.

The economic growth of Montreal, on the other hand, was not large enough to help create a conurbation. Montreal's growth contained itself within the city and its suburbs. That is why it's deceptive to compare population sizes of the two cities and jump to the conclusion that not until the 1970's had they become more or less equal in economic terms. Toronto supplanted Montreal as Canada's chief economic centre considerably before that, probably even before 1960. Whenever it did happen, it was another of those things that most of us never realized had happened until considerably afterwards.

Because Toronto was growing more rapidly than Montreal in the 1940's, '50's and '60's, and because so many of its institutions and enterprises now served the entire country, Toronto not only drew people from many other countries but from across Canada too. The first two weeks I lived here, back in the late 1960's, it seemed to me that almost everyone I encountered was a migrant from Winnipeg or New Brunswick. Had Montreal remained Canada's pre-eminent metropolis and national centre, many of these Canadians would have been migrating to Montreal instead. In that case, Montreal would not only be even larger than it is today, but—and this is important—it would have remained an English Canadian metropolis. Instead it has become more and more distinctively Quebecois.

In sum, then, these two things were occurring at once: on the one hand, Montreal's growth in the decades 1941-1971 shook up much of rural Quebec and transformed Quebec's culture too. On the other hand, Toronto and the Golden Horseshoe were growing even more rapidly. Montreal, in spite of its growth, was losing its character as the economic centre of an English-speaking Canada and was simultaneously taking on its character as a regional, French-speaking metropolis.

These events, I think, are at the core of Quebec's changed and changing relationship with the rest of Canada. Things can never go back to the way they were when an English-speaking Montreal was the chief economic centre of all of Canada and when life elsewhere in the province was isolated and traditional. These changes are not merely in people's heads. They cannot be reasoned away or even voted away. Nor are they merely intensifications or extensions of the old French-Canadian grievances.

A culture can persist without its own metropolitan capital, as Quebec's did for so long, but it cannot flower and thrive without one. Quebec does have its own cultural metropolis now. But Montreal, to continue thriving as a cultural capital must also thrive economically.

Yet as a regional Canadian city, Montreal's economic future is unpromising. To understand why this is so, we must be aware of Canada's customary view of economic life and its traditional approach to economic development. The Canadian approach emphasizes exploitation and export of resources, to the neglect of industry and services based on manufacturing.

The experience of Canada has been that the largest and most quickly obtained fortunes, whether public or private, come from resources—furs, timber, apples, fish, coal, iron, nickel, gold, silver, grain, cobalt, uranium, aluminum, potash, hydro-electric power, oil, to name some of the most influential. Societies, like individuals, are shaped by their experiences. Canada's get-rich-quick economic experiences have helped mould all the country's major institutions: the national government, the provincial governments, the banks and other financial establishments. They have shaped the way venture capital is used, the ways subsidies are used, the kinds of development schemes considered most attractive, and the thinking of almost everyone in authority. These are not easy things to change. Even most of the Canadian nationalists who object to foreign ownership of branch plants here do not seem to be aware that ownership is a superficial matter if Canada, in reality, does not create industry and develop branch plants of its own.

When one dominant approach to economic life and economic wealth has been pursued as consistently as it has been here, and for as long as it has been here, the experience gets thoroughly built into the way things work. It especially gets built into the uses of capital. Dazzling sums of money are available for resource exploitation and export, and for a few other schemes, usually of grandiose proportions. But although there are some exceptions, especially in Toronto, almost no capital goes into development of the many, many smaller, humdrum and more humble kinds of work. It is this kind of work, taken altogether, that builds up creative city economies and, along with them, an industrially and commercially strong national economy.

Canada's regional cities have their traditional role. They work primarily as service centres for the exploitation of resources from their hinterlands.

To be sure, all have some manufacturing, even the small ones like Halifax, Thunder Bay and Saskatoon, as well as the larger ones like Winnipeg, Calgary, Edmonton, and the largest, Vancouver. But large or small, they have not served, at least so far, as creative economic centres in their own right. That is why so many Canadian inventors and creative entrepreneurs must traditionally leave

Canada for other countries to put their ideas to use. That is also why Canada, taken as a whole, has developed so little manufacturing, and why so much of what we do have is undertaken in branch plants spun off from other countries. That is also why Canadian regional cities boom while the exploitation of their hinterlands is booming, as is happening in Alberta—but then characteristically stagnate when the resource exploitation reaches a plateau.

We now have a difficulty unprecedented in Canada. We have never before had a national city which lost that position and became a regional city. We have one now. Montreal cannot sustain the economy it had in the past, or retain its many other unusual assets, if it subsides into becoming a typical Canadian regional city. If that is all it does, it will stagnate and decline economically, and probably culturally too.

In short, Montreal cannot afford to act like other, uncreative Canadian regional cities. It must be the kind of place in which enterprises can develop new, innovative city-made products and services, and can take to producing locally wide ranges of former imports, and can find capital to help this happen. If Montreal cannot be that sort of place, it will be in grave and gathering trouble.

The chances are small that Montreal will be able to transcend the usual inertia of Canadian regional cities if Quebec remains a province of Canada. As Montreal's troubles deepen, Quebecois are certainly going to believe they would do better by taking their economy into their own hands. They might not do better, of course. They might cling to the traditional Canadian approach to economic life, themselves, and neglect other possibilities. But the point is, Quebec is now headed for trouble because of Montreal's situation, and the traditional Canadian solutions are not going to help. Inevitably, whether or not they would do better on their own, the Quebecois are going to think they could. Perhaps they even might.

This is why the issue of sovereignty, now that it has been raised, is not going to evaporate. The changes underlying that issue are irreversible and *they* are not going to evaporate. Until the issue is somehow resolved, it is going to be raised again, and again, and again. In one guise or another, it will go on, and on, and on. Thus, it seems to me that we'd better think about it, emotionally painful though it may be.

II

The Separation of Norway from Sweden

We know little from actual experience about peaceable separations. To be sure, Canada, Australia, New Zealand and Iceland all became independent in peace, as did a few of the still newer nations that formerly were colonies. But those were overseas possessions of empire. With only one exception—the separation of Norway from Sweden—new nations that were former provinces or regions of another country have come to birth in violence. They have either won independence after armed insurrection, highly disruptive terrorism or civil war; or else, like the Balkans or East and West Germany, they have emerged as a sequel to military defeat, prostration and dismemberment by conquerors. It is difficult, if not impossible to sort out the repercussions of such disasters from the practical consequences of the separations themselves. This is only one of many reasons that the singular case of Norway's peaceful separation is interesting.

Although the separation occurred in this century, in 1905,[8] it seems to be little remembered. Perhaps precisely because the tale lacks blood and thunder it has become forgettable. But it does not lack conflict and struggle. The kinds of emotions at work in all cases of separatist sentiment were present in all their force.

Offhand, it might be supposed that Norway was a special case because once upon a time, long ago, it had been an independent kingdom. But think of Scotland, Ulster, Wales, Burgundy, Aquitania, Catalonia, Bavaria, Sicily, Saxony, the Ukraine. . . . one could go on and on. Nothing has been more common than the reduction of kingdoms or powerful dukedoms to provincial status. Norway lost its independence in fact in late medieval times, and then lost it officially in the 16th century when the Danish King decreed that Norway had ceased to exist as a realm and was hence-forth part of Denmark.

This was how things stood until 1814 when Norway became one of the chips lost and won in the Napoleonic wars. It was given to Sweden. Denmark was out of luck because it had sided with Napoleon.

At this time Norway was a poor and undeveloped place. Although its economy improved somewhat over the next ninety-one years while it belonged to Sweden, it was still very poor in 1905, at the time of the separation. So we must visualize Norway's struggle for independence as taking place in two small provincial cities, Oslo and Bergen, a few poor and old towns, and the scattered and isolated settlements of subsistence farmers where most people eked out their livings. Norwegians today marvel at the succession of their great men, generation after generation, who emerged from the narrow, drudging, tradition-bound life and built the country's independence.

At the time Norway was transferred from Denmark to Sweden there happened to be a few months' hiatus between the signing of the treaty of transferral and the assumption of rule by Sweden.

During this moment of accidental freedom, a group of Norwegians proclaimed independence and called for an assembly representing a cross-section of the population. That assembly, held in the small town of Eidsvold just north of Oslo, went to work feverishly. In ten days it managed to write and adopt a constitution, and authorized itself to create a national bank and a currency. The constitution provided for a constitutional monarchy and a national legislature to be called the Storting, meaning "Great Thing." At the time, the constitution was the most democratic in Europe. It was also so well constructed and so workable that it still serves as the Norwegian constitution today.

But grand as all this sounds, it was pitiful too. Sweden had made its own very different plans for Norway. In Swedish eyes, Norway was now in effect a province. The arrangement in form was that Sweden and Norway were two kingdoms under one crown, like Scotland and England in the United Kingdom. Indeed, the form was proposed to Sweden by the British.

The actual rule was set up this way. In Stockholm the King appointed a cabinet of Ministers for Norway, composed of Norwegians. They lived and worked in Stockholm and served at the King's pleasure. On matters affecting both Sweden and Norway, these ministers joined with the Swedish ministers in one cabinet. On matters affecting only Norway, the Ministers for Norway and the civil servants on their staffs were the Norwegian government. So these ministers constituted both the provincial government of Norway and a portion of the national government. In Oslo, a governor-general was ensconced to represent the King and to see that the will of his government was executed.

In view of all this, the Storting and the Norwegian constitution would seem to have been rather in the realm of folk fantasy. Perhaps that is the way the Swedish government thought of it. Let them have their fantasies if it amuses and occupies them. At any rate, Sweden, to its credit, never forbade the Storting or tried to suppress its elections, never arrested or otherwise harried its leaders and members, never attempted to censor its debates or interfere in its communications with the Norwegian people, and did not poison Norwegian political life with spies, secret police, bribers or informers.

By means of persuasion during the first two years of Swedish rule, the Storting managed to pry loose two little fragments of autonomy. Sweden had made what seemed a generous offer, and probably was: the opening of military and civil appointments in both realms to people of both on equal terms. The Storting rejected the offer, and the rejection was respected by Sweden. This closed off to Norwegians the prestigious and ample opportunities of public life to be found in Sweden, but of course it also meant that Swedes could not occupy government posts within Norway, and the members of the Storting evidently thought that was worth the sacrifice.

The other point won was that Sweden agreed to separate its own debts from the debts incurred on behalf of Norway. In this way the Norwegians limited their own financial responsibility for Sweden but at the same time they insisted on taking their full share of a national debt without also having powers to determine the size of the debt, the way the money was raised or what it was to be used for. The Norwegians were also determined to use their own bank and currency which that hasty meeting of the constitutional assembly had authorized, and amazingly enough they did so for a period, although later Sweden tied the money to its own. After independence, Norway again had an independent currency and still does.

Thus two persistent themes were set from the beginning and thereafter ran through Norway's entire struggle. One was the Norwegians' lack of fear, poor though they were, about taking financial responsibility for their own affairs—indeed their positive eagerness to do so. The other was their strategy of seeking and grasping whatever bit, piece or symbol of independence they could find, no matter how irrational it might be, given their subordinate status.

They did not win another of those fragments until 1821 when they got themselves a flag. Not a national flag, which they would have liked. That was denied them on grounds that Sweden's flag was their flag too. Nevertheless, they got permission to use this flag of theirs on their mercantile ships, as a commercial emblem in northern waters. Years later they won the right to use the trade flag on all the oceans. Thus things went in the Storting, symbol or substance, push, push, push over the years, always for a little bit more. In 1837 they won another fragment of financial responsibility, the right of local taxpayers to govern local expenditures for purely local matters. Not all the ideas came out of the Storting. Early on, a poet conceived the idea of celebrating the adoption of the constitution by the Eidsvold assembly. His idea caught on, it soon became a great Norwegian national holiday, and still is.

Up to 1859 the conflict, though earnest, was on the whole very tame. But the Storting was turning balky, digging in its heels. That year it managed to hold off two governmental changes adopted in Stockholm and also asked Sweden to abolish the office of governor-general. Sweden refused. Now, before we plunge into the political crises that are going to follow, we need to be aware of other excitements brewing.

Norway had lacked, or thought it lacked, a language and culture of its own. The language of the pulpit, the press, the schools, the government, the capital city, all educated people and many who were uneducated too, was Danish owing to the centuries-long Danish occupation and rule. The Norwegians pronounced it in a distinctive way; nowadays it is called Dano-Norwegian. Even in

Dano-Norwegian, Norwegians had produced little literature, so the Norwegians assumed they had no culture of their own, as that word is usually understood.

Then, beginning in the 1840's, two young Norwegians started publishing folk tales they had picked up by travelling among the villages and listening. Their work created a sensation in Oslo. In the first place, the stories themselves were a revelation. Their originality, fantasy and beauty revealed a side of the national character Norwegians themselves had hardly appreciated. But the real bombshell was the language. The authors incorporated into Dano-Norwegian as much indigenous Norwegian vocabulary and idiom as they could, while keeping the work understandable to city readers. A new style had been born, based on a preference for selecting words of Norwegian origin. The style produced a new language over the course of time, called Neo-Norwegian, which by the 1890's became a second official language, making Norway bilingual, which it still is.

About the same time the folk tales were published, a battle shaped up between improvers and preservationists over whether to tear down the ruins of an ancient cathedral in Trondheim. The preservationists, who won, were headed by Norway's leading historian, who used the battle as an opportunity to educate his countrymen in the achievements and civilization of medieval Norway.

In sum, beginning about the middle of the 19th century, Norwegians began to understand they had a history in which it was possible to take pride, a language it was possible to enjoy, and the beginnings of a literature of their own. The excitement and pride this generated was rather overdone, if anything, both then and later. According to an English historian of modern Norway, "anything done by a Norwegian in the arts and sciences, commerce and even sport had always to be vociferously acclaimed as the triumph of a specifically Norwegian culture. . . ."

Alongside the nationalist ferment rose another movement, also idealistic and exciting, which ran counter to independence, a movement called Scandinavianization. Its object was the unification of Denmark, Norway and Sweden into a single nation. The Swedish king favoured the movement, so did many people in all three countries and many Europeans outside them. Unifications were in the air everywhere. The German principalities were uniting into the North German Confederation which became the German Empire. Austria and Hungary were sealing the union that was to hold the joint empire together for half a century. Here in Canada, the time was nearing for Confederation and the British North America Act. In the Scandinavian countries the movement for unification flourished for some twenty years; then abruptly in 1864 it collapsed when Norwegians refused to enter a war with Germany on Denmark's side.

Now let us get back to the Storting which we left in 1859 when Norway had been turned down on its proposal to abolish the governor-general. The Swedish government had remained a good deal more placatory and patient with the cantankerous Norwegians than the Swedish people had. One can see why Swedes were becoming impatient. Sweden had acted very decently toward Norway within the framework of the conception that Norway was a province; but the Norwegians would not meet the Swedes half-way by taking some pride and pleasure in the association. When the issue of the governor-general was raised, the King had been willing to agree but he was stopped by angry Swedish public opinion.

Instead of backing off from this hostility, the Storting continued to press the issue of the governor-general so persistently that finally, after fourteen years, it got its way. The King abolished the post and in its place created a new office, Minister of State for Norway, a position analogous to that of prime minister. The gain for Norway was the implication that the centre of Norwegian authority was now in Oslo, not Stockholm.

This change was only the first step in a much more ambitious Norwegian scheme: attainment of responsible government under a true parliamentary system. The Storting passed a bill providing for ministers to sit with it and be responsible to it. It was promptly vetoed by Sweden. Hostility between the two peoples mounted further, and tensions increased to the point that during the next thirty years, until separation, there were at least three occasions when it appeared that either Sweden or Norway might take up arms against the other.

During a good part of this perilous period, opinion in Norway was split, although separatists were always in the majority. Within the Storting a split existed that was tailor-made for dissension. In election after election the party favouring separatism was returned with decisive majorities. But the quasi-prime minister, the new Minister of State for Norway who had replaced the governor-general, was a unionist. The government civil service consisted of unionists too. The actual leader of the Storting majority, who was the leader of the separatists, was without formal power. Crisis of some sort was inevitable and it came.

What happened was that the separatist majority proceeded to amend the constitution to require responsible government. Of course the measure was vetoed. So the Storting passed it twice more, each time after elections that returned larger and larger separatist majorities. After the third passage, which the separatists claimed overcame a veto according to the constitution's own formula for amendment, the Storting ordered Stockholm's Norwegian ministers to obey the amendment, come to the Storting, and start being responsible to it. Of course they refused.

A legal wrangle of stupendous complexity followed. Overruling the courts, the Storting proceeded to impeach the ministers, convict them, levy fines against them, and declare their offices forfeit and vacant. Through all this, tempers in Sweden rose and so did tempers in Norway. This was one of the occasions when violence appeared probable. The Norwegians feared a royal military coup, which had been rumoured. Volunteer rifle clubs began organizing to resist a coup.

All along, the Swedish government and King were voices of moderation. But now they had only two choices. Either Sweden must enforce its rule by military means, which clearly meant civil war, or else it must accede to the Storting's demand for responsible government.

Sweden chose the peaceful course. The King asked the leader of the separatist party to form a cabinet. Government of Norway by Norway, the grand and pitiful public fantasy of Eidsvold, seventy years before, had actually become a reality.

The uses to which the Storting put its new powers were on the whole exemplary from a democratic point of view. It concerned itself with such things as introducing the jury system for criminal cases, improving the school system, providing for locally elected school boards, extending suffrage. More ominously, it reorganized the Norwegian army on a more democratic basis. From this point on, the Storting could count on the army.

Things calmed down for about a decade. The unionist accepted responsible government as a fact of life and even won an election or two because of splits in the separatist party over personalities and strategies.

But beginning in 1888, the conflict flared up anew, this time shifting to economic issues. Norway was poor. Sweden, although better off, was underdeveloped and relatively poor too, and in an effort to encourage manufacturing it adopted a policy of very high tariffs. It directed those tariffs quite as much against Norwegian imports as against those from other nations. Perhaps there was some element of satisfaction here, some element of retaliation against Norway for having won the great tussle over responsible government. The Norwegians, with an economy already so close to the bone, felt as if the bone itself were being gnawed.

The only way Norway could compensate for losses of its trade with Sweden was to find more customers abroad for the work of its merchant marine fleet. But here Sweden had Norway in a bind too. As far as foreign affairs were concerned, Norway was still a part of Sweden. It contributed to a joint consular service. Norway now desperately needed consular help in finding and servicing new markets for its cargo shipping, and Swedish consuls were not that interested in hustling for Norway. So the Storting resolved to withhold its consular contributions and to establish unilaterally a service of its own. The King vetoed the measure.

The veto had to be countersigned by the ministers. But these were no longer unionists and would not ratify the royal veto. The government was dissolved and a cabinet of unionists was then appointed by the King, but it could not govern a Storting and a people who would not be governed by it. Its attempts to do so were a shambles. In Sweden, public opinion against Norway was again rising and again there was talk of war.

Now it was the Norwegians' turn to realize they had only two choices. They could make war to establish their independence or they could pay up their contribution and try to negotiate more attention to their needs. Norway chose the peaceful course. It paid up and negotiated. But no agreements could be reached and the talks broke down. Tempers in both countries grew uglier. The Norwegians embarked on a strong rearmament program for their military forces. Again war looked imminent.

This time it was Sweden's turn to back off. It did so by suggesting a compromise permitting separate consular services under a single diplomatic staff and negotiations began again. In reality, however, the Swedish position was hardening and the talks got nowhere. By this time even the Norwegian unionists, who felt betrayed by the Swedish negotiators, were ready to embrace secession. Plebiscites were called in Norway, great demonstrations were mounted, the country was in an uproar, and in the spring of 1905 the Storting, now organized into a coalition government of all parties, unanimously passed a bill demanding thoroughly separate consular services.

This was the final crisis. It was over and done with swiftly. The form it took was a legalistic deadlock, a kind of Gordian knot. When the King vetoed the bill, the ministers refused to countersign the veto and resigned their offices. All this was somewhat familiar. But this time the King refused to accept the resignations because that move had worked out as such a mess the last time. In refusing, he said, "No other ministry can now be formed."

The words of the King meant one thing in Sweden: that Norway must now knuckle under. But in Norway they were chosen to mean something different. There the prime minister, a Bergen ship owner much admired among his countrymen for his quickwittedness and efficiency, quickwittedly used the King's remark to mean that the King himself had dissolved the union. His argument was that the King, by announcing no ministry could now be formed, had announced he could not constitutionally rule Norway and so had dissolved the union himself. This went over as a great idea in the Storting which passed a resolution on June 7, 1905, that Norway's union with Sweden was at an end and then proceeded to act as the government of a fully sovereign state.

Of course this did not quite end the matter. As you might suppose, a tense time followed. But once again Sweden recognized that it was a matter of war or peace, and so it resolved matters in this fashion: if the Norwegians would agree to meet certain conditions, then Sweden would be willing to negotiate for dissolution.

The chief conditions were that Norway should dismantle its border forts and create a military neutral zone where its lands and waters abutted Sweden, and that Norway must hold a referendum to see whether its people actually did want dissolution.

The Norwegians had already scheduled a referendum. It produced an outpouring of votes overwhelmingly in favour of Norwegian sovereignty, and negotiations promptly started. They were complex and difficult, but now Sweden had accepted the fact of secession and Norway, for its part, recognized it was being dealt with in good faith. In this atmosphere the arrangements moved rapidly, and were readily accepted in both countries. In Norway, a historian has written, "the feelings of relief and of enhanced self-respect were comparable to those which other peoples associate with the winning of a major war."

It is difficult to say whether the outcome did greater honour to Sweden or to Norway. Let us say that it not only did honour to both, but also to civilization.

The separation, as it turned out, harmed neither country. On the contrary, it was probably helpful to both. The conflict, which could only have grown uglier and more dangerous, was disposed of. Sweden was better off economically in the years to follow than if it had had to carry on its back a poverty-stricken province, as likely would have been the case. Norway, although it went through hard times in its struggle to develop a modern and prospering economy, did succeed in doing so, and with a verve and inventiveness that it is hard to imagine Norwegians could have exercised had the government and people been preoccupied with bitter political grievances. Today each country is the other's best customer.

Here in Toronto, in two different office buildings, one on King Street, the other on Yonge, are to be found two trade commissions, one Norwegian, one Swedish. To me, the two establishments seem more than pleasant, busy, competently run commercial offices, staffed by cheerful, alert people. To me, they seem the concrete evidence of a miracle—a separation achieved without armed rebellion, without terrorism, without military defeat of a former ruler.

In the Swedish office I recently asked one of the civil servants how Swedes really feel toward Norwegians today: Do they harbour any feelings of resentment about the secession? He looked shocked at the idea. "Of course not," he said. "We make jokes," and he blushed. "The same jokes you tell in Canada about Newfies. But the Norwegians are good neighbours, good customers, our best, and they have made a fine country for themselves." Then he added reflectively, "We wanted them to like being with us, but—" and he shook his head.

There are many obvious differences between Quebec and Norway and between Canada and Sweden. Quebec, for one thing, is better developed economically and richer than Norway was at the time Norwegian sovereignty hung in the balance. Nor is the form of sovereignty-association that René Lévesque has been proposing as thoroughgoing as the sovereignty Norway achieved.

But there are similarities too. Quebec, for some years, has been taking step after step toward autonomy and these moves, as in Norway, jumble symbols with substance; demands for responsibility with claims to cultural pride; economic concerns with political concerns. Canada, for its part, is similar to Sweden in its recoil against the idea of civil war or use of military force to keep Quebec in its place. Canada is also similar to Sweden in not wanting its province to separate, and in wanting Quebec to take pleasure and pride in being Canadian. The government in Ottawa, like the government in Stockholm, is a voice of moderation, in comparison with the anger and hostility against Quebec vented in such places as letters-to-the-editor columns, many newspaper editorials, or on the part of some of the provincial governments. If Quebec does insist on moving toward sovereignty, I have an unshakable feeling that Canada's behaviour, like Sweden's, will do honour to civilization. That conviction is one of many reasons why I happen to identify emotionally, very strongly, with my community of Canada.

One of the real differences between Norway and Sweden on the one hand, and Quebec and the rest of Canada on the other, is that Norway and Sweden are so small, which brings up the question of whether it is an economic disadvantage for a nation to be small.

III

SOME PARADOXES OF SIZE

The idea of Canada becoming smaller than it is now, and Quebec being an even smaller sovereignty than that, seems economically threatening to many people. On the one hand, although we hear "Small is Beautiful," we also hear "Bigger is Better." Is either of these sayings enlightening as far as the quality of a nation's economy or government is concerned?

Norway and Sweden are plausible cases to support an argument for smallness. While both countries do have their problems, as things go in this world they are both successful economically. They produce amply and diversely for their own people and diversely for export, too. Their economies are up-to-date, productive, efficient and innovative, providing wide ranges of opportunities for their people. Yet Norway has a population of only four million, about two-thirds the size of Quebec's. Sweden has slightly more than eight million, about the size of Ontario's population. Each is small in comparison with Canada's 23½ million.

With that in mind, consider this economic argument that Bigger is Better. It comes from a fact sheet, as it's called, put out by the Minister of Industry of one of our provinces.[9] It could just as well have been plucked from any of hundreds of Canadian speeches, reports or panel sessions.

"Canada has the smallest domestic market of any major industrialized nation. That market, in addition, is more deeply penetrated by import goods than any of the other industrialized nations.

"These factors make it difficult for Canadian manufacturers to achieve sufficient scale of operation to support world scale technology, to permit adequate research and development activities, or to compete effectively in world markets."

It sounds plausible. But if we lift our eyes from Canada, doubts must creep in. Not only Norway, Sweden and Denmark, but Switzerland, Belgium, the Netherlands and Austria all have very much smaller populations than Canada. Small size does not seem to have handicapped their economies. And of course many very large nations have underdeveloped economies and great poverty—India, China and Nigeria are obvious examples.

Suppose we were to look at Norway or Sweden in comparison with the Soviet Union; or at the Netherlands in comparison with much bigger Spain or even Britain. And then suppose we were to decide that the differences among these nations' economies must be caused by the differing sizes of their domestic markets. In that case, we would have to come to exactly the opposite conclusion from the one endorsed by the minister of industry I quoted. We would have to conclude that a small domestic market is an important asset and a large domestic market a severe handicap.

Obviously, the size of a nation doesn't determine how vigorously its economy develops, or how prosperous the economy is. Other things are more important than size.

The trade between Canada and Norway is, in microcosm, much like the trade between Canada and the United States. That is to say, only 15% of what we send to Norway is processed and manufactured goods. But half of what we get from Norway is processed and manufactured.[10] So here is Canada behaving like a semi-colonial nation, and little bitty Norway, which isn't even a member of the European Economic Community, behaving like a nation with a more highly developed economy.

We send Norway nickel ores and ore concentrates, raw material. Norway sends us back nickel anodes, cathodes, ingots and rods, more than $100 million worth in 1979.[11]

Some of the processed and manufactured goods traded between the two countries are similar in kind. For instance, Norway sells us thermometers, we sell Norway thermostats; we trade each other mining equipment, sound amplifiers, semi-conductors, carpets, mittens, toys, hockey equipment and quite a few other things. But Norway sends us 29% more *kinds* of manufactured and processed items than we send Norway.

Moreover, of the twelve chief items each country trades with the other, only three of Canada's are manufactured goods, while six of Norway's are. Norway's biggest exports to us include items like skis, farm machinery and commercial fishing equipment. Yet Canada is a much bigger farming country than Norway, with a much bigger domestic market of farmers and we also have big domestic markets for commercial fishing equipment and skis.[12] Why, then, are we importing these things, and in big quantities, too?

As for what the minister I quoted calls "world scale technology," Norway does fine. Glancing through the news items in the Export Council of Norway's 1979 annual,[13] I find, for instance, that a Norwegian company is exporting to the United States and to Sweden a computer controlled system for maintaining a vessel in exact position without need for anchors; another is building and equipping five fertilizer factories for the Soviet Union; another is selling underwater seismic equipment to China for geophysical survey work. Still another has built a branch plant in Brockville, Ontario, prepared to supply about 100,000 pairs of skis annually for the Canadian domestic market.

Norway makes tools of the trades for its own domestic producers, then exports those tools, too. We get fish canning machinery from Norway.[14] There's a big difference between simply canning fish on the one hand, and also making the machinery to do it, on the other.

Norway struck oil after Alberta did, but Norway is already one of the world's most advanced countries in the invention and manufacture of several items used in oil production,[15] and is a leader in the creation of new safety procedures and techniques.[16] One of Norway's many growth industries during the past decade has been the production of non-polluting electric smelting furnaces. First they were developed for Norway's own producers; now hundreds of them have been supplied to other countries as well.[17]

Now hear J. J. Brown, the historian of Canadian technology:

"Canadians have made contributions to world science and technology out of all proportion to their small numbers. Some Canadian inventions made possible major world industries, but we have ended up importing from England, Belgium, Italy and the United States billions of dollars worth of equipment invented here. This is our basic problem as a nation . . . If not corrected soon, it will leave us unable to compete as an industrialized nation in the modern world."[18]

To be sure, small nations can have miserable economies. Many do. So do many big nations. Norway, throughout its whole economy—consumers' goods as well as producers' goods like those I've mentioned—takes a creative approach. Canada, concentrating mainly on exploitation and export of resources, by and large does not take a creative approach. Sheer size is quite irrelevant in this area; size is not the Canadian economic problem. Economic arguments for or against the independence of Quebec cannot stand on the issue of size alone.

Is it a step backward or downward to make smaller things from bigger things? Is progression from big to small a sign of decline and disintegration?

Clearly, sometimes it is. The Chrysler motor company, if it survives as an entity, is going to be smaller than it used to be. Indeed, it is already smaller. Chrysler's share of the automobile market has been shrivelling, its deficits have been growing. Once the company was young, vital, growing, on the ball. But its recent history is a glum tale of failure—failures in judgement and forecasting, failures to learn from its competition, failure to understand the limitations of what it was doing, failure to consider other possibilities and pursue them.

Getting smaller often means things like that. As we all know, sovereignties, like automobile companies, can shrink or collapse because of inner decay or because they are nibbled and eroded by rivals, or both. That has always, so far, been the eventual fate of great empires; at the very moment when their power seemed most invincible, their wealth most enviable, their achievements most astonishing, the worm was already at work, the decline was in the making, the centre was no longer holding, things were beginning insidiously to disintegrate. For a country, getting smaller, or being cut up into smaller pieces, can certainly have connotations of dwindling, ebbing, sickening, decaying, disintegrating, failing.

But let's go back to industry for a minute, this time to the Standard Oil Company instead of the Chrysler Corporation. Back at the turn of the century, Standard Oil was not only a huge American corporation, but an outright monopoly. So ruthless were its methods of squeezing out or taking over competitors, and so powerful had it become, that in 1911, in a famous anti-trust judgement by the U.S. courts, Standard Oil was dissolved into more than 30 different companies. I'm not going to list all the new corporations that came into being this way, but four of them are among the largest oil companies in the world: Standard Oil of New Jersey, which became Esso, now Exxon; Standard Oil of California; Standard Oil of New York, which became Socony, now Mobil; Standard Oil of Indiana, which became American or Amoco. Some of the others were Atlantic Refining Company, Anglo-American Oil Company Limited, Colonial Oil, Continental Oil, Standard Oil of Ohio, ten pipeline companies, and a railroad tank car operation.[19]

In short order some of the progeny became more profitable than the original company, and many of them individually came to exceed or rival it in size. The first three offspring I mentioned by name, Exxon, Standard Oil of California, and Mobil, taken as a group, today absolutely dwarf the original Standard Oil.

I for one don't wish the oil companies well—or, rather, I don't wish well their function of providing oil for fuel. I hope that particular function shrivels, dwindles and ebbs in the future, succumbs to the rising use of safe renewable forms of energy. But whatever happens to the oil industry in the future, that does not change this fact: when Standard Oil, a big entity, was reduced to smaller entities, the process at work was not at all the same as Chrysler getting smaller.

Looking at an amoeba under the microscope, we may happen to catch it disintegrating. Or we may see it being engulfed, eaten up whole, by another organism. But we may also see it dividing. Look, two amoebas where there was one. Making little ones out of big ones, then—whether amoebas, Standard Oil companies, or new nations like Norway—can mean not disintegration but birth, with the chance for new vigor that birth implies.

In all vigorous economic life, division like this happens constantly. Perhaps it will surprise you as much as it did me to learn that restaurant employment is one of the largest categories of employment in Canada. In Ontario alone, over a quarter of a million people are employed by the restaurant industry.[20] But once I knew that the restaurant industry operated on such a scale, I was not surprised to learn that the industry is rife with amoeba type division. Here are a very few examples from Toronto: a chef from Winston's started Corner House; the manager of Café de L'Auberge and his brother, the maitre d' at the Constellation Hotel, started Quo Vadis; the maitre d' from Le Provençal started Casa Baldo; a chef at Auberge Gavroche started Jacques' Omelettes; a chef from Truffles started Cafe Jurgens; the manager of Three Small Rooms started Fenton's. All are thriving, the children as well as the parents.

In creative, developing economic life, the amoebas don't always divide into more amoebas. The people who manage to spin off new organizations out of their experience in older ones don't always reproduce that older enterprise. They often are able to build new ideas into their previous experience and create new kinds of enterprises. This is a chief way an economy diversifies and retains its vitality. When that process stops in an economy, the economy stagnates.

"Big things turning into smaller things" thus has two different and opposite meanings. One implies decay and disintegration, the other implies birth and renewal of vigor. Once we recognize this, we can make more theoretical sense out of Norway's separation from Sweden, and the vitality that both countries and their economies displayed afterwards. And we can at least hope, with reason I think, that if Quebec does insist on separating at some time in the future, the kind of division at work will be new birth.

I have tried to keep away from speculative thinking for the most part, sticking instead to how things are in real life. But to conceive of new nations as being spin-offs from existing nations does raise a speculative question about some of today's large nations. When we look through the lens of history at big sovereignties of the past, we see that they reached a time when they behaved like decaying and disintegrating organisms. Must this always happen? What if they had behaved in time, while they were still reasonably vigorous, like dividing amoebas? Is this a means by which nations, like so many other organisms, could renew their vitality instead of stagnating and withering?

Bigness means power, as long as the bigness is combined with vitality. Power is the great attraction of bigness. Practicality is not at all its long suit. For one thing, big units make such big mistakes with such big consequences. Small things make mistakes and fail too, but in the sum of things these can more easily be absorbed, written off, taken in stride. The Chrysler company, it's said, is too big to let fail; the consequences are too big, even if in fact it has failed.

An old English nursery rhyme says this:

"If all the seas were one sea,
What a great sea that would be.
If all the trees were one tree,
What a great tree that would be.
If all the axes were one axe,
What a great axe that would be.
If all the men were one man,

What a great man that would be;
And if the great man took the great axe
And cut down the great tree
And it fell into the great sea,
What a splish-splash that would be."[21]

Yes, what a splish-splash the big empires make when they fail, and big companies make when they fail, all the big things make when they fail.

Bigness has another hazard, perhaps less obvious. The English biologist, J. B. S. Haldane, about half a century ago wrote a delightful short essay called "On Being the Right Size."[22] He pointed out, among other things, that sheer size has much to do with the equipment an animal must have. Insects, being so small, do not need oxygen-carrying bloodstreams. The oxygen their cells require can be absorbed by simple diffusion of air through their bodies. But being larger means an animal must take on complicated oxygen pumping and distributing systems to reach all the cells.

Haldane presents us with an interesting principle about animal size: Big animals are not big because they are complicated. Rather, they are complicated because they are big.

Haldane's principle, it seems to me, also applies to institutions, companies, governments, organizations of all sorts. The larger they are, the more complications they require: coordinators, liaison people, prescribed channels of communication, administrators, supervisors of supervisors, whole extra departments devoted to serving the organism itself. A small organization can get along without a bureaucracy. A big one cannot.

Big organizations are not big because they are complicated. Rather, they are big because they produce a huge output of telephones or have a lot of welfare clients or govern a very big population. But they are complicated because they are big.

Complications have their price, but can be worth it. For instance, the human brain, with its incomprehensibly numerous cells for storing, sorting, cross-referencing and retrieving words, and doing so many other things too, is so complicated that my own brain cannot understand its own complications. There are many prices exacted by our brains' large capacities, which animals with smaller brains escape. We must use exorbitant amounts of fuel to maintain our brains and the services for them; we seem to be subject to more mental illnesses than chickens or cows; we have to be born in an exceedingly helpless state in order to emerge before the head is too big for the birth canal; we have very extended childhoods compared with other animals, which can be hard on parents, and so on.

Just so, many jobs in this world can best be done, or can only be done, by large units. It would be too bad, or so I think, if we could contend only with the simplicities of little villages or towns. But there is a price to be paid for the size of big cities: the physical, economic and social complications they require must be respected and constantly kept in working order, on pain of breakdown.

People who don't understand what I'm calling Haldane's principle are forever being disappointed that making big units out of many smaller units does not necessarily save money. They think consolidation will give economies of scale, and will eliminate unnecessary duplications. Sometimes this works, if the consolidated unit is actually rather small. Otherwise, the costs of complication can exact their own high price. When the Metro government of Toronto was formed, combining some of the otherwise duplicated functions of what is now the city and five boroughs, costs of government did not show economies of scale. Costs rose. If all the functions, instead of only some, were to be amalgamated in a single all-purpose Metro government, we may be sure costs would soar.

One of the worst costs of large size is that sometimes the complications it requires become so excessive they're stifling. They interfere with the very reasons for being of the organizations and functions they're intended to serve. A hospital architect has told me that a hospital in Canada can be designed, built and put into operation in roughly two years' less time than a comparable hospital in the United States. The added costs of those extra two years' time and effort are of course large. The differences in red tape, he says, are in large part owing to the fact that in the United States the huge Federal government gets into the act with all its own extremely complicated ways of doing things, and these are added to whatever complications are injected by the state, the municipality and the hospital administration itself. In Canada, the provincial governments, not Ottawa, take responsibility.

An Ontario civil servant told me a few years ago a similar tale about complications, this one concerning the clean-up of Lake Ontario. On our side of the border the work proceeded according to a timetable set up by international agreement. On the American side work fell far behind the timetable. The problem, he said, wasn't lack of money for the American part of the work, nor lack of will. People there had been working, in their own way, quite as hard as the Canadians. They were struggling with red tape. Red tape is the way we commonly describe complications of size that have become stifling.

Many jobs for which we've come to think very large outfits are necessary—just because that's the way they're being handled—can be done just as well by smaller organizations, indeed can often be done better. When the Canadian postal system was smaller, and had less mail to handle, it delivered the mail more swiftly and reliably. I think our postal system has become like the human brain in the sense that the post office itself is no longer able to understand its own complications.

One of the things I look forward to if Quebec ever does separate is two smaller postal systems instead of what we have. Small countries have their own postal systems; we don't see that as economically alarming. Much important Canadian mail is now being handled by relatively small courier services that are reliable and swift.

Many Americans take it for granted that telephone service has to be consolidated in a huge organization to be efficient. When I tell American acquaintances that the province of Alberta has long owned a separate telephone system, and that I can vouch from experience for its first-class efficiency, they're amazed. They become downright incredulous then they hear that within Alberta the city of Edmonton owns yet a different and separate telephone system and that it works with first-class efficiency too.

In New York, people have been pointing out for a couple of generations that the amount of money spent per pupil in the public schools is larger than the amount per pupil spent in many fine private schools with smaller classes. At first thought it's hard to imagine, short of assuming embezzlement, how the discrepancies between what is paid for and what is delivered can be explained. But if you explore the New York public school system's administration and see the vast burden of overhead the vast consolidated system supports, the costs become understandable. These are costs of size, not corruption. Perhaps we can speak of the corruption of size. Decentralization of the school system was undertaken about a decade ago in New York. But in practice, decentralization meant new layers of administration and complication within the central organization, because the central organization was retained too. As Marshall McLuhan has said, you can't decentralize centrally.[23]

Where national governments are concerned, a traditional way of keeping size and its complications under control has been federalism. Most large nations have employed federal systems in one form or another, and so have some very small ones, like Switzerland. Of course there have been other reasons for federalism too. But one use of it has been to try to keep big government and centralized government in hand.

Federalism has been falling on bad days in many places. The Soviet Union has federalism in form, but in fact is exceedingly centralized in its management and decisions. The United States has federalism in form, but in fact has been converting itself rapidly into a unitary state where all but the most minor and inherently local matters—and even some of those—must be traipsed through centralized corridors of power.

Centralization of national governments has been gathering force most of this century, and has been intensifying swiftly in our own time. When centralization is combined with increased responsibilities taken on by government, as has also been happening, the result is very big government and thus very complicated government.

Not all countries have embraced this combination. Switzerland and Japan, for instance, have relatively few programs which are the responsibility of their national governments or are paid for by their national governments. Canada has resisted extreme centralization because of insistence by Quebec, Ontario, Alberta and British Columbia on considerable provincial autonomy. Nevertheless, elephantiasis at the centre threatens us too. Ottawa's employees have increased by more than 50% just since 1968.[24]

Almost everywhere in the world bureaucratic complications are now intractable. Many intelligent, industrious and well-intentioned people in governments are spending their lives creating messes, futilities and waste because they cannot avoid doing so. The mistakes are big mistakes. The complications are labyrinthine. The red tape is stifling. The vast organizations are inflexible, impossible to put on the right track when they have nosed onto the wrong. Arrangements like this do not seem to me to offer a promising future.

Some functions and responsibilities taken on by governments seem to do more harm than good. But many are functions we have come to require or desire. If we take Haldane's principle seriously, as I think we must, increased centralization should not be combined with added or multiplied responsibilities. On the contrary, added governmental responsibilities should be combined with looser federalism, or else with separation.

Perhaps the only workable arrangement for busy governments is smaller nations. If that reasoning is correct, then sovereignty-association is a valuable idea, quite apart from being a possible way of dealing with the problems and discontents of Quebec.

IV

SOVEREIGNTY-ASSOCIATION: CONNECTORS

Sovereignty-association. The phrase has two elements meaning "independent" and "connected." Thus it is a thumbnail description of the human condition itself as we are born and brought up in it. As we all know, it's not easy for us as individuals to juggle those elements "independent" and "connected," juggle our individual natures and our social natures without doing unacceptable damage to either. Customs, traditions and philosophies of innumerable sorts help us in this juggling act. Even so, we have to practice and work at it as long as we live, forever trying to keep some balance between our independence and connectedness.

The organizations we have, including our governments and nations, are like all the rest of life in needing ways of being both independent and connected. If we were to try to find a synonym for René Lévesque's phrase, sovereignty-association, we might easily hit upon this rather neat translation: Allied Powers. But that phrase is already used up; it was once appropriated for a different association of sovereignties. Or we could try other synonyms, United States, United Nations or United Kingdoms. All appropriated already. It is the same with League of Nations. We might try Group of Independents, except that it sounds like a society of separate and connected artists or perhaps an organization of retail grocery stores. Or we might try Canadian League except that it sounds like a hockey association; or simply Confederation, except that in Canada, and some other places too, this already has its own meaning in the juggling act.

We seem to be running out of ways of saying "independent and connected governments." But we can always invent new names for new kinds of ties, as René Lévesque has done with the phrase sovereignty-association.

Governments, like the rest of us, have the help of customs and traditions too: practices already worked out for carrying on federal relationships and international relationships. But governments, like the rest of us, need constant readjustments. Otherwise, their relationships are liable to do unacceptable damage either to independence or connectedness. Governments aren't good at this juggling act. Mostly, they do not make readjustments and corrections successfully, when they make them at all. Their connections with one another often break down, usually very messily. Or the connections are drawn too tight. Then damage is done to independence and we get the insanely overcomplicated, highly centralized governments I used as examples in discussing the built-in hazards, wastes and weaknesses of great size.

An association meant to balance independence and connectedness of governments, and to keep that balance, must have two main attributes. First, it must have some means of feeling its way to that balance and some way of trying to keep it thereafter. In federal systems, constitutions are often meant to serve that purpose. But in the case of a sovereignty-association, such as René

Lévesque proposes for Quebec, the appropriate means is negotiation followed by treaties. Second, the basic framework aimed at must be suitable for the purpose of achieving *both* independence and connectedness. This is the point of view from which I am going to look at Lévesque's proposals and reasoning. My chief source is his book, *My Quebec*, published in an English-language edition in March of 1979.[25] His ideas, with little change, are incorporated in the Quebec government's white paper on sovereignty-association.[26]

What does he propose as connectors? He suggests five of them. I will say, right off, that four of them seem to me to be right on the mark. But the fifth seems so ill-considered and unworkable that I am convinced it would give rise to frictions and new hatreds, and would also undermine any actual independence for Quebec. I think I see a possible way of overcoming the difficulty, which I will suggest. First, let's look at the four connectors that ought to work.

The first connector Lévesque proposes, and by far the most basic, is free trade between the associated sovereignties.

We are much preoccupied in Canada with the subject of foreign export and import trade. We have far more statistical data about our foreign exports and imports than about our own internal trade. That is true of most other countries too. But Statistics Canada has made two surveys of internal trade. These were analyses of the destinations of Canadian manufactured goods. One survey was made in the late 1960's, the other in 1974.[27] Here is what they tell us.

By far the chief markets for Canadian manufactured goods are within Canada itself. Taken overall, in 1974 more than half the goods found their markets in the same provinces where they were made. In addition to that, more than a quarter found their markets in other provinces. Only 21% of Canada's manufactured goods were exported, chiefly to the United States. But to most provinces, the foreign exports were of little importance, because the lion's share of manufactured exports were produced in Ontario. Ontario alone accounts for 82% of all Canadian manufactured goods exported to the United States and for roughly comparable proportions of Canadian-made goods exported to other countries too. But even for Ontario, Canadian markets are vital. They absorb two-thirds of the province's manufactured goods. Much of that market, of course, is within Ontario itself.

The trade among provinces follows just the pattern one might expect from looking at a map. Neighbouring provinces tend to be each other's best inter-provincial customers for manufactured goods. Beginning at the west, British Columbia and Alberta are each other's best inter-provincial customers. The central west is split down the middle. Saskatchewan's best customer for its meagre production of manufactured goods, apart from itself of course, is Alberta. Manitoba's best customer is Ontario. Ontario and Quebec are each other's best customers. Nova Scotia is the best customer of Prince Edward Island, Ontario the best customer of New Brunswick, Quebec the best customer of Newfoundland and Nova Scotia.

The biggest inter-provincial trade in manufactured goods is that between Quebec and Ontario. It has grown a good deal in recent times. It doubled in value between 1967 and 1974. Of course, those increases are partly owing to inflation. If there were figures for increases in volume, they would be less. Nevertheless, the increases in value of manufactured goods traded between Ontario and Quebec go far beyond gains in value of manufactured goods exported to foreign countries. Quebec is no province's poorest customer for Canadian-made goods, not even British Columbia's.

The trade links between Quebec and the rest of Canada—especially with Ontario and the Maritimes—would still exist if Quebec were to become independent. They would have to continue to exist. The alternative would be intolerable economic privation for all concerned, perhaps even economic collapse or something close to it. There is no point in fantasizing how Canada could cut off trade with an independent Quebec, treating it the way the United States treated Cuba after the Cuban revolution.

Of course some people do talk as if an independent Quebec could be blockaded, ignored or isolated. From time to time the press reports sentiments like this: A proposed new corridor road across Maine would speed truck and tourist traffic between the Atlantic Provinces and Central Canada and it would take on added importance—here is the kicker—in the event of separation of Quebec from Confederation.

The man who said that is the past-president of the Atlantic Provinces Chamber of Commerce.[28] Of course, much traffic between Quebec and the Maritimes already runs through Maine because the route is shorter and more convenient in spite of the nuisances of crossing international boundaries. There spoke a man who accepts such border crossings with equanimity, even with some enthusiasm, yet boggles at the thought of people and goods traversing an independent Quebec. I think we must assume such remarks are cries of emotion, not rational remarks about trade. Yet even premiers and finance ministers make spiteful and frivolous remarks in this vein. They must think it is good politics, or perhaps their own emotions get the better of their reason.

Owing to the geographical position of the Maritimes, with Quebec lying between them and central Canada, free and unimpeded flow of trade back and forth through Quebec, as well as into and out of Quebec, would be especially important to the Maritimes.

On every count I find Lévesque is quite right in identifying free trade as a practical connector in sovereignty-association. Because it would be mutually beneficial, and certainly workable, it would also be a powerful connector.

The second connector he proposes is similar in principle: free travel of persons, meaning that Canadian citizens and Quebec citizens could travel back and forth as a right, without passports. He also proposes, as a possible point for negotiation, dual citizenship with joint issuance of Canadian-Quebec passports for foreign travel.

Both of these connectors, free trade and free travel, would leave present trade and travel arrangements essentially as they are now. So would customs union, or partial customs union, if that were included, as he suggests.

The next two connectors he proposes do entail some changes. They're meant, as I read their meaning, to give assurances to Canadians that Quebec sovereignty would not threaten their lifelines.

The St. Lawrence, over much of its course, runs solely through Quebec territory, yet of course, it is vital to Ontario directly and to all the rest of Canada indirectly. So Lévesque has proposed a maritime community, which the white paper spells out as a membership for Quebec alongside Canada and the United States on the International Joint Commission for the St. Lawrence Seaway.

The fourth connector he proposes is military, and therefore deals with an inherently touchy subject. He proposes that Quebec participate in the same military alliances as Canada, which means participation in NATO and NORAD. Offhand, such a suggestion might seem logically to fall into a category of cooperative programs, but he includes this proposal as part of the framework of association, as does the white paper. I think he is correct to include it as a basic connector. A sovereignty such as Canada simply could not permit an associated sovereignty, such as

Quebec, to take a different military line, or no military line, where defense arrangements are concerned. Nor could it possibly be in Quebec's interest to do so either. Thus this is another essential of the framework.

Now we come to Lévesque's last connector, his proposal that Canada and a sovereign Quebec share the same currency.

Such a proposal might have seemed plausible between 1945 and 1971, during the period when what was called the Bretton Woods agreement on international currencies operated. That system, which was dreamed up in the United States, was adopted by Canada and much of Europe. It was an attempt to eliminate fluctuations in the exchange rates among currencies. All the currencies involved were rather firmly pegged to the U.S. dollar. Thus they fluctuated very little in relation to one another or, of course, in relation to the dollar. It was thought that international monetary stability would be achieved by this scheme.

But under the cover of this artificially imposed stability, discrepancies among the real values of currencies were building up, and in 1971 the system collapsed because it had become so out of touch with realities that it could no longer work. For one thing, countries that had been experiencing rapid rates of inflation at home were, in effect, exporting their inflation to other countries. Their currencies, although actually declining in value, still commanded high exchange rates. The United States was not the only offender of this sort but it was the most serious offender because the U.S. dollar was the anchor currency. In addition, the United States began running big deficits in its balance of trade and this led to a vast over-supply of U.S. dollars in Europe. That made nonsense of European monetary reserves, because U.S. dollars were included among the bank reserves against which European loans were made. From the mid-1960's, the system was thus heading for serious trouble, and the collapse, when it finally came, created a financial crisis. It also initiated a period during which many currencies had to be abruptly and drastically revalued.

Changes and adjustments which should have been taking place gradually over a period of a quarter of a century had been dammed up. Nowadays, when it is convenient to blame all inflation on the oil exporting countries, we sometimes forget that the serious depreciation of the U.S. dollar actually began in the 1960's and created havoc internationally.

Now here is the important point we need to understand when considering the advisability of shared currencies. National policies of many kinds influence the value of a country's currency. For instance, if incomes within a country are increased—by any means whatever—and at the same time there is no corresponding increase in production and productivity, then the money loses real value. We say too much money is chasing too few goods. Although non-governmental factors influence a country's balance of trade and also the domestic buying power of its money, national policies are among the most important influences in most countries today, including Canada.

René Lévesque wants Quebec to have full sovereignty over taxation and social problems. He also wants Quebec to have control over policies concerned with investment, borrowing, use of savings, and subsidies, as well as many other matters that directly and indirectly can inflate a currency or have an influence on a country's balance of trade, or both, and therefore can affect both the domestic and international value of a currency. These are powers now largely, although not entirely, held by Ottawa. Indeed, Lévesque complains of just exactly that when he says Quebec does "not control the real economic levers, which remain in the federal domain."

Suppose Canada and Quebec actually have become associated sovereignties, and suppose each actually is exercising the kinds of power that I've mentioned. Nowadays, when our currency is ravaged by inflation or otherwise seems badly managed, we blame Ottawa. Under the arrangement proposed by Lévesque and the Quebec white paper, Ottawa and Quebec would be blaming each other. Unless everything went very well indeed, they would likely be furious with each other.

Both Lévesque and the white paper say the answer to that is that the two governments could cooperate on matters affecting the currency. Yes, so they could. But there goes independence.

The trouble is that the governmental powers which affect a currency are the very core of sovereignty. Lévesque himself recognizes this whenever he talks about them in other connections. If I were a negotiator for Quebec, I would certainly want to aim at having and keeping the very core of independence. Or, if I were a negotiator for Canada, I would feel the same way about protecting Canada's sovereignty and independence. I would be afraid for Quebec to have sovereign powers whose use could jeopardise Canadian currency, yet I would see no point whatever in Quebec having sovereign powers if it weren't going to use them. And I would reason much the same way if I were a negotiator for Quebec.

Lévesque's general remarks on currency, both in his book and in his public comments after the white paper was tabled, sound as if at some time in the past he became a fan of the Bretton Woods agreement and has not given the matter further careful thought in recent years. His comments, including those on European currencies, are so out-of-date. Bretton Woods, before its messy breakdown, was supposed to lead to a shared European currency. It led to no such thing. Lévesque does not seem to understand that the members of the European Economic Community have excellent reasons for not proceeding toward a shared currency.

In his book, Lévesque introduces his comments on currency by saying, "As you know, this subject belongs in an area about which, as a whole, public opinion very easily becomes nervous. There is an aura almost of black magic to the word 'monetáry.'" The impression I get is that Lévesque himself is easily made nervous by the subject. Here I am conjecturing, but perhaps he fears that derogatory predictions about the probable value of a Quebec currency could easily be used to panic people in Quebec, no matter how ill-founded or unfounded the predictions might be.

But be that as it may, two of the things Lévesque wants for Quebec—sovereignty and a shared currency with the rest of Canada—are simply irreconcilable. Is there any way around this?

The experience of Ireland suggests a possibility. To see why, we must make a brief and sketchy sortie into some Irish economic history. At the time Ireland wrested its independence from Britain in 1922, it wanted free trade with Britain and it also wanted its own currency and central bank. Britain would agree on free trade, but only if Ireland agreed to keep the Pound.

Of course Ireland did not participate, in the years that followed, in British decisions that either directly or indirectly helped influence the fate of the Pound. And of course Ireland itself was so small a part of imperial Britain that nothing done by Ireland could much affect the value of the Pound. But because Ireland had wanted its own money, for reasons of pride if nothing else, a fiction was arranged. Irish coins were minted, very handsome coins with their own pictures: harps, pigs, sailboats. No British royalty on them. Bills were printed and called the Irish Pound. But the Irish Pound was the British Pound by a different name just as the Scottish Pound is to this day. The Irish coins were British coins with different pictures. The Bank of Ireland was a branch of the Bank of England.

In 1973 Ireland joined the European Economic Community, but the Irish Pound remained the British Pound. Then in January

1979 an interesting thing happened. Ireland joined the European Monetary System and Britain did not. That move severed the Irish Pound from the British Pound. Now Ireland had its own currency in fact. The new, independent unit of currency was named the Irish Punt.

Under the European system, national currencies now float against each other, fluctuating up and down within certain specified ranges for each. When a given currency transgresses those limits, the central banks buy or sell it in large quantities, whichever is appropriate, to prevent more massive fluctuations, especially those that could be triggered by currency speculators. Of course similar devices are used, when needed, to calm down the U.S. dollar, the Canadian dollar, the British Pound, and various other currencies as well. Every so often in Europe, when it is clear that realities are changing, the ranges of float for various currencies are altered. That lesson of Bretton Woods has been learned.

When the new Irish Punt joined the European Monetary System, it was assigned a range of fluctuations through which it was expected to float, below the value of the British Pound. The Punt was generally expected to fall rather badly and not to be stable. The Punt did drop very briefly to 91 British pence. But then it swiftly rose in value and hovered close to the top of the fluctuation range assigned to it, much to the surprise of many experts.[29] Through 1979 the Punt's value remained at about 97 British pence, which is as if the Canadian dollar had been worth 97 U.S. cents, instead of the 84 or 85 cents which was its usual 1979 value.

Even more interesting has been the Punt's stability. Throughout the year it remained more stable than the British Pound. Although the Punt is a minor currency—the population of Ireland is less than half the size of Quebec's, after all—it has behaved like

Europe's strong currencies, as one expert at the Bank of Canada's office here in Toronto put it.

The Irish, obviously, had developed confidence that they could depend on their own currency. Otherwise they would not have severed their connection with the British Pound.

My suggestion is this. If Canada and Quebec do construct a framework of sovereignty-association, it might best be done in stages, like the way Norway achieved its self-government and independence from Sweden—in stages. The complete framework of sovereignty-association might require too much adjustment for either Quebec or Canada to make at one time. If the changes were made progressively, then during the period when Quebec was in the process of achieving more autonomy and independence it could arrange a fictional currency like the old Irish Pound. This would actually be a shared currency, that is, Canadian currency under a different name. Then in due course, as Quebec gained both independence and self-confidence, it could convert the symbolic currency to its own actual currency, much as the Irish have done.

Fluctuations in currency can be helpful, especially among close trading partners. It depends, of course, on what causes the fluctuations. If the causes are changes in trade balances, then fluctuations can work very well as correctives. That is, a drop in the value of a small country's currency can help it boost and diversify its export trade precisely at the moment the boost and diversification are needed. The drop means the country's exports become cheaper. It also means imports become more expensive, and so the drop can help stimulate replacement of some imports by locally made goods, precisely at the moment the stimulation is most needed.

In a big country like Canada, embracing many and widely differing regions, currency fluctuations cannot serve those corrective purposes the way they can in a small country. That is because one region of our big country may badly need its exports boosted at the same time that trade surpluses in the country, taken as a whole, are pushing up the value of the currency, therefore making the exports of the region in question more expensive, not making them cheaper which is the help the region needs. The reverse also happens; then a region with a trade surplus must pay more for imports than it would have to if its own currency were at work. The more important the foreign trade of a region, relative to domestic trade, the more serious and regionally harmful these contradictions are.

This is a built-in economic difficulty. The value of Canadian currency that may be beneficial at a given time to Alberta, say, may not be the value beneficial at the same time to Nova Scotia. The value beneficial to Ontario may not be the value beneficial at the same time to Quebec, and so on. Indeed, it would be rather a miracle if the currency's value at a given time were actually beneficial across the country. It does not distinguish among the widely varying realities in the varying regions, or reflect them.

If in due course an independent Quebec were to acquire a currency of its own, Quebec would have a built-in economic advantage it now lacks, an advantage that countries like Norway and Ireland have. That would not solve the problem of Canada's less sensitive currency, but at least it would help a little by diminishing the range of regions our Canadian currency must try to serve so clumsily.

V

Sovereignty-Association:
Separateness

Quebec is the only province for which independence is realistically possible in the foreseeable future. The chief reason for that is equalization. Under our equalization policy federal tax yields from all the provinces, rich and poor, are pooled and then redistributed. They help pay for public services and social programs the poor provinces could not maintain on their own. In addition, Ottawa tries to help out the poor provinces with special, and usually very expensive, development schemes.

In theory, equalization is not charity. It has been intended to rejuvenate the economies of the poor provinces and to help them become self-supporting. But it has not really worked out that way. The poor provinces remain poor. Nevertheless the funds distributed from Ottawa do make poverty easier to bear and do help disguise the economic stagnation in the poor provinces.

The poorest are the Atlantic provinces, but Saskatchewan and Manitoba are also on the receiving side of the ledger. In any conference among provincial premiers, those from Saskatchewan, Manitoba, New Brunswick, Nova Scotia, Prince Edward Island and Newfoundland can usually be depended on to support strengthened central government. Quite apart from the emotional attachments of these provinces to Confederation, strong federalism is their bread-and-butter.

Ontario and Alberta are of course the two richest provinces, but British Columbia is also on the giving side of the ledger. In any conference of premiers, the three from these provinces can usually be depended on to press for greater provincial autonomy, more leeway to run their own affairs and make their own decisions, meaning looser federalism.

Neither the have-not provinces nor the haves are in a position to think seriously about independence. The have-nots are too dependent on the federal government. The federal government is too dependent on the haves. Ontario, Alberta and British Columbia are thus somewhat in the position of family breadwinners who have taken on heavy responsibilities for their dependants. They may complain about the burdens, they may grumble and insist on having their own way sometimes. But morally and practically, they cannot walk out on their dependants. The dependants, for their part, may grumble and envy, may even accuse their benefactors of having trapped them into economic dependency. They often accuse Ontario of having done just that. But the dependants can't walk out, either. What would they live on?

The bookkeeping of equalization is so complex and confused it is literally beyond understanding. And in addition to equalization payments, the federal government distributes many other funds and services. Nobody, whether in Ottawa or in the provinces, knows exactly what the balance sheets are, exactly what the difference is between tax revenues sent from any given province to Ottawa and the revenues and services received back.

Even so, the discrepancies between what is yielded and what is received are great enough in nine cases so there is no doubt about their financial roles in Confederation: three breadwinners, six dependants.

Quebec, the tenth case, is different. The Parti Québécois claims Quebec yields up more revenue to Ottawa than it gets back, and makes out a plausible sounding case to support that claim. Their opponents, on the other hand, say Quebec gets more than it yields, and make out a plausible sounding case to support that claim too. The very fact that both can argue this way shows how close the balance sheet must be. Walter Gordon has said that ten years ago, when he was federal finance minister, Quebec had roughly a quarter of the population, yielded just about a quarter of federal revenues, and probably got back just about a quarter.[30] Things may have changed somewhat since, one way or the other. Nobody knows.

The point is, that whatever may be the exact truth concealed beneath the impenetrable bookkeeping, Quebec is clearly singular. At present, it could become independent without forcing serious financial sacrifices on either the other provinces or itself.

Sovereignty is many-sided. Its various aspects overlap and interlock. But keeping that in mind, we can think of René Lévesque's sovereignty proposals under three headings: cultural, economic and political.

Cultural sovereignty revolves around language. That is to be expected because language is at the heart of any people's culture. What Lévesque wants culturally for Quebec is sovereignty over powers concerned with communication, immigration and language.[31] He defines communications as television and radio broadcasting. This seems to mean he wants a Quebec broadcasting company independent from the Canadian Broadcasting Corporation. As for immigration, he complains that for generations "the federal government has maintained a very active network of immigration offices in England, Scotland and Ireland, while there has never been one in France."

When he speaks of language itself, he regrets that, as he puts it, "a fortress of laws" protects the rights of Quebecois to use their own language. He says one of the reasons he has dreamed of political sovereignty is "precisely so that we will not have to legislate on questions which should be as clear as the air we breathe." In matters concerned with language, he wants Quebec to have, as he puts it, whatever is normal to a national community which administers its own affairs.

As to whether this is a good or bad cultural aim, I for one cannot help but think it is good. While I have been writing this, I have been entertaining myself after work by reading the translation of a charming Japanese novel written in 1913 about the Japan of the 1880's, and a novel about the pageant of English history, by Virginia Woolf. I love living these multiple lives. It is possible only because many different cultures have become wonderfully articulate, enriching us all. For the culture of French Quebec to languish rather than flourish on its own terms—which is the only way a culture can flourish—would mean some impoverishment for us all.

But those sentiments do not tell us why Lévesque and many other Quebecois have now become so aggressive about the elbow room their culture needs. The most thoughtful comments I have come across are those of David Cameron, an economist and political scientist at Trent University.[32] He points out that before "the quiet revolution" of the 1960's, French Quebec's culture had managed to preserve itself behind a shell of isolation and unchanging tradition. It did little more than survive, but it did find the security to do that. Now, he points out, there is no security for the culture in resistance to change. Too much else has changed.

The only possible way to insure its own future is for Quebec's culture to initiate changes and ride with them. It has to develop or die.

Cameron and the authors he quotes have some interesting things to say about changing views concerning uniformity and diversity. I am going to comment on this point because it has a bearing not only on cultural sovereignty but on economic sovereignty too.

A few paragraphs ago I remarked that every different articulate culture enriches us all. That is such a cliché we might suppose it has always been self-evident. Not so. It expresses a rather recent point of view.

During what we call the Enlightenment, the European intellectual climate that dominated the 18th century and prevailed well into Victorian times and in many ways into our own, people took a view of Nature which has since been turned upside down. The Enlightenment view was that Nature itself seeks standardization, uniformity, universality, immutability. Spinoza, a forerunner of the Enlightenment, put it in so many words. He wrote, "The purpose of Nature is to make men uniform, as children of a common mother." People always seem to want to believe they are in harmony with the world as it is ordered by Nature or the gods-that-be. Perhaps such a belief is necessary to human morale. At any rate, the concept of a natural order seems to wriggle into our thought about all kinds of things, and so it was with the thought of the Enlightenment. Universality and uniformity, as ideals, subtly influenced thought about education, politics, economics, government, everything.

In the meantime, naturalists went on studying Nature. What they found made it impossible to continue thinking of Nature as a force promoting uniformity. On the contrary, what they learned revealed Nature as a force which is forever wiping away uniformity and casting up diversity. Today we think of standardization, and immutability too, as being unnatural. Thus an American paleontologist can now remark, with every expectation of being understood by a general readership, that evolutionary biologists like himself, "tend to equate goodness with the correlation between unconstrained smallness and innovation, and the sheer exuberant diversity of life."[33] As you may have noticed by now, that sort of view has worked a strong influence on me. It did so long before I was conscious of its source in the thinking of naturalists. One cultural historian quoted by Cameron says that in the entire history of thought there have been "few changes in standards of value more profound and more momentous" than the shift from belief in natural uniformity to belief in natural diversity, a belief he sums up this way: not only are there diverse excellences in many, or in all, phases of human life, but "diversity itself is of the essence of excellence."[34]

That idea has not yet been assimilated into all the nooks and crannies of our thoughts, let alone our actions. We still find many cultural lags. But the belief that diversity is both natural and wholesome has come to influence thought and action in a thousand everyday ways. And we may be as sure as we can be of anything that as long as our current understanding of Nature's nature prevails, the belief that diversity itself is excellent will continue to be a powerful and growing influence on thought about all kinds of things.

At the time the underlying cultural rules for Canada were laid down, the ideal of uniformity and universality was still operating full force. As a heritage, it has left us with a deep uneasiness about the separateness of English and French Canada, and a feeling that our inability to dissolve the differentness has been some sort of social or political failure. That idea has been dinned into us by novelists, politicians, and especially by English-speaking Canada's historians.

But looked at in light of changing and changed ideas about uniformity on the one hand, and diversity on the other, the sense that we should dissolve the differentness of English and French Canada is antiquated. Looked at in that light, official bilingualism is an instance of cultural lag, a sort of last gasp of the Enlightenment ideal. We force English-speaking civil servants with no gift for languages to qualify in French, and we legislate the bags of macaroni and the announcements of postal rate increases into saying everything in both French and English, even where Italian and English, or Ukrainian and English, or Chinese and English or Italian and French might be more to the point. If we have failed at uniformity, well then, the bilingual policy tells us, we can at least still try for the standardization of universality.

But once we have come to feel in our bones that diversity is valid, then the vision of an artificially and uniformly bilingual Canada simply becomes arbitrary and silly. Then the separateness and differentness of English and French Canada no longer seems cause for uneasiness and regret on anyone's part. On the contrary, the whole stubborn tale comes to seem a triumph for the splendid principles of life itself. Lo and behold, here in our midst is differentness that simply would not be squelched, and that is now insisting on its right to flourish and flower, root and branch. Three cheers for the dogged persistence and mysterious vitality of diversity.

An important practical virtue of diversity is this: many independent institutions, even those with similar purposes, are bound to develop different aims from one another too. Under uniform control or centralized control, experiment increasingly comes hard, and eventually improvements come not at all. The chance of hitting on fresh ideas and fresh methods is thus the chief value of the Lévesque proposals for economic sovereignty; or at any rate, that is the chief value of them for the rest of us in other parts of Canada.

Almost all Lévesque's proposals for economic sovereignty concern investment, ownership and control. He wants Quebec savings and other capital to be invested in Quebec's own development. He would thus apply to Quebec much the same rule for control of banks that is now applied by Ottawa to Canadian banks. That is, he would like to allow non-residents of Quebec to hold no more than 25% of the voting shares of a bank operating in Quebec. Similarly, Canadian law now requires Canadian insurance companies to reinvest fixed proportions of their incomes in Canada. Lévesque would leave the ratios undisturbed, but the insurance companies operating in Quebec would have to reinvest in Quebec. By these means he would attempt to stem what he calls the haemorrhaging of Quebec capital. His name for this policy is repatriation of the Quebec economy.

Behind that idea are many specific worries. He worries over Quebec's huge borrowings from outside the province and the country, and the huge costs of servicing those debts. The interest payments drain money away. He worries that so many Quebec industries and resources are owned and controlled from outside.

He also worries over Canadian agricultural policies, about which he has this to say: "The Federal Minister of Agriculture very often follows policies which to us are undesirable and which sabotage the Quebec agricultural markets. This is the case very frequently in the milk industry, which is traditionally the backbone of Quebec agricultural production and which feels itself literally strangled."

As a consumer of Ontario's excellent and varied cheddar cheeses, I worry about the milk board, too. Its policies, the press informs us, are destroying all but the largest Ontario cheese producers. I will not be happy with nothing but Kraft and Borden Ontario cheeses.

Many people in other parts of Canada are, of course, worried about some of the same things that worry Lévesque. They worry that Canada has become perhaps the largest borrower of foreign funds in the western world; that almost half of Canadian manufacturing capacity is owned by U.S. companies; that Canada lacks venture capital or else does not know how to use it; that Canada's share of manufactured goods in world trade keeps dropping.

Lévesque's proposals for economic sovereignty are not concerned with concrete questions or issues of how economies develop. I have commented that Norway takes a creative approach to development and that Canada, with its fixation on the exploitation and export of resources and the attraction of branch plants, does not. Lévesque seems to take for granted the traditional Canadian idea that wealth is based on natural resources, not on the inventiveness of people. His notions about development seem to be essentially the same as Ottawa's. Nor am I impressed by the Lévesque government's pronouncements on scientific and technological research.[35] They sound just like every other bureaucracy's pompous nonsense on that subject.

In that case, we may well ask, what is the point of having two economic sovereignties where there was one before? Is there any value in this possibility, at least for those of us outside Quebec?

There is practical value. In the first place, Quebec's repatriation of banking and capital actually could amount to significant change in Quebec, and in economic life when any one thing changes, other things start to change too. In the second place, just the fact of different people being in charge in the two different sovereignties, and having two different constituencies, would increase the chances for fresh judgments and fresh approaches. And finally, the fact that Quebec really does have a different culture means an increased chance that things might be done differently there. At worst, we would learn nothing useful from Quebec's experience with economic sovereignty. At best we might learn a good deal. The milk board might learn something.

Now we come to political sovereignty. With one exception, Lévesque's proposals on this subject are easily stated. He would like the Quebec National Assembly, which is the provincial parliament, to be a national parliament with all the usual powers over taxes and laws that national parliaments have. He would like Quebec to have a seat in the United Nations, and probably membership in the Commonwealth. He would like Quebec to take its place as a nation on appropriate international commissions, and to cooperate with Canada as an equal on joint scientific projects or other joint ventures of mutual interest.

All that is straightforward, and simple and normal enough, at least in concept. But whenever Lévesque touches on the subject of a political structure to handle customs union and a common currency, his proposals become tortured. His usual lucidity turns muddy and his usual eloquence flounders.

On the one hand, he expresses fears that direction of Quebec's affairs might revert back to Ottawa. And as a general principle he fears that associated sovereignties face the danger of falling into what he calls "merely a multinational, multicultural federalism."

On the other hand, when he attempts to describe joint management of the currency and matters affecting the currency, he conjures up exactly the sort of centralized power structure that would make his fears come true. He proposes joint Canadian-Quebec bodies at what he calls the technocratic level; and centralized special ministries; and possibly also, in his words, "a delegated parliament to which both sides would delegate members who are already elected to their parliaments, and which would meet once or twice a year. . . ."

And then he adds, "It could go further if necessary, but on one condition: that, when the time comes, sovereignty in all its defined dimensions is neither affected nor restricted by exterior structures." Indeed? Then why have all those exterior structures?

The Quebec government's white paper conjures up an even more elaborate superstructure: a joint council of ministers for the two countries, Canada and Quebec, plus a commission of experts to act as a general secretariat for both countries, plus a monetary authority to coordinate some of the policies and actions of the two countries' central banks, plus a court of justice to interpret the treaties setting all this up and to keep both countries in line. The court's decisions would be final and binding on both Canada and Quebec. If Canada would like to have, besides all this, a super-interparliamentary assembly for the two countries, Quebec would be willing to consider it a matter for negotiation.

Two of Lévesque's aspirations for Quebec—sovereignty and a shared currency with Canada—are not reconcilable, for reasons I have explained. Here we see that same contradiction rearing its head again. The elaborate super-government would leave Quebec with only a pretense of economic and political sovereignty. It would be a fancy way to construct "a multinational, multicultural federalism," to use Lévesque's own description of what should be avoided. And it would saddle us all with additional layers of bureaucracy and with a new layer of central government and centralized control even more remote from us than what we have now. This would be a high price to pay for what I can only understand as Quebec's timidity about a currency of its own.

In sum, then, looking at sovereignty-association as a whole, Lévesque's concept seems to offer much that would be advantageous to both the rest of Canada and Quebec, but because of the illogical and unworkable proposal for a shared currency, the concept is flawed. The flaw is so serious that it would undercut all the potential advantages of sovereignty-association for Canada and most of the advantages for Quebec.

Does this mean, then, that sovereignty-association should be dismissed out-of-hand? No, not at all. Here I will offer a fable which happens to be true. Some years ago, the Ontario government joined with a West German corporation to try to develop a new form of transit—quiet, very rapid and efficient in its requirements for energy and space. Electromagnets were used to move the vehicles without friction on a cushion of air above a narrow, elevated track. Unfortunately, the thing wouldn't work on curves. After some $25 million had been spent, Ontario and its German partners dropped the project. Who wanted a train that can't turn corners?

The Japanese did. Japan Airlines took up the idea and spun off a new organization to work on it, under the premise that even if the system's track had to be straight there were plenty of good uses for it. This was reported in the Toronto press, along with the comments of an Ontario transportation expert who had visited the first Japanese test track. He said it was "so straight it's almost unbelievable," and that the absence of curves "simplified the project enough to enable the Japanese to get going."[36]

Soon afterwards further word reached Toronto from the head of the Japanese project's engineering group. He reported that they had finally found a way, after all, to overcome the trouble at the curves. Test vehicles in Japan, he reported, were now running successfully on two curvilinear sections of track.[37]

The moral of the fable, of course, is that you don't start with what you cannot do. You start with what you can do, if the doing has worthwhile advantages. Then if you can, you evolve improvements on that foundation. This is the commonsense approach to all creative endeavours of any difficulty. Indeed, it amounts to virtually a law of development, whether we are thinking of the way things are successfully developed by human beings or of the way development happens in Nature.

René Lévesque's concept has a flaw. It doesn't turn corners. But it can do other useful and worthwhile things. There is much to be said for it, both from Quebec's viewpoint and from the rest of Canada's. In any case, independence or sovereignty for Quebec would have to be introduced in stages and steps. By the time it became necessary for Quebec to confront the need for its own currency, it would likely have built up the necessary self-confidence, and a way of introducing the change could be worked out—either by means of a two-stage process like Ireland's or some other device. The problem is not nearly as difficult, technically, as putting those curves in the track, nor is the introduction of a new currency for a new sovereignty an unprecedented sort of problem. It has often been done successfully.

One of the hang-overs of the Enlightenment is the notion that immutability is natural. Of course it isn't; everything changes. No governmental arrangements last forever. The best we can hope for is that changes be constructive and flexible. We might think of sovereignty-association as an experiment, rather than as a solution for all time.

All of us, if we are reasonably comfortable, healthy and safe, owe immense debts to the past. There is no way, of course, to repay the past. We can only pay those debts by making gifts to the future. We are all worried, I think, about our bequests to the future, worried that we may be presenting the generations to come chiefly with heavy burdens and terrible unsolved problems, rather than new gifts.

Among the burdens we have contrived are the stifling, wasteful and all but uncontrollable centralized bureaucracies that have proliferated so wildly and rapidly in our time—even in Canada. What a mess. What a load for the next generation to bear.

Perhaps right now, and right here, we can do a little something to lighten that burden. If we were to work out a kind of sovereignty for Quebec, and a kind of association that really does combat centralization instead of increasing it, that would be a presentable gift to the future.

Nobody has quite done what we would have to do. Sort out and keep only the connections Quebec and the rest of Canada would need to trade with each other and cooperate on projects of mutual interest, and discard the connections that would require Quebec and the rest of Canada to try to run each other's governments as well as their own. If we could do that, we could say what people say of the gifts they're proudest to give: "We made it ourselves."

It could be our Canadian way of answering a question that Virginia Woolf has posed like this:[38]

"Look at ourselves, ladies and gentlemen! Then at the wall; and ask how's this wall, the great wall, which we call, perhaps miscall, civilization, to be built by orts, scraps and fragments like ourselves?"

GLOBALISM AND THE NATION-STATE

by
ERIC W. KIERANS

Foreword

Williamsburg provided, as Professor Abraham Rotstein has pointed out, an excellent metaphor for dealing with concerns that have engaged me since the Honourable Walter Gordon's budget of June 13, 1963—the vulnerability of the Canadian economy and the recognition that our status, in American eyes, was simply that of an economic and political satellite.[1] While I had vigorously opposed the minister's budget, it became clear to me in December, 1965, when the United States government imposed guidelines on their subsidiaries operating in Canada, that Mr. Gordon had been right to express his anxieties. For the guidelines had involved a principle—the principle that the American government had the right to dictate the investment and reinvestment policies, the purchasing practices, and the financial operations of Canadian companies in which Americans had more than a 10 per cent interest. What price Canadian sovereignty and jurisdiction in such a state of affairs?

Canada was later granted an exemption from these particular directives by a foreign government, but this is beside the point. The brutal fact of Canada's vulnerability to a neighbour's economic and political pressures had been bared for all to see. Henceforth the issue became—"Is Canada sovereign or is it not?"

When David Ricardo formulated his doctrine of comparative advantage, he was writing about trade between sovereign and independent nations, each choosing its own areas of specialization. He was not talking about trade between a motherland and its colonies where the size of the home markets and the direction of investment made the colony a supplier to the needs of the heartland. This was not trade but rather an in-house transfer of resources. In an imperial federation, the colonies and dependencies have no room to pursue the balanced growth of their own economies. Their role is to consolidate and strengthen the empire by undertaking those patterns of development that will converge with the needs and objectives of the empire.

If one wants to create a world economy, one does it in the Soviet manner. One creates a bloc, a collection of nations and peoples ruled over and dominated by a powerful state. The centre is supreme and imperial and all the rest are satellites. Then, and only then, can one speak of a collective world, a world economy in which the factors and resources of all the member nations are integrated in the pursuit of one set of goals, the goals of the governing bloc. The cohesion of the bloc is effective when the goals of the satellites—balanced growth, as an example—are sacrificed to the imperial aims of the bloc itself. Then the supreme power in the heartland can speak of combining the labour of some members, the minerals and petroleum resources of another, with the technology and capital of the centre to produce an optimum output geared to heartland objectives—world domination or whatever. In such an integrated economy, East or West, we can be certain of two results—the subordination of consumer interests in all parts of the bloc (including the dominant centre), and the vulnerability and dependence of the satellite members as their own specialized contributions to bloc production creates imbalance and distortion at home.

Within the Soviet world economy, the nation-state, as an independent political unit free to choose its own principal directions, no longer exists. The argument in 1983 seems to be, at least in the current Washington orthodoxy, that a similar cohesion must be assented to, if not imposed, in the West. The emphasis is tilting from the alliance outlook, all for one and one for all, to the imperial view—all for one and the one *is* all.

Economists who speak of a new world economy are thinking of the world, or the Western part of it, as one vast production line, turning out so many machines or gallons of paint or whatever. It is international production, using "the capital of one nation, the land of another, the labour of a third." The economic region is not a nation but the world itself.

The same people generally think of themselves as the core, the heartland, with all the rest a periphery. American economists, in particular, who describe the concept of international production as a breakthrough replacing classical (Ricardian) trade theory and salute it as a profound insight of great intellectual power forget, or do not know, that the Soviet bloc has been organized in this fashion since the days of the first five-year plan. Canadians, of course, see nothing new in all this, since Great Britain organized her colonies in this fashion and, at least since 1854, the United States has so regarded Canada as its economic appendage.

Extending the Monroe Doctrine to cover Europe and Japan made the commitment to the policies of international production and a supranational allocation of resources seem as natural as the night following the day. The result would be an economy of the

Western world via the restoration of the hegemony of the United States. This unified conception of the world is not an economic arrangement of production, consumption, and distribution patterns designed to satisfy the varying needs and objectives of nations in differing circumstances, but rather an arbitrary and ruthless imposition of productive processes geared to securing nuclear supremacy and undisputed world dominance as the first and major objective of a tightly controlled Western bloc.

Efficiency in international (or national) production of anything is easy. Settle on what it is that you want to produce and then produce it. The economic problems do not lie in the production process. They surface later in the exchange process, in the market place, in the consumption and consequent distribution of incomes arising from the particular production if it is consumed. The pattern of production in a market economy is dictated by the adding up of the choices of consumers, which, being infinitely varied, do not admit of less than numberless producing units—from family units and selfless communities willing to work for no reward or very little, the growing informal (bartering-services) economy espoused by the Vanier Institute, to the local, provincial, regional, and national markets that integrate the myriad decisions to exchange and the even greater number of decisions not to exchange.

In a world-command economy, which is not a market economy, the organization of production and consumption obviously lends itself to international production. Nuclear missiles come to mind. But in this instance, production may be divided between a Soviet bloc and a United States bloc. Surely, according to the logic of the one-world economists, the two should then get together and meld their technology, resources, capital, and labour and produce at optimum efficiency, say, fifty thousand nuclear missiles. Since this production is its own consumption, they could each take twenty-five thousand missiles home, to do with as they will, so long as they leave the rest of us with the freedom to look after our own problems of poverty, unemployment, inflation, and pollution of the environment.

To withstand the Soviet might, it is not necessary for the nations of the West to regroup themselves into provinces within a great United States empire and so become the very thing that we despise. Yet there are many in the corridors of power in Washington who bitterly regret the decline in the capacity of the United States to control and direct the course of political and economic change, as it was able to do in the two decades following the Second World War.

The following lectures were recorded prior to the United States intervention in Grenada. The circumstances surrounding the invasion make clear that the United States has little faith or confidence in alliance systems (and even in some allies) and is in fact determined to play a role that emphasizes its power, both military and economic, to control events—and this with or without the consent of members of the alliance.

To have power is to use it. The sources of United States power are the nuclear force, a market well in excess of three trillion dollars, and a veto power over IMF decisions on the granting of loans and credits to nations.

The nuclear umbrella is of incalculable benefit to Europe and important to Japan. Canada would be severely damaged by even a partial closing of the American market to our goods. The less affluent nations, living with the burden of monstrous debts and interest repayments, depend on U.S. good will as they plead their case for further loans. These are strong cards, and, in the game of power politics, there should be little doubt that the United States can and will play them.

The view from Washington holds that the policies of the

nation-states of the West *must* conform to the needs of global security as defined by the United States. The use of such terms as "alliances," "participation," and "interdependence" has been abandoned as foolish rhetoric that influences no one. The remaining nation-states of the Western alliance, therefore, face the double challenge of maintaining their own sovereignty and independence in face-to-face confrontation with their dominating partner while, at the same time, making clear to the Soviet bloc that there is in this diversity the real strength that comes from knowing that freedom is worth defending and that it will be defended at all costs.

Twenty-two years ago a director of a large Swiss bank gave me his view of Canada as seen from his boardroom in Geneva. "Your country is all but faceless," he said gently, describing our passivity and inertia in the face of American initiatives.

Later, in the rather long discussion, he mused, "You do have cards of your own to play, if you would only act instead of being always acted upon. After all, if the United States cannot get along with Canada, who can they get along with?"

If we do not want to live in the bipolar world of perpetual confrontation, we, as a people, should say so—loud and clear.

PROFESSOR ERIC KIERANS
Department of Economics,
Dalhousie University,
Halifax, Nova Scotia.

I

The Meaning of Williamsburg

The theme of these lectures reflects an anxiety for the continued freedom and independence of the constitutionally governed nation-states. In 1983, military security demands the close collaboration of the nations of the West, but does it require the formation of a totalitarian bloc to match the satellitic cohesion of the Soviets? Secondly, given the increasing pressure for ever-greater levels of economic integration, how much freedom will nation-states have to set their own objectives and to choose their particular policy instruments and institutions?

Military security in a nuclear age and the alleged efficiency of economic interdependence are the arguments used to force the industrial nations of the West along the road to political unification. At Williamsburg, Virginia, the seven leading industrial nations put their stamp of approval on American defence proposals as well as the U.S. program to promote the convergence of the economic policies and performance of the group.

The meaning of Williamsburg is quite simply that the global community has arrived and that the industrial nations of the West are transforming themselves into a superbloc to match the cohesion and forced unity of the members of the Warsaw Pact. NATO, the OECD, the IMF, and GATT are organizations without authority or the power to make decisions. Making recommendations, searching for consensus, dialogue and debate—the time for all this is past. Government of the Western world, under the hegemony of the United States, is a distinct possibility by 1990.

The summit statement on arms control of May 29, 1983,[1] agreed to by all seven nations, contained the following declaration: "the security of our countries is indivisible and must be approached on a global basis." President Reagan, in supporting the declaration, effectively extended the protection of the Monroe Doctrine from North, Central, and South America to Europe and Japan. With this single sentence, the industrial nations of the West became a single, homogeneous bloc, and the six members underlined their gratitude for and submission to the absolute dominance of the United States by agreeing to "proceed with the planned deployment of the U.S. systems (Cruise and Pershing II) in Europe at the end of 1983"—unless the Soviet Union agrees to meaningful and constructive concessions in the negotiations on strategic weapons, intermediate-range nuclear missiles, and chemical weapons.

Confirming the objective "to maintain sufficient military strength to deter any attack, to counter any threat, and to ensure the peace," the conference studied the American proposals for the integration of the national economies and the convergence of economic policies. Military strength depends on productive power, and the optimization of productive power requires the clear recognition of the bloc's priorities, the organization, acquisition, and development of the resources of all the members, and the allocation and budgeting of the total resources for maximum efficiency and output.

Ignoring the desire of each nation to retain as much freedom as possible in setting its own priorities and the policies necessary to the resolution of its particular problems, the conference placed the needs of the bloc itself ahead of the requirements of the merging members. "East-West economic relations should be compatible with our security interests," states the declaration,[2] thus placing a large question mark on the future of European-Soviet trade, though not necessarily on American grain exports.

The path to economic unification is spelled out in an annex detailing the necessary "near-term policy actions leading to convergence of economic conditions in the medium term."

In the realm of monetary policy, all nations are agreed on a "disciplined non-inflationary growth of monetary aggregates and appropriate interest rates," a clear assumption that the relative position of the members is in equilibrium.

The nations will pursue a deflationary fiscal policy by exercising restraint over government spending, by reducing structural budget deficits, and by keeping in mind the impact of tax and expenditure policies on interest rates and economic growth. Since the seven members are also expected to increase their support of NATO and military expenditures, it is clear that the interests of consumers are being subordinated to the objectives of the military union.

Just as restrictive of national freedom to make one's own choices as the monetary and fiscal packages is the agreement to pursue greater stability of exchange rates and policies of convergence and co-ordinated intervention in exchange markets. This attempt to introduce a 1983 version of the Bretton Woods monetary system is bound to fail for the same reason that Bretton Woods failed. One cannot packet together nations of unequal size, resource wealth, and productive power except under military and economic pressures.

It is sensible to agree that for some purposes, such as military security in this nuclear era, nations must join in collaboration and alliance. It is a question, however, if the creation of a supra-national bloc on the same model as the Soviet system is called for. Internalizing all military power in a single high command would be the surrender of the very values and traditions that we cherish, the freedom to choose the principal directions of national life. For military security inevitably demands the inte-grated economic community, and this adds up to the loss of national autonomy. Countries that have no control over their monetary system, their tax and expenditure policies, and their exchange rates are not sovereign.

Collective action under the leadership of the superior power, the United States, has been the Western option, but it has, until recently, taken the form of alliances and treaty organizations in which all partners are heard and presumably their views taken into account. The motivating principle behind the degree of central-ization accepted at Williamsburg seems to be a conscious longing within the American leadership for the same terrifying accumula-tion of powers and degree of cohesion and political conformity in the West that is the Soviet reality. One has to ask if it is necessary to convert an organized system of alliances into a cabinet of satel-lites and so degrade the very system of Western traditions of pluralism and liberty that we proclaim, in order to achieve the alleged advantages of the efficiency and discipline that we impute to the members of the Warsaw Pact.

Centralization of power and authority that begins with the military and economic sectors leads inevitably to pressures for the integration of all decision making and a degree of commitment and obedience to the bloc's objectives that leave only marginal room for the national purposes. Such a commitment can hardly be expected of democratic nations possessing a long history of freedom to set their own goals and to choose the instruments of policy necessary to their achievement.

To create a Western bloc involves the location of the foundations of military and economic power in a single authority, the most powerful member being the United States. The foundations are the centralization of all decision making; the unification of the total resource base of the member nations; the control and allocation of all resources, human and material, to achieve maximum output; forced resolution of conflicts between the bloc's objectives and national goals; and finally the subordination of the interests of consumers and the standard of living generally to the goals of increased productive power and military security. Efforts to regiment the Western world in this fashion would require, if not the terrorization practised in the East, enormous economic pressure and the terrifying threat to abandon the recalcitrant to the nuclear nightmare.

Before we proceed further in the substitution of the present system of international relations, the pluralism of the Western alliances, for the tightly knit bloc control that typifies the Soviet monolith, we should examine very carefully the pressures that are being exerted. One virtue of the present international system is that, while the United States is clearly the leader of the West, it has to take account of and bring into consensus or compromise the views of its partners. The creation of an American-Japanese-European superbloc under American hegemony allows no such flexibility or dialogue. We become more and more the satellites, forced to subordinate national priorities for the interests of the bloc system.

If we go this route, we have to ask ourselves how different would the two systems of political control over the lives and times of our citizens then be. The major difference would appear to be the greater diffusion of property and private power in the West, but how quickly could that be eroded in the new system of centralized decision making?

Given a superbloc in the West, the two political systems would have much more in common than is supposed. Each could annihilate the other with its nuclear power. Each would emphasize the growth of industrial and productive power as a priority. Each would subordinate the interests of the consumer to military and economic growth objectives. As the people of the Soviet bloc are powerless before the bureaucratic authority, so too would the people of the West lose power to our corporate and public monuments of stone. The difference would be one of degree.

The argument for military globalism is that only then would the West have the cohesion, discipline, and the nuclear inventory and configuration that could effectively oppose the Russian menace. Experts, however, such as Admiral Robert Falls of Canada, Rear Admiral LaRocque of the United States, and field Marshal Lord Carver of the United Kingdom, tell us that we have more than enough nuclear weaponry already in position to inflict untold casualties and destruction on the Soviet Union. Since the enemy can do the same to us, both sides are in the same position—no possible victory, only complete and utter defeat.

It is a good thing to know that the Western alliance has more than enough nuclear missiles; the bad thing is that we keep on building more; the worst thing of all is not to know why—why more production, why more deployment, why a superbloc of the West. If we are not satisfied with the power to annihilate, what will we be satisfied with?

NATO officials have themselves maintained that the 1979 decision to station intermediate-range nuclear missiles in Europe was psychological and political rather than military. The NATO generals, in their venture into psychology, argue that the highly visible death-dealing Cruise and Pershing II missiles deployed on European soil will comfort the populations of Europe. It is at least arguable that fear, despair, and hysteria at the sight of some 572 of these monsters of destruction may be the paramount response, with Europe facing a hot and riotous period as installations go forward.

NATO and the Warsaw Pact are the instruments of their respective masters. They are neither political nor executive in respect of their powers. Both NATO and the Warsaw Pact are genuine deterrents against perceived threats. We have here the classic instance of two bureaucracies leaning upon each other for nourishment. As each screams its defiance, they guarantee the continuity and growth of the functions and purposes of the other. Russia uses the belligerence of NATO to maintain its grip over its Eastern satellites, while the Warsaw Pact serves as the rationale for stripping the industrial nations of the West of sovereignty in their military and economic policies and creating the United States supranational bloc.

The summit conference is now an established coming together with the purpose of stopping the Russian threat. With this objective there can be no dispute. In a nuclear era, we can hardly find security on a nation-by-nation defence. The meaning of Williamsburg, however, is that we intend to create the identical military and economic monolith in the West that exists in the East. Thus there will be two, and two only, supranational powers facing each other, each power believing that the other is all black while absolute right and justice remains with it alone. Williamsburg brings not a movement toward the foundation of a true international order but the absolute polarization of two political crusades treading a head-on collision course.

Williamsburg has brought us back to the bipolar world of the

1950s and John Foster Dulles, with Moscow speaking for the East and Washington speaking for the Canadians, Europeans, and Japanese. In the fluid, unpredictable, nuclear atmosphere of violence, the polarization can only deepen the tensions and expand the areas of conflict, making reassessment and negotiation all the more difficult since neither side will want to risk the possible humiliation of retreat and loss of face.

Williamsburg reaffirmed the deployment of the intermediate-range nuclear missiles in Europe; it announced the creation of a Japanese-American-European superbloc. We already live in a world that faces annihilation in the event of a nuclear war. Our future will be, as Jonathan Schell describes, "the republic of insects and grass." The superbloc set forth at Williamsburg adds little if anything to the military unification that already exists at NATO. It makes little sense to add to the arms or improve the system when you have already passed well beyond the point of mutual annihilation. If more arms are redundant, more food, water, education, health, and housing for the underprivileged of this world are not. Reducing the production of arms by two weeks would enable us to double our spending on these vital elements in the world's standard of living.

Despite all the headlines, all the editorials, all the meet-the-press and week-in-review commentaries, there is no evidence that the danger of nuclear war is growing. There can be no winners in a nuclear holocaust. There is something fundamentally irrational in the confrontation of two powers that keep their citizens in anxious suspense even though each has brought the other to a standstill. When victory is not possible, when further action means utter defeat, it is time to accept the deadlock, relieve the tensions, and create the environment that will enable all peoples to pursue the ways and means to creative living.

An American-Japanese-European economic bloc to support the

military stance makes good sense from the American point of view, if it can be obtained under the terms outlined in the Williamsburg agreement, which in effect defined the basic economic unit as the Western world. Given the total commitment of the United States to guaranteeing the security of the industrial West, including Japan, the fusion of economic policies as they converge with American objectives follows as the necessary condition.

Thus President Reagan outlined the agreement as "policy actions leading to convergence of economic conditions in the medium term." Essential to the agreement is the understanding that East-West economic relations should hinge upon and be compatible with the security interests of the West. This restores the United States to the unquestioned political, economic, and military dominance that it enjoyed in the two decades prior to its involvement in Vietnam.

That the United States should be the heartland, the core, of Western values and principles is not in dispute. That it should exercise leadership, persuasion, and direction by example is again not the issue. That the United States should be in a position to impose and to dictate policies and priorities for the other nations of the West would be the end of the politics and pluralism of the Western world. It is this that is unacceptable.

Williamsburg not only defined the industrial West as a global community, it outlined some of the terms of global governance. The leaders agreed to maintain appropriate interest rates and to avoid the inflationary growth of monetary aggregates. They further agreed to reduce their budget deficits by exercising stringent control over government expenditures—at least in the areas of housing, education, health and welfare, and social security, but presumably not in the area of military and defence expenditures, where all members are expected to increase their shares of spending. Equally fundamental is the agreement to work for stabilized exchange markets and, by restricting the use of exchange-rate policy to solve critical national problems, so to strip away the flexibility open to sovereign and autonomous nations and their elected leaders. In other words, the needs of the bloc take precedence over the particular priorities of the member nations.

The problem with extending the concept of interdependence from the military to the economic sector is that we are dealing with the creation of a bloc composed of nations which are now sovereign, which vary in resource wealth, size of markets, needs for capital, and are unequal in productivity and overhead costs. The policies of convergence leave no room to manoeuvre for the solution to these imbalances and the problems that they bring.

The heightened anxiety caused by the increasing polarizations of the two superpowers prevents people from arguing the unsupported and unproven claims that economic interdependence will yield a greater output and that maintaining the benefits of their greater efficiency is vital to Western survival. The blunt facts are that economic interdependence demands the integration of national economies and, therefore, the denial of freedom to an elected government to address a nation's problems and priorities.

A nation will then be defined quite simply as an area, the part of a greater entity, an area where resources are plentiful or an area where labour is cheap or an area where capital is plentiful. In the relevant market of the West, some regions will specialize in steel production, others in chemicals, pulp and paper, cars, agricultural products, etc. Engineers, using technical principles of location theory, will put populations, money, and land in their computers and position the producing facility accordingly. Unstated is the basic assumption that, to make economic interdependence work, there must be a perfect mobility of labour—that is, people must be willing to follow capital, the more perfectly mobile factor, as it moves across nations and continents. Equally unstated and undebated is the pretence that immigration laws and other restrictions do not exist.

The free movement of goods, services, capital, and persons across borders—"what an arrogant and pretentious statement." And what a peculiar definition of freedom when the price of a job requires workers to leave home, heritage, culture, tradition, language, and the community of friends and family.

Globalism is defined in economic terms as the optimal allocation (use) of men and women, resources and capital, across the broad spectrum of the bloc. Globalism, therefore, is specialization—but specialization means an ever-growing dependency. Nations become famous for making the wings of a plane but not the fuselage, for mining the ore but not milling it, for cutting down the trees but importing the furniture. Gone is the balanced growth that would enable a state to offer the wide range of career opportunities to a youth educated at great expense.

The specialization process imposes a planned dependency on a nation. Specialization makes interdependence necessary after it has first made the nation vulnerable by creating an unbalanced economy at home. Specialization in resource exploitation makes the nation subject to the terms and conditions imposed by the industrial powers for its manufacturing needs. The converse is also true.

Consider the logic of international economic interdependence, that is, the deployment of the resources of the globe according to a single most efficient scheduling, an abstract idea at best. Putting the mental image to work, planners then talk glowingly of a gross world production that is greater than the sum of the national outputs. Therefore, there are benefits for everyone that remain to be divided, although this is never spelled out.

If we accept the assumption—which, incidentally, has never been demonstrated—that there will be a greater world output, how is it to be shared? Who will decide the distribution? What percentage will go to improving the standard of living of consumers? What percentage will be invested to increase the military power of the bloc or to validate the perennial promise of a better tomorrow? Will the developed or less developed nations fare best? Which nations will benefit now and which in a distant future?

More fundamentally, who in our brave, new global world will make the decisions? Since each nation's resources have been placed in an international pot and its manpower assigned some partial and specialized role, the nation's freedom to create the instruments necessary to the achievement of its own priorities has been sharply reduced. As the scope for national decision making declines, the instructions coming from the supranational authority increases. The professionals in the international bureaucracies will save the nations of the world from politicians and democratic politics with "all those noisy and incoherent promises, the impossible demands, the hotchpotch of unfounded ideas and impractical plans. . . ."

The new reality with which Canadians must deal is simply this—the United States considers the security of the Western world to be indivisible with its own. Given this purpose and its acceptance by the leading industrial nations, the United States government believes that the task it has undertaken requires that it obtain the unqualified support of the Canadians, the Europeans, and the Japanese in all things political, economic, and military. This is the commitment that was demanded at Williamsburg. This is the commitment that was given.

Williamsburg created the superbloc of the West. Is that superbloc to be America and the six satellites or America and the six allies? In any event, Canada's interests are being poorly served by maintaining the pretence that we are a leading industrial power. We are not. We will never develop the set of strong domestic policies needed to give us control over the directions of our economy until we accept that fact.

Neither Japan nor Europe nor the United States has any intention of helping Canada to become an industrial power. These three industrial giants are each fully capable of supplying a whole range of manufactured products, cars, televisions, steel, radios, capital equipment, tools, and so on, to world markets. Canada's manufacturing potential is neither needed nor will it be welcomed in a world that is moving, despite all protestations, toward increasing protectionism. As these three powers divide the world into industrial spheres of influence, Canada's role will be the supplier of raw materials and energy resources.

Canadian economic policy has, since Confederation, rested on the twin pillars of resource exploitation and capital imports in the colonial form of direct investment. Both policies have been used to such excess that Canada is presently the most vulnerable nation in the world, with its abnormal dependence on export markets, trade cycles, and corporate-capital flows.

To bury ourselves in the bosom of the American superstate is to condemn Canadians forever to the role of suppliers of raw materials. The current trade conflicts between our two countries are an example of the challenge that we face. The United States has always insisted on at least an equilibrium in their balance of trade with us. As we continue to ship billions of dollars of petroleum and mineral resources, they will insist on an equivalent return flow in manufactured goods. For every million dollars in wages and salaries that we export, we will be importing three to four million dollars in American or Japanese or European wages and salaries. In employment terms, we import the labour and effort of three to four workers for every Canadian employed.

How are we as a nation to counteract age-old policies? Are we nasty nationalists if we try? Moving Canadian economic policies into line with those of the United States—consequences, as President Reagan phrased it at Williamsburg—means that we are serving the interests of the bloc rather than our own. It means that Canada will continue to concentrate on the extractive export industries and that domestic and imported capital will abandon the pursuit of industrialization. No industrial policy for Canada but rather the age-old specialization in primary production, with this difference—that it will no longer be the result of market forces and inept government leadership but will be the outcome of the political pressures imposed on us by our trading partners at Williamsburg.

There is no abstract set of international policies that can simultaneously satisfy the needs and requirements of nations as unequal in wealth and power as Canada and the United States. Each nation in the world must define and pursue the strong domestic policies tailored to the development of its own material and human resources. Free trade was the appropriate policy for Great Britain at the zenith of her power in the nineteenth century, but, as Bismarck remarked, "free trade is the policy of the strong," suitable for the nations that were industrial leaders but not necessarily for nations that wanted to be.

Canada's tariff policy of 1879 was a national policy, although it turned out to be counterproductive. Infant industry protectionism can be made to work if it is accompanied by strong industry creation, as the policies of both the United States and Germany have shown. But Canada failed to create the industries that the tariff was designed to protect, and so the foreign investment and the branch plants took over.

Reaganomics, the emphasis on military power and economic hegemony, is clearly a new national policy designed to establish in the West the measure of cohesion and unification that has existed in the Soviet bloc. Those searching for Canadian policy options in the eighties are not nasty nationalists (what nation blindly places the interests of others before its own?), but Canadians genuinely concerned with the vulnerability of the economy that they are turning over to the next generation.

President Reagan was elected on the promise to make the United States strong again, to restore American prestige and power to the level of the 1950s and the 1960s. He has done so. At Williamsburg, with U.S. nuclear might as the lever, he guaranteed the security of the West on condition that they follow American economic initiatives, and then—less tactfully—become American satellites. A weak and uncompetitive American economy is back in the saddle again, dictating objectives, formulating policies, and assigning roles to the leading nations of the West.

Hyping the unthinkable, the threat of nuclear holocaust, has brought great dividends to the rhetorician of the White House. He cannot lose. When the nuclear tensions lessen, as indeed that insanity must, the United States will have regained undisputed economic leadership of the West, and this is what the exercise is all about.

If Williamsburg is to be Canada's future, that future is bleak indeed.

II

SHOULD THERE BE A NATION-STATE?

Wallace Stevens, an American poet, wrote "Anecdote of Men by the Thousand," in which he speaks of the influence that the land has on people.

> *The soul, he said, is composed*
> *of the external world.*
> *There are men of the East, he said,*
> *Who are the East.*
> *There are men of a province*
> *Who are that province*
> *There are men of a valley*
> *Who are that valley. . . .*

The roots of a community are two—the land and the people who come to it. A society is born when a sufficient number of people gather together in a particular place. Each person will have his own reasons for settling in a region—the escape from poverty and oppression, the attraction of a greater freedom and liberty, the hope and promise of greater opportunity. In time, the people of the region will develop their own ethos, the spirit and dispositions that will provide the set of norms and moral postulates that will govern their economic affairs and their political relations. A community, above all else, expresses the tone, the outlook, the vital force and spirit underlying the living reality of people at work and leisure.

To a great degree nature itself defines and imposes the scope and range if not the limits of opportunities open to the people. It is certain that over the generations there will be in the community a gradual harmonization of values, of expectations, of viewpoints, and of purposes. Thus defined, the community has no problem with its identity.

The external world, as Wallace Stevens writes, affects us, forms us, and commands our work. The challenges facing the east-coast fisherman are not the causes of concern to the prairie farmer or even to the west-coast fisherman. Nor will the responses be the same.

Each accepts his environment for what it is and strives to shape it and to use it rationally and consistently within the limits that nature itself imposes. In this unity of man and environment there is the continuity that will survive even the greatest social upheavals. A better example of survival can scarcely be found than the preservation of French Canadian identity and nationalism after military defeat and political catastrophe. As Canon Groulx has written, *"La même entité humaine continue sa vie, sur la même terre, dans le même environnement géographique."* The strength of the Quebec culture lies in the historical fact that the spiritual beliefs, the outlook, the language, the social institutions, and the political forms remain rooted in the same soil that shaped past generations. And this is true of all communities.

A community, established in its particular living space, soon develops the principles and norms of conduct, the laws and form of government that reflect the beliefs and value systems of its people and guide both internal conduct and a collective approach to the outside world. Local government is a necessity for the members of a community who wish to attain the good of order and the possibility of the collective definition of goals and purpose. Fundamental to this creation of meaningful civic relations is the individual's surrender of his own use of force and the assignment of monopoly powers of coercion to the civil authorities. Without this transfer there could not be community. There would be confusion and anarchy.

Out of the creation of local government by people in particular places flows the range and nature of the specific choices to be made and the goals to be pursued—the third element of the complete society. At the level of community, the horizons embrace all modes of man's existence: the religious, the economic, the social, the scientific, and the cultural. And it is principally at this level, while all the principal directions of living and intending are still open to them, that men and women have the greatest freedom of choice. I take the community to be the solid core of the social system.

What does society lose when successively higher forms of political integration, inspired by unproved and doubtful claims of commercial and financial efficiency, are introduced?

Community economics is an uncomplicated but rational system. The logic of the community requires that the power to produce be matched with an equivalent capacity to consume. The community priority is a standard of living.

David Riesman's question, "Abundance for what?" is not a relevant question at the community level, where "sharing" is the distinguishing feature and no one need feel alone. If the question were raised, the answer would be clear and unequivocal—a large production and a fair distribution of that production go hand in hand. The circle of economic activity is complete.

Economics was born in the minds of men who lived in a world of court privilege, mercantilism, monopolies, national objectives of empire and trade surpluses, and hated what they saw. "No man produces for the sake of producing and nothing further," said James Mill. "Things are distributed as also exchanged to some end. That end is consumption." As for Adam Smith, "Consumption is the sole end and purpose of all production." And that was that.

As we move to more complex and larger social groupings, Riesman's question raises troubling issues. Production is not necessarily for a good distribution but for more production. Future growth and wealth itself become goals that insert themselves ahead of equitable distribution and improvements in sharing and the present standard of living. Here we are on sensitive ground! John Stuart Mill, writing of the growing abundance provided by the American economy, continued as follows: "and all that these advantages seem to have done for them is that the life of the whole of one sex is devoted to dollar-hunting and of the other to breeding dollar-hunters." This brutal passage, which appeared in the first (1848) edition of Mill's *Principles of Political Economy*, was deleted from the following editions. It is dangerous to suggest that investment in a better tomorrow may leave the living generation hooked on money and nothing else.

Repeating our definition, a community is a sufficient number of people in a particular corner of the world who form a government empowered to define and enforce rules of conduct so that man may know and be free to choose among the principal directions and modes of his existence. In short, the community has no problem with its identity, is the first expression of social humanism and freedom, and is the mould that shapes character, choices, and careers.

The problem of Canadian unity, for example, is to find a way in which the primary importance and fundamental values of community can be maintained in the face of escalating concentration and regimentation at both the political and economic levels. I do not see how this can be accomplished unless our political leaders start from the beginning with the objectives of strengthening our communities and reinforcing our provinces. This will be no simple task in an age of technological, industrial, and financial integration. What the computer imposes upon us is a social discipline, conformity, and homogeneity unknown in all previous history, for corporate and public bureaucracies, if their aims are to be achieved, must define and program the individual in functional terms—man becomes a means to an end, not an end in himself.

This raises the problem of the survival of the individual in a growing bureaucratic society. If power is centralized, the individual loses the protection and security of his community, those who know him and those whom he knows. He is isolated and vulnerable, and the community that once provided the base from which he could develop and make a contribution itself declines in authority and the capacity to support him.

Mill had hoped for the day when "minds ceased to be engrossed by the art of getting on." He wrote that in a stationary state "There would be as much scope as ever for all kinds of mental culture, and moral and social progress; as much room for improving the Art of Living, and much more likelihood of its being improved." His philosophy and sociology were correct, at least in my view, but few economists agreed with him. The historical context, the height of the Industrial Revolution, was not sympathetic.

Similarly, those who speak out against centralization and concentration of power, political or economic, feel instinctively that they are whistling against the wind. Centralization, however, is not a new evil. As Sir Halford Mackinder, famed British geographer, reminded critics of his balanced-economy concept: "You tell me that centralization is the 'tendency' of the age: I reply to you that it is the blind tendency of every age—was it not said nineteen hundred years ago that 'to him that hath shall be given'?"

Centralization, concentration, the accumulation of power and property may well be the tendencies of the age, but they may also be blind tendencies wherein communities are ignored and individuals lose their identity. The governed no longer know their governors.

Nationalist- or provincial-rights movements do not begin with power-mad Politicians bent on Balkanizing or "Iranizing" a country. They arise out of dispositions and sentiments that already exist, most often among young people anxious to live a life of challenge and achievement at home. They know that the world moves on, that communities form regional groups which grow into provinces, and the provinces unite to form the federal state. The anxiety centres on the costs of regionalism, nationhood, and now globalism. How much control over their lives and freedom is lost along the way? The land may be strong, but if this foundation of economic independence and personal freedom is owned abroad, what remains of effective, political freedom and the community's capacity to solve problems and to satisfy needs? It is through politics that the spirit of the times is captured, reflected in the polling booths, but then ignored by the elected and the servants of the state.

If I were a political leader, I would find it increasingly difficult to accept the doctrine that Canada, with its distinct economic regions and cultures, should be a strong, centralized country—a heartland centred on Ottawa, Montreal, and Toronto and with all the rest a periphery. In effect, I would be telling the best young people of my province, the educated and the intelligent, to go away. There is no room for you at home.

To make provinces and communities more important is to insist that they strive for more balance in their economies. An economic heartland, the metropolitan centre of colonial days, organizes an economy from the core outward and assigns specialized roles to the outlying regions, which lose their balance and sovereignty and become dependent, lopsided, and vulnerable to change. If you wreck the economic balance of a community or region, can social frustration, cultural poverty, and political ineptness be far behind?

If the roots of a community are its people and its land, then the primary factors of production must also be the people and the land. Capital, then, is a secondary affair derived from the surpluses arising from the utilization of land and labour. Capital is not an original factor of production, however useful and necessary it may be in accelerating the pace of growth and development.

Growth begins with the land and the services of people. If the land is attractive and the yields are good, many will come and stay. If the yields are retained, the community will grow and prosper. If, however, the surpluses are drained away, the community will stagnate and decline in an increasing dependence.

Land and labour are indispensably bound together as the basis of society. Isolating land and forming markets out of it is as great a crime against community as slavery is against humanity. Land is not a product for sale but part of a life-support system which, with labour, precedes the market economy just as it exists prior to the formation of the institutions, laws, and norms of the society. From the point of view of the community, the land and resources must be considered as inalienable, one of the reasons for coming and one of the reasons for staying, the root of sovereignty and the foundation of policies which determine future directions as well as current standards of living.

When we debate the question "should the nation-state survive," the discussion centres around growth, efficiency, the benefits of an international assignment of the factors of production; that discussion is carried on in chambers of commerce, at conferences of economists and bureaucrats both public and private. We seem to forget that economics has to take into account social attitudes, the quality of politics, traditions, language, and human endowments. Above everything else the participation should include people under thirty who will be the more affected than aging corporate executives.

The young are also the ones most likely to have something new to say for, as Keynes remarked, "in the field of economic and political philosophy there are not many who are influenced by new theories after they are twenty-five or thirty years of age, so that the ideas which civil servants and politicians and even agitators apply to current events are not likely to be the newest."

A half-century ago, Berle and Means wrote in their seminal book *The Modern Corporation and Private Property*:

> The rise of the modern corporation has brought a concentration of economic power which can compete on equal terms with the modern state . . . where its own interests are concerned, it even attempts to dominate the state. . . . The law of corporations, accordingly, might well be considered as a potential constitutional law for the new economic state, while business practice is increasingly assuming the aspect of economic statesmanship. . . .

In 1975, discussing the power of large corporate groups and their control of markets, Prime Minister Trudeau was an eloquent witness to the truth of the Berle and Means prophecies—"People are wondering who is in charge of the economy, who's in charge of the society, and they're concerned, they're worried. And they have cause to be."

In a similar vein, President Eisenhower, in his farewell address to the nation, "Liberty Is at Stake," had warned of the dangers to the very structure of American society in the growth of "the total influence—economic, political, even spiritual—" inherent in the size of the military and industrial corporate establishments.

> In the councils of Government, we must guard against the acquisition of unwarranted influence, whether sought or unsought, by the military industrial complex. The potential for the disastrous rise of misplaced power exists and will persist. We must never let the weight of this combination endanger our liberties or our democratic processes. We should take nothing for granted.

Size of firm, economies of scale, efficiencies of concentration, multinational corporations, all are justified by the more productive possibilities assumed to exist in global markets. This conception of the *economic* unification of the world has been justified by George W. Ball, former undersecretary of state in the Kennedy administration, in the following terms:

> In order to survive, man must use the world's resources in the most efficient manner. This can be achieved only when all the factors necessary for the production and use of goods—capital, labor, raw materials, plant facilities and distribution are freely mobilized and deployed according to the most efficient pattern. And this in turn will be possible only when national boundaries no longer play a critical role in defining economic horizons.

And again in the same article:

> Conflict will increase between the world corporation, which
> is a modern concept evolved to meet the requirements of the
> modern age, and the nation-state, which is still rooted in
> archaic concepts unsympathetic to the needs of our modern
> world.

So there we have it—the modern era has witnessed the progress
of civilization from feudal manor to nation-state. It is now, in
1983, time to move on to the emergent world economy, i.e., a
unified commercial and corporate view of the world, the organization of production on an international scale.

Economics has as its object the most efficient use of resources
at the disposal of a decision-making unit, whether that unit is
Aristotle's household, the classical firm, or the corporation or the
nation-state. When the world itself is taken as the basic economic
unit, the assumption must be that the world is a great anonymous
pool of resources both human and physical, yielding goods and
services in accordance with their most efficient allocation and
without regard to nation-states concerned with their own problems, priorities, and even prejudices. That is the death of the
nation-state.

The "archaic" concepts of which Ball speaks are only as
"archaic" as the last century. The difference between the 1983
theory of international production and the nineteenth-century
theory of international trade is the profound respect that classical
economists held for people and for community. A political philosophy is embedded in classical trade theory, for our predecessors
were not merely economists but were possessed of a political
philosophy as well. Men and women were citizens, the foundation
and source of national strength, custodians of the traditions,

beliefs, language, laws, and customs of the nation. They were the substance of the state, not mere instruments and factors of production to be transferred to foreign lands at the dictate of capital flows and feedback systems.

No one knew better than David Ricardo the extent of capital exports and emigration from England, but this was not the national purpose. He wrote approvingly of the "natural disinclination which every man has to quit the country of his birth and connexions, and intrust himself with all habits fixed, to a strange government and new laws . . ." The theory of free trade, so suitable for that period of England's hegemony, was designed to build financial power, employment, and industrial strength at home.

In a similar vein, Germany under the influence of the doctrines of Friedrich List and Chancellor Bismarck adopted the opposite policy of protectionism in intense efforts to keep her manpower from emigrating by providing employment at home. Limiting imports to materials containing little labour and few skills, and promoting exports with high wage content soon provided the employment that caused net emigration from Germany to disappear.

Trade in goods, unlike trade in persons, adds to the level of real income in a nation, which leads in turn to an increase in the standard of living and wealth. Nations gained from trading the goods and services in the production of which they had a natural or comparative advantage. They did not gain from draining each other. It would not have occurred to Ricardo, for example, when he spoke of trading English bolts of cloth for Portuguese pipes of wine, that England would be even better off if English capital bought out the vineyards of Portugal and managed their production. Such actions would have invaded a neighbour's sovereignty and reduced its economic independence and, in the long run, was bound to be counterproductive. Such, at least, was the nineteenth-century view. Sovereignty depended not only on a strong citizenry proud of their rights, it also depended on the control of all one's resources. Unlike our political leaders and the current network of civil servants and economic advisers, classical economists believed that the citizenship of those who owned and controlled the land and its natural resources was fundamental to a strong society. A state that is not the master of its own environment can hardly aspire to great status and importance in the assembly of nations. Classical economists incorporated into their principles the society's institutions (private property), national aspirations and objectives, human motivations, drives, and needs, and looked upon the national economy as an ongoing process.

In 1983 the logicians of the world enterprises refuse to recognize that nations are autonomous entities. The world is one, a global system in which each area interacts with the others, and behaviour in any region has repercussions throughout the world economy. Those who refuse to accept the new model of ordering economic activity are labelled nationalists, xenophobes, parochial monopolists, socialists, protectionists, and anti-American.

No one, to my knowledge, of those concerned with the problems of retaining independence in decision making and control over their own choices and value systems has ever held that anyone or any nation can exist apart, or that there would be great value in such isolation if it did exist. Progress is only possible through interaction and interdependence; the diversification that exists between communities adds to the vitality and quality of each.

This acceptance of the worth of other cultures, outlooks, value systems, and social structures leads to an interdependence that is profitable in more than the material sense. Something new is added to one's culture which conserves as it broadens and is subtly changed. There is no dependence in this effect, for nothing is

imposed. As Bernard Lonergan has written, "If one is to communicate with persons of another culture, one must use the resources
of their culture. To use simply the resources of one's own culture is
not to communicate with the other but to remain locked up in
one's own." There is no one culture, as anyone from Quebec
understands full well; just as there are differences within Canada,
so we are entitled to believe in and support a Canada that has a set
and shape of values that is distinct from other systems and nations.
This does not mean that we would refuse, in the name of independence, to subscribe to a set of moral principles that would
serve as the basis for international relations and international law,
but it does mean that we contribute what we can of our own values
without surrendering our sovereignty, objectives, and policies.

Internationalism can be carried too far, as Keynes pointed out.
International trade can become economic warfare as nations
attempt to export their unemployment by subsidizing the exports
of goods and services on unwilling friends and neighbours. "But if
nations can learn to provide themselves with full employment by
their domestic policy . . . there need be no important economic
forces calculated to set the interest of one country against that of
its neighbours. There would still be room for the international
division of labour and for international lending in appropriate
conditions." The international community is something added
after a national order has been achieved and a society organizes its
activities to bring all its citizens a satisfactory standard of living. A
nation is entitled to defend itself and its citizens against the power
drives of those nations that are willing to risk class warfare at
home in order to finance the exports and investments that will
secure balance-of-payment surpluses and commercial supremacy.
The instability of such competition and economic conflict would
effectively block all hopes of achieving a higher unity standing
above but rooted in the sovereignty of individual nations. Interna-

tional rules of conduct arise from a proper respect for the particular genius and character of one's neighbours and are defeated by the unrestrained pursuit of one's own interests.

The idea of the world economy is based on the assumption that there exists a one, true, efficient allocation of all the world's human and material resources. This purely mechanistic vision of efficiency, unproved and undemonstrable, cannot accept the intervention of the nation-state with its own ideas of how output and distribution should be pursued. More fundamentally, globalism cannot tolerate politics, the system by which people express their preferences and determine their priorities as a community.

Economic globalism will create a heartland and a heartland creates peripheries, the vulnerable outposts which no level of regional development assistance can reverse. The centre and the heart of the unification zone become strong and affluent as the outlying regions and countries decline in importance and in the capacity to control their own directions. The drain of material resources and skills accelerates, the flow to the core broadens and deepens.

The trouble with the superbloc thesis and the dream world of global efficiency is that it is neither a political nor an economic concept. It is planning, regimentation, bureaucracy. It eliminates initiative, incentive, and the famed freedom of opportunity for new men. One is reminded of Mussolini's grandiose vision of "the complete organic and totalitarian regulation of production with a view to the expansion of the wealth and political power of the Italian people." Williamsburg goes further. It envisions the convergence of policy, planning, and production not for Italy alone but for Italy and the six other leading industrial nations in the proposed Western bloc.

When power is accumulated at the centre, nations are not through, as Professor Kindelberger suggests—they become merely economic units. They are through as political units. The societies become pure economies, the quantitative and mechanical domains of technical coefficients, the inputs and outputs, a world which becomes a great pool of goods and services where the services of labour are separated from the will or needs of the labourer, the services of land and resources from national goals, and the services of capital from the motivations, ambitions, and desires of the proprietor.

Once political power is accumulated in a heartland, is it reasonable to expect that power will then be redistributed back again? Each nation has its own particular set of resources to deal with problems of inflation, unemployment, and poverty. Each nation must maintain its freedom and power to deal directly with them. It cannot be satisfied to wait the day when those who have the power have achieved their objectives nor can it expect that an affluent core will ever willingly decentralize.

Stagnation and inflation, unemployment and poverty are problems that must be faced at the level of the nation-state. The political power to combine and direct its resources, to define the priorities, must remain with the state.

There is a great and immediate urgency for growth and development everywhere. For this to be distributed fairly among all regions of the world, each nation-state must be able to do this job itself. Aid, capital, and technical assistance can be provided by others in supporting but not controlling roles.

Few can believe in a single, global, best allocation of inert and passive factors of production to achieve a purely material growth. Even fewer can expect that a nation can be self-sufficient in so complex and interrelated a world.

Canadians will agree to alliances and arrangements that will add to the strength and security of the Western world, but they will at the same time insist on maintaining the political power and economic freedom to manage their own affairs. Canada must not become a periphery in a superbloc, a supplier of resources to a global centre. Centralization, whatever the advantages—and I see none—drains nations, checks their development, and thwarts their efforts to build the balanced economy that alone can provide sufficient scope and opportunity to our people.

Canada, by insisting on the distinction between the adaptations that are necessary to the security of the West and the pressures that serve simply to centralize power, will be a better ally by remaining an independent nation-state.

III

Is Canada a Nation-State?

During her 1983 visit to Canada, Prime Minister Thatcher of Great Britain sharply reminded Canadians that they were members of NATO and had agreed at the summit meetings at Williamsburg in May of that year to support NATO policy and particularly the deployment of the Cruise and Pershing II missiles in Europe. It followed that we had no choice but to agree to the testing of the Cruise on Canadian territory; the visiting prime minister implied that that was little enough.

In fact, we agreed to a great deal more than the complete integration of Canadian defence policy with that of the United States, including the latter's stance in the negotiations on arms control with the Soviet Union. We also agreed to make our trade relations with the East compatible with the security interests of the West as defined at Williamsburg. The definitions of compatible economic relations remain to be spelled out.

In the economic field we agreed to align our policies with those of the United States to promote an integration of economic performance in the two economies, as well as with the other leading industrial powers. This alignment included the acceptance of the American lead in restraining the growth of money and credit and in maintaining appropriate interest rates. We further agreed to reduce budget deficits by curtailing government expenditures in areas other than defence, since this would not be compatible with our NATO obligations and, since fluctuating exchange rates might provide a convenient escape hatch from the above onerous restrictions on Canada's freedom to operate independently, that door also was closed by the inclusion in the declaration of a commitment to move toward greater stability in the exchange markets.

A nation that agrees to all of this cannot be called an independent nation-state. Canada has agreed to all of this. Walter Stewart in *Towers of Gold—Feet of Clay* quotes a Mackenzie King statement of 1935 as saying, "Once a nation parts with the control of its currency and credit, it matters not who makes the nation's laws." Canada's longest-serving prime minister was arguing against the control of the Bank of Canada, resting at that time in the private sector. Re-elected in the fall of 1935, he set in motion the legislation that would place the central bank and monetary policy firmly in the hands of the federal government, or so Mackenzie King thought.

Mr. King argued that the major function of a central bank is to regulate credit and currency in the best interests of the economic life of the nation. And he also believed that the best interests of the country could only be defined by the government of the day, elected by the people in response to the policies and platforms that had been put forward by that government. It certainly did not occur to him when he vigorously debated the Bank of Canada Bill in 1935, or moved the nationalization of the bank in 1938, that technocrats in the Central Bank would, or could, determine where

lay the best interests of the Canadian people. It was the King position that the problems facing a nation ultimately and always
demand political, not technical, solutions, and monetary issues
could not in any way be an exception.

A governor of the Central Bank accepts the mandate, the terms
of reference, and the policy directions laid down by the government, or he can resign. The goals of the institution define the
range and limits of its operations, and these goals are given by
elected governments. If the group of seven industrial nations lays
down the policy directions that will bring together interest-rate
movement, growth of monetary aggregates, produce co-ordinated
fiscal measures to reduce government expenditures and budget
deficits, and stabilize exchange rates by controlling rate changes,
then where is the freedom of elected governments to address the
problems peculiar to their community? And yet this is the situation in which Canada finds itself presently. Can Canada, or even
the others, be called independent sovereign states?

Confederation gave some three-and-a-half million Canadians
political control over four provinces of British North America.
While the Fathers of Confederation would have little faith in an
ideological choice to develop the Canadian economy by government action, this option was not available, since none of the
three levels of government had the money or credit available
through domestic sources necessary to achieve reasonable rates
of development.

Alexander Galt and George Brown in particular had pushed for
Confederation on the grounds of a Canadian market of three-and-
a-half million people, but such a market simply did not exist. Nova
Scotia and New Brunswick were within the geographical space of
New England manufacturers, and tariff protection could not
match the disparity in transportation costs facing the fledgling
industry of southern Ontario. Montreal, with its intimate links to

metropolitan England and a surrounding province with largely rural, agricultural, and subsistence economies in fact, did not provide that thriving level of demand that would justify investment in large- or even small-scale productive facilities.

The federal government could do little to promote growth of the general economy because it was swept up in the desperate urgency to build the transcontinental links in both the West and East needed to reinforce the political unification. In 1874, for example, we only spent the pitifully small sum of $206,000 in the mining, the forestry, and the fisheries sections of the economy. Megaprojects, then as now, captured the attention of our political leaders.

The provinces were even more feeble instruments of growth than the federal government. In 1874, the seven provinces spent the grand total of $10,000 on promoting mining development and $10,000 on strengthening agricultural production. In addition, the provinces had seen their revenues collapse from a total of $16 million in 1866, the year prior to Confederation, to less than $7 million in 1874, after seven years of settling into the new federal system. Of that $6.7 million, $3.8 million, or 58 per cent of provincial revenues, came in the form of federal subsidies. To underline the utter dependence of the four original provinces in the early years of Confederation, Ontario depended on federal grants for 47 per cent of its current revenue, Quebec for 48 per cent, Nova Scotia for 81 per cent, and New Brunswick for 92 per cent. Thus, provincial intervention to get the economy moving was simply not feasible. Vulnerability and dependence was the lot of the provinces in 1874, and vulnerability and dependence are not conducive to development.

With hindsight, it is still difficult to believe that John A. Macdonald, the Conservative prime minister of Canada, could have adopted any policy other than the so-called American solution, protectionism and the Tariff of 1879. The challenge facing the Fathers of Confederation was to give economic substance and direction to the political structure of the new nation. By 1867, however, Canada was already fully integrated into the continental economy of the United States, for the free movement of persons, capital, and transfers of resource ownership was a daily experience. The complete mobility of factors is a much greater threat to sovereignty and national freedom than free trade in goods and services. In 1867, there was no significant barrier to the mobility of the factors of production, either resources or Canadian manpower. Thus the Macdonald government had to live with a Canada set in its economic ways, a supplier of raw materials to Great Britain until free trade in 1846, and then the supplier of largely the same resources to the United States under the terms of the Reciprocity Treaty of 1854-1866. When this was not renewed, the Canada of 1867 had cause to believe itself isolated and insecure.

Macdonald's tariff was mistimed, a hundred years too soon, by which I mean that it would be a more appropriate policy in 1983 than it was in 1879, when there were few industries and little domestic capital available for entrepreneurs and risk takers, and few Canadian entrepreneurs who remained in the country. In any event, the richer, more rapidly expanding—one could say exploding—American economy was an attraction for the best and brightest in Canada, and the flow of emigration to the south swelled dramatically in the last two decades of the nineteenth century. Our loss, of course, was the American gain.

On the other hand, protectionism in the United States and Germany had worked because there were large markets and mature industries to protect. In Canada, there were no strong industries except the resource and financial sectors. Protectionism is designed to support the infant firm, but given the size of markets, not even the infants that were to be helped by the tariff could advance far beyond their local markets. Internal tariffs and transportation costs quickly limited expansion in an east-west direction, and south-north traffic remained heavy to the benefit of federal customs revenues.

In brief, tariffs protect the strong and the established. They may protect viable infant industries where these exist, but these infant industries should have growing markets that will yield surpluses for reinvestment and further growth, and financial institutions that will be sufficiently imaginative and entrepreneurial themselves to support initiative and risk taking. All these conditions existed in Germany, or were provided by government in the last four decades of the nineteenth century. They all came together during the same period in the United States, a period in which the United States emerged as the most powerful industrial nation in the world. In these conditions, protectionism will work. In the conditions existing in Canada from Confederation to 1900, they did not exist; the dependence of the Canadian economy was firmly established at that time.

The United States' growth rate could not have been sustained in those years without the heavy flow of British capital, but flows were in the form of bonds and debentures placed by the wealthy and their investment trusts. The form of the capital flows was the important difference between the Canadian and the American experience. Canada has been the recipient principally of direct investment funds in its industrial and resource sectors, equity and ownership flows carrying property rights to perpetual streams of income. Thus the equity in and the control of basic sectors of the Canadian economy remained and remain firmly in the hands of foreign investors and entrepreneurs.

The United States, on the other hand, never lost control of its own economy, nor was it drained of the surpluses needed to maintain and expand its productive base after it had redeemed the bonds and debentures on which it had borrowed. It was the American determination to keep control of its own economy that constituted the difference between the two economic policies. The United States grew an economic strength and military power financed by the surpluses that it kept at home.

Confederation had laid down the groundwork for the political control of British North America by the people of Canada, the new nation. With political control assured, the challenge to acquire control of the economy followed. The question is not whether a new nation should or should not acquire control of its own economy, but how it should do so. Political unification would have little significance or meaning if economic control did not come with it. Ideology comes into the equation when the government rules on the method and means of acquiring that economic control. Does the new nation utilize the private sector or the public sector to develop and to expand the economy? And if the private sector, will the major responsibility rest with domestic investment or with foreign investment, or with some combination of both?

The government's choice, in the heyday of laissez faire and unlimited faith in the individual, could only be to rely on the self-interest, efficiency, and profit motivation of the private sector. In practice, however, this meant reliance on the foreign private sector, for there were neither the markets, the domestic capital formation, nor indigenous entrepreneurship of sufficient quality and quantity available to spark the Canadian economy. As a result, Canadian growth languished for an entire generation while the government of Canada, struggling with the finances of railways and other megaprojects to span the continent, had no funds for development, and the provinces struggled to stay afloat on the subsidies provided by the Dominion.

The framers of the tariff policy extolled it as a protectionist measure to preserve the Canadian market for domestic infant industry. They did not realize that a tariff could not possibly ensure national control of an industrial sector in a continental economy—Canada and the United States—where there was already a free movement of persons, capital, services, and goods. A tariff on goods, then, could raise revenues for the federal government, but it could not protect. In fact, imports from the United States, as a percentage of total imports, doubled between 1870 and World War I.

The Canadian experience with continental integration following upon Confederation provides clear evidence that the assumption of a greater wealth upon the allocation of factors of production in a larger market, perhaps even a world market, may be valid, but that there are still bound to be winners and losers. As Canadian resources and people moved southward, the reallocation of these factors of production strengthened the American economy significantly, while leaving Canada weakened by the loss of much of its resource and manpower strength. The mobile Canadians did well as they strengthened and enhanced the growth rate in their new homeland, but at the cost of the stagnating and increasingly dependent economy in the land of their birth. From 1860 until 1900, Canada was not a land of hope and immigration, but a land of frustrated ambition and emigration. This was the period when we set ourselves firmly in the role of economic satellite and suppliers of our resources, our land, and our labour, to the American economy, a role that we still play and that Williamsburg intends us to play in the future.

Given the free movement of Canadian factors of production to the south, what did Macdonald's Tariff of 1879 really accomplish? Basically, it increased the cost of living by reducing the incomes of Canadians, and little else. The tariff was a revenue-gathering device, not a protective instrument. Few of the industries that did exist could qualify as infant industries worthy of protection. They were small, single-product, and community-based firms in a largely barter environment, fully protected by transportation costs and local loyalties, and themselves indifferent to expansion and larger markets. Markets in Canada were not national, as the Fathers of Confederation had vociferously and confidently predicted, but a jumble of separate markets sustained by geographic barriers and transportation costs, plus the fierce regional and cultural loyalties that made market penetration a costly affair.

If the tariff had been effective as a protective measure—that is, if it had succeeded in preserving Canadian markets for Canadian entrepreneurs—one could have expected a flow of the new American branch plants during this period. In fact, there was little direct investment during the next twenty years, indicating that Canadian markets were too small and scattered to justify investment and that the most efficient way to supply the meagre market was still the shipping of American goods, not capital, over the tariff wall.

It was only when the frontier in the United States had been closed that American capital turned its attention northward. Confederation, to repeat, was a political union that never became a nation in control of its own economy. The national policy of 1879, often touted as Canada's declaration of economic independence, was nothing more than a sales tax on the Canadian consumer, a source of revenues to shore up declining customs and excise revenues and to avert national bankruptcy.

A protective tariff appealed to the national sentiment for a protected market and the desire to build a more balanced, diversified—hence less vulnerable—economy. The assumptions were: a) That there was a strong and concentrated market to justify domestic investment and to support industry; b) That there was a sufficient number of infant industries and firms to protect;

and c) That a banking and financial community existed, ready and willing to devote resources to the financing of industrial growth in preference to the less risky short-term commercial financing at which they were adept. All three assumptions were mistaken.

The continuing pilgrimages to Washington that are a feature of our own times commenced before Confederation and continued in the years after, as Ottawa strenuously tried to have the Reciprocity Treaty renewed. But it was useless and—from Washington's point of view—unnecessary. They already had all the control over the Canadian economy that they required. More fundamentally, the Fathers of Confederation found the institutions and elements of the Canadian economy to be completely subject to the needs and wants of American market mechanisms. Thus the purpose of political unification—the control of one's land, resources, and capital to achieve an improving standard of living for the people—was beyond them.

The growth of the Canadian economy, then as now, depended on decisions taken elsewhere. Canada was, for all intents and purposes, a market in real estate and raw materials, without large enough markets to throw off surpluses nor domestic capital sufficient to finance a greater share of our own growth.

The course of Canada's dependence on foreign investment took form in the first decade of this century, although the pattern itself had been set well before Confederation. In 1983, Canadian economic dependence is without parallel in the developed world. An analysis of the operations of some 220,000 non-financial corporations in 1980 showed that 36 per cent of the equity ownership and 38 per cent of all the profits in the group accrued to foreign-controlled companies. Such is our present vulnerability to outside pressures.

By comparison, the total sales of foreign subsidiaries in the United States amount to approximately 2 per cent of their GNP.

Does the United States take a relaxed view of this 2 per cent direct-investment problem? By no means. The findings of various research groups in the United States are widely publicized and debated in their media, and this has increased the activity of American agencies in the areas of trade and commerce, banking, oil and gas, justice, the securities-and-exchange commission, communications, and defence procurement. In fact, as one consultant has noticed, the scope of United States restrictions on and barriers to foreign investment is so vast that it has taken almost three volumes just to set them out. Very simply, no comparison is to be made between the measures and practices introduced by the United States to restrain a foreign investment that touches only 2 per cent of their gross national product and the single timorous investment-review agency that Canada has put in place after more than a third of her economy has been found to be in foreign control.

A strategy for greater independence means that the Canadian economy must be switched into new directions—not overnight, since one does not overcome the errors and inertia of more than a century with a brutal turnaround. The damage to the present structure would be immediate and biting. But slowly, perhaps over a generation, we can accomplish new directions that will give an assurance of a more promising and sovereign future.

Sweden faced much the same dilemma, and introduced a policy in 1916 whereby the Swedish parliament insisted that the ownership and control of natural resources, lands and forests, markets and manufacturing must remain firmly in Swedish hands. This policy contains many lessons for Canada. The Swedish government argued, and the people agreed, that to have permitted foreigners to own and control Swedish lands and resources, the life-support system of their economy, would have been detrimental to the interest of the nation. Such a policy would have, of course, made the Swedish consumer vulnerable to exploitation by Swedish manufacturers and industrialists, but Sweden also introduced at the same time a free-trade policy which forced her businessmen to meet world standards of performance. In sum, Swedish economic policy reversed the road taken in Canada by insisting on free trade in goods and limiting the movement of her factors of production.

The beginning of economic wisdom is the control of our own money and credit, as Mackenzie King pointed out. An independent monetary policy does not mean that we can ignore the policies and practices of our neighbour to the south, but it does mean that we do not blindly accept its objectives and policies as our own. We should not be the thirteenth federal branch of its reserve system, nor should we adopt practices in the interest of harmony with the International Monetary Fund at the expense of efforts to resolve domestic problems such as inflation and unemployment. We need to reject the follow-the-leader practices that have kept us dependent for more than a century.

Money and credit policies can force the direction of all other elements of economic planning—fiscal, trade, energy, employment, and industrial—into a monetary framework. A monetary policy totally aligned with that of another nation means that all economic policies will be similarly contained. But a central bank is not responsible for the definition of the best interests of the nation. It is the government, elected by the people, that alone can decide on the economic, political, and social objectives of the community. As an agency, the bank must accept and adapt to the directions laid down by government. It is not the other way around, as is now the case.

No other nation in the world is so controlled by foreign capital and multinational corporations as Canada. The problem posed by the threat of the corporate cathedrals to the processes of democracy are immediate and urgent. One cannot expect nations such as the United States, Japan, and Germany, which benefit from the number of multinationals headquartered in their capitals, to raise questions about the role of these monoliths in the world community. The international legitimation—that is, freedom from national sovereignty—that these commercial giants seek is not an acceptable answer. It will not be tolerated by nations whose objectives of a fair distribution of what is produced in their country, and a rising standard of living for their people, are not compatible with corporate goals of concentration of wealth and power in the private sector.

Philosophically, politically, socially, economically, and culturally, society has yet to examine the awesome impact of these self-determining, self-propelling, perpetual money-making machines. Whether they are foreign owned or not is beside the point. Who is to ask the real questions about corporate growth? To whom are you responsible? To yourselves alone, to the people who own you, to the nations in which you operate? What are your goals and are they ethically justified?

More than any other nation, Canada has a stake in the answers to these questions. Until they are answered, Canada will remain a country that cannot answer the question, who is in charge here?

IV

THE NEW CATHEDRALS

Peter Drucker accurately reflected the euphoria and awe surrounding global corporations when he wrote: "Multinationals, whether corporate or communist, put economic sovereignty ahead of political nationality; the multinational corporation is by far our most effective economic instrument today and probably the one organ of economic development that actually develops. It is the one non-nationalist institution in a world shaken by nationalist delirium. It puts the economic decision beyond the effective reach of the political process and its decision makers, national governments."

However much one may be astonished by Mr. Drucker's eulogy, he speaks what is for many the simple truth. The dominant and dominating institution of our time is the commercial corporation. Few suspected when the act of incorporation for commercial purposes became, in the nineteenth century, a simple right, that the chartered company would ever attain its present importance and strength.

Drucker puts his point of view very well. In essence, he is saying that it is economics that determines the directions that a community should take, because the corporation knows best what are the priority needs and problems facing the nation. The nation-state has become an outmoded and archaic institution unable to deal with the mounting complexities and decisions of the world.

While attempts at military, religious, and revolutionary domination of our social institutions are in fact the history of the Western world, the commercial attack on the role of politics, the open discussion of directions and the possibility of choosing freely, is now the dominant threat to our liberties, as President Eisenhower foresaw.

The heart of the problem lies not in the multinational corporation or the giant conglomerate as such but rather in the concept itself of the corporation as a social institution.

The multinational is not a non-nationalist institution, as Mr. Drucker puts it, but is, in fact, the supreme national instrument of the industrial powers. American economic power is based on hundreds of huge international corporations operating in all corners of the globe. As Mr. Fowler, secretary of the treasury under President Johnson, described them, they were "mighty engines of Enlightened Capitalism." He then went on to declare that "for this nation—the United States—they have not only a commercial importance but a highly significant role in U.S. foreign policy." That is blunt enough! The occasion was the imposition of guidelines on the operations of American subsidiaries in Canada, December, 1965.

To emphasize the point, the secretary went on to say that "much more is involved than the economic advantages of investors of capital and the return to profits." While Canadians have been repeatedly told by their political leaders that the citizenship of those who own and control Canadian resources and Canadian markets is a matter of little or no importance, the secretary of the United States Treasury lays down the doctrine that American multinationals are expected to serve the interests of United States foreign policy. While Canadian economists were teaching that the essence of free enterprise lies in the pursuit of profits and maximizing the return on investment, a member of the U.S. cabinet says not so.

As a colleague of mine, Dr. John Dales of the University of Toronto, pointed out at the time, "We did suppose that American subsidiaries were business enterprises, run by businessmen intent on making a profit. If they really are a herd of little Trojan horses under the control of Washington, economists have nothing to say about them. We know nothing whatever about the behaviour of Trojan horses."

The 1965 imposition of guidelines on subsidiaries of American corporations operating in Canada, while later rescinded, illustrated the extent of Canadian vulnerability to American priorities. In this instance, controlling their balance-of-payments deficits limited United States multinationals, who were told to require their branch plants abroad to import more of their requirements from or through the American parent, to declare larger dividends, and to return excess working capital to the home office. Drucker's point that multinationals put economic sovereignty ahead of political nationality is wrong on two counts. When the United States Department of Commerce orders hundreds of American multinationals to force an expanded repatriation of funds from abroad to reduce the severity of balance-of-payment deficits, we are no longer dealing with the economic sovereignty of multinationals or even with the large numbers of economic theory, but rather with a single, directing political voice—not with the disparate and independent decisions of thousands of businessmen acting in their own corporate interests but with deliberate and hard government policy in Washington. Secondly, it is not economic sovereignty and decision making that rides over the political sovereignty of the host country but the demands and political priorities of the investing nation.

Of even greater concern to Canadians than Mr. Drucker's views should be the attitude of the federal government and its agencies such as the Bank of Canada to the whole question of ownership and control. Briefly, the opinion has always been that, as long as investment funds flow in and incomes are rising, the citizenship of those who own and control major sectors of the Canadian economy does not matter.

With respect to the imposition of the guidelines on Canadian business in December, 1965, there was more resistance from the managements of the Canadian companies (who saw their freedom to buy in the best market and to reinvest funds in such projects as they deemed to be in the best interests of the company dramatically reduced) than there was from their American parents or the Canadian government.

The American parent, of course, could not afford to antagonize the federal government and the Pentagon, particularly by opposing U.S. policy, given their dependence on the enormous market for goods and services in Washington.

As for the Canadian government and the officials in the Department of finance, together with the Governor of the Bank of Canada, they did not comprehend in the slightest the significance of this serious infringement of Canadian sovereignty and the national interest. It remained for an American economist, Professor Fritz Machlup of Princeton University, to point out that the introduction of guidelines to control economic activity abroad meant that the "United States has taken an enormous step away from our systems of free enterprise."

Contrary to Mr. Drucker, the world of the multinationals is

no longer the world of private capitalism but is, in fact, the world of a guided capitalism wherein the leading industrial governments transform the managements of multinational corporations into lengthened arms of the home governments. It is this consistent invasion of the political authority of the host nations that is creating the hostile environment to the concept of an emerging international organization of production and specialization with consequent political and economic vulnerability for the smaller countries.

When Mr. Drucker speaks of the multinational as "probably the one organ of economic development that actually develops," he is talking nonsense. There is an immediate investment period that gives construction jobs; but the purpose of any investment is to show a profit, i.e., to take out more from a market or an economy than one puts in. In the case of the multinational, a one-time investment of capital, often a minimal contribution, has secured control of a resource or a share of a market with the rights to an indefinite flow of income arising therefrom. Investment by the multinational takes place only when the opportunity exists to take more out of an economy than is put in. A multinational pursues the surplus in any situation and leaves the social problems to governments.

Equity flows of foreign capital with absolute and perpetual rights to future surpluses drain the recipient nation of the very sums needed to maintain and to expand its own economy. The objective of each investment is to take out of the zone of operations more than has been committed, and inevitably the investing nations expand at the expense of the less-developed ones. More importantly, since the debtor nations have sold the control of future as well as the present streams of revenue to their creditors, they never do get back control of their economies.

When the Kennedy administration conducted hearings in 1961

on tax recommendations governing the operations of global companies, hundreds of pages of testimony proved the point that the United States multinationals brought back far greater sums than they invested abroad. Thus Standard Oil of New Jersey had a cumulative surplus of $1.5 billion over a five-year period. Procter and Gamble, during a ten-year period, sent abroad $11 million and brought back to the United States $290 million. And on and on.

Once established and in control of a market share or a resource endowment, the subsidiary is in a position to exert the power that comes from the property rights that it has acquired, for property is sovereignty and the right to income flows. Sovereignty over its activities enables the foreign corporation to insist on the laws, privileges, and concessions necessary to encourage its expansion and control.

Everyone agrees to the free flow of international capital and particularly to developing nations. In its equity form, however, the absolute ownership and property rights attached to their investments enable multinationals to accumulate the surpluses out of each market in which they operate and to dispose of them as they will. Thus a minimal income to labour may remain in the host nation, but the surpluses such as royalty and management fees, interest, dividends, and retained earnings accrue to the creditor nation through its multinational firms.

To declare, as Drucker does, that multinationals put economic sovereignty ahead of political nationality is to assert that the nation has lost all power to limit the rights of private property in the interests of the conservation of exhaustible resources, and the provision of social services such as education, health, welfare, and acceptable working conditions based on the reconciliation of the needs of future generations with the greed for immediate capital gains. But this cannot endure; it invites growing hostility and the certain destruction of the multinational system as we know it.

The dominance of multinationals begins initially with the exploitation of their domestic markets and the consequent accumulation of surpluses. Capacity soon comes to exceed domestic markets and, eventually, the export markets that are not protected by effective tariffs and quotas. One could ask whether the excess capacity was not bad investment and suggest that the funds might have been better distributed to share owners in the home country who could pursue their own consumption and investment patterns. But the capital is retained and moved abroad as direct investment to capture the protected markets for the same technology. The technology that is exported is the technology of the advanced economy. It has to be because the parent, denied the profits on the export of final products, is looking for the profits inherent in the export of the same basic raw materials, equipment, and component parts that it has produced to satisfy its domestic market.

Cosmocorps, then, do transfer advanced technology widely. But a suitable technology for a highly industrialized nation may not be and likely will not be appropriate for a developing nation. The supply of the factors of production in the two economies will certainly not be the same. In the more advanced home economy, capital will be more abundant and its price cheaper, while labour will be relatively scarce and wages much higher than in the developing nation. The transfer of a technology based on a high capital-output ratio to an economy where capital is scarce and expensive and ignores the employment of the labour that is abundant and cheap distorts the pattern of growth and is bad economics, however advanced the technology. As Professor Schumpeter has stated, "This explains why technically backward methods of production may still be the most rational ones, provided the more perfect methods would require less of a plentiful factor and more of one which is less plentiful, and why the technically most perfect method of production is so often a failure in economic life." As Keith Marsden has pointed out, it would be easy to substitute a high-technology bakery employing 60 workers at double their daily wage for traditional methods in West Africa, thereby rendering redundant 565 workers, but the burden of caring for and finding employment for the displaced labour falls upon the economy.

Slower and steadier improvement of existing technologies in the backward nations would enable all sectors of such an economy to advance in concert, but this is not what the multinational has to sell.

The global corporation sells mass-production techniques, even in their branch-plant version. To be profitable, however, mass production requires mass consumption—that is, the homogenization of the tastes, needs, values, and priorities of all the nations within which the firm and its subsidiaries operate. In the name of technical efficiency, we erase the differences among persons, the style and the art of their living. People of different cultures and nations in varying stages of development are made, through enormous selling and advertising pressures, to want the same things. The freedom of the individual to choose, to maintain his own preferences, and to search for satisfaction, is reduced. So it is with nations. If their governments believe that their resources, human and material, are appropriated and applied to objectives other than those of their own choosing, on whom do they turn? The end results are easily foreseen, and therein lies the tragedy. The developing nations will inevitably reject the final and complete Americanization, Japanization, or Europeanization of their economies. The multinationals, as the vehicles of that domination, must face at best control of their operations, if not expropriation. And this brings the governments of the powerful industrial economies, determined to protect the wealth of their corporate citizens, into open conflict with the developing nation-states.

The multinational does not transfer ownership of its methods and technology in its foreign activities. There is no export or sale of these assets to an arms-length entity in the host country. The specific advantage, together with the invested capital, remains the property of the parent as the parent absorbs foreign assets—resources and/or markets—via its branch plants. What happens is not a transfer but an extension of the firm's existing property rights and control over a stream of revenues to new markets and political jurisdictions. The theorist of international resource allocation and the multinational president then assert, without proof or demonstration, that there is a superior efficiency in this global allocation and investment of resources, which must be protected from the political interference of national governments acting in the name of the interests and priorities of their citizens. If the nation-state is to have no place in the board rooms of the global corporation, then the community is indeed in the grip of an industrial autarchy.

The use of the corporate form for commercial purposes is a late product of the Industrial Revolution. We tend to think of the concept of the corporation as an ancient form of organizing business activity, whereas in fact the legislation creating limited companies in Great Britain dates back to 1855 and 1856. The Industrial Revolution had changed economies from the emphasis on agricultural to commercial and industrial activity, with the consequent changing composition of assets and private wealth from land to liquid and current assets. More formal procedures of accounting and administration were clearly needed to protect property. Since the corporate form had been used for centuries to co-ordinate and control non-profit-making activities—monasteries, bishoprics, universities, highways and canals—its adoption by commercial profit-making activity seemed a natural move. Few could foresee at the time the extent to which the corporate form would be used for the making and accumulating of profit.

In a famous case relating to the responsibilities of the Board of Regents of Dartmouth College, Chief Justice Marshall of the U.S. Supreme Court had defined, in 1819, a corporation as "an artificial being, . . . possessing among its most important properties immortality and individuality, properties by which a perpetual succession of many persons are considered as the same, and may act as an individual."

Until the nineteenth century, incorporation had been a privilege granted by the Crown or state for achieving national purposes or social objectives, privileges that could be and often were taken away. Social institutions—universities, for example—are continually called upon to justify their stewardship and so to continue their work long after the original founders have left the scene. The existence of the institution and the validity of the institution are continually legitimated by the interlock of their services with the objectives of the community. The immortality of the social institution was and is a contingent immortality, conditional on serving the public welfare.

The attributes of the public corporation—continuity, personality, and individuality—were not extended to the private corporation until the Industrial Revolution was well under way. From Adam Smith through to John Stuart Mill writing in 1849, economists viewed the firm as a proprietorship or partnership, mortal like the owners and operators, certain to disappear in time, thus providing the openings for new men, new initiatives, new ideas. If entry was not easy, exit at least was certain. It was this constant turnover in a dynamic, evolving economy that theoretically prevented a large number of firms from controlling prices and production. This is not the appropriate manner of looking at the economy of 1983 or the multinational, although the model still survives in economic theory.

A commercial corporation may be endowed by the law with

immortality, but somehow this attribute has to be supported by adequate sources of funds. Unlike universities or bishoprics, which depend on gifts and alms from their supporters, or municipalities and states, which depend on taxes, the commercial corporation can only prove its claim and right to perpetual operations by gaining and maintaining a control over consumer markets and/or natural resources. Such a control or near monopoly will enable it to survive more confidently through time, growing and accumulating all the way.

The half century after the passage of the limited-liability and corporate legislation saw an unprecedented concentration of industrial power that led to consolidations, mergers, and trusts. The Sherman Act, designed to slow down concentration and the creation of trusts, was rendered virtually harmless by an act of the New Jersey legislature in 1888 that permitted corporations to buy each other out, a movement that reappears regularly as takeovers and consolidations reach billion-dollar proportions in 1983.

Their control of their markets, their absolute size (measured by assets and material strength), and their independence from those who own them means that society has created institutions that can grow without limit through time. As they grow, they burst through national boundaries and demand the right to range across the world—anonymous institutions that acknowledge no citizenship and would be free of all responsibility except the single objective of accumulating wealth.

In 1970, the Royal Bank of Canada was a hundred years old and had accumulated $11.4 billion in assets. Twelve years later, in 1982, its wealth and power had increased to $88.5 billion.

The CPR, founded in 1880, by 1970 reported assets of $2.3 billion. By 1982, its assets has risen to $17.3 billion, partly financed by government generosity permitting the deferral of $1.8 billion in corporate tax.

Imperial Oil was founded in 1880 and had collected assets of $1.6 billion by 1970: By 1982, with the federal government amiably deferring the payment of $1.3 billion in taxes, Imperial Oil had amassed the grand total of $7.5 billion in assets.

Corporate capitalism is not a competitive system when 608 corporations reported taxable income of $15.5 billion in 1980, 53 per cent of the taxable income of the $29.5 billion reported by the Canadian corporate community of 451,567 firms. These are the firms that administer prices in their markets, control output of goods and services, and generate the funds from their operations that ensure the "immortality" that the law accepts.

A government can be dismissed by voters, a church affected by the scepticism of its adherents, or a university deserted by a community for losing touch with its needs or goals. Each of these institutions is bound by the purposes and priorities of its constituents.

The sole concern of the corporation, however, is with itself. Being a new legal person, it is possessed of an identity and form that is distinct from that of the people who own it, who work in it, and who deal with it. What happens to the corporation if a number of shareholders decide to sell their shares? Nothing. Others take their place through the facilities of the stock exchanges; management, which considers owners to be speculating in and outers, is indifferent to the change.

Managements come and go as do the workers. There is a little ceremony, a wristwatch, or a television set. The corporation, of which these men and women were a part, carries on undisturbed. The whole is not only greater than the sum of its parts—owners, management, workers—it is completely separate from any of them. If the corporation is linked to anything, it is not to people.

In 1973 Barclays Bank Limited of London, England, had a record year, a gross profit of £199 million. The chairman, in an advertisement in the *Economist*, announced that £96 million would be retained by the bank to increase the wool on its back, that £88 million had to go to the government for taxes, and £15 million in dividends to the stockholders. He stated: "It is also worth recording that of the three parties who make up a bank, namely stockholders, staff, and customers, none has gained much from these profits." And, indeed, they had not. In a year of 10 per cent inflation, the salary increases were limited to 7 per cent, the dividend increase to 5 per cent, and customers had to pay higher rates of interest.

These facts apply right across the corporate spectrum. The Barclays chairman was simply being frank. The corporation has simply one concern, to make full provision for its own continuity and growth.

Corporations have become ends in themselves when they were never meant to be more than efficient means of grouping the factors of production, land, and labour with the support and thrust of capital saved, to expand the output of goods and services and thus establish a higher standard of living for the whole community.

Unwilling to accept the goals of those who own it—although private property is the core of the value system in which it flourishes—struggling to free itself from the priorities and purposes of the community, the sole concern of the corporation is with its future. Self-perpetuating, self-determining, independent of time and space, the object of the corporation's existence is itself.

To be wealthy, said Aristotle, is no problem, even for a philosopher. He related the story of Thales, the astronomer-philosopher born in Miletus. Observing the stars, the philosopher judged the conditions appropriate for a great olive harvest. Whereupon Thales bought up all the olive presses in Chios and Miletus. There was a great harvest, but no olive presses—except those belonging to the philosopher, who rented them out at prices that soon made him rich. Control a market, be a monopolist.

Aristotle told another story. A man in Sicily bought up all the iron that was available. When merchants came to buy, he was the only seller, and with little difficulty he soon gained 200 per cent. Dionysius, the tyrant of Syracuse, called the man before him and told him that he could keep his money but that he must leave Syracuse. Dionysius feared that the man's wealth would soon be dangerous to his own political authority.

Aristotle established clearly the supremacy of politics over economics. Dionysius, wrote Aristotle approvingly, had recognized immediately and clearly that the accumulation of wealth can be a threat to and victor over political authority. For Aristotle, politics—even when practised by a tyrant—was to be preferred to the tyranny of wealth, for it is by politics that people decide on their priorities and their future directions.

Laissez faire was the spirit of the age when the acts of incorporation were adopted, permitting the right to incorporate with a freedom and lack of control that was clearly irresponsible. One hundred and twenty-seven years later, society is still paying for its failure to impose safeguards, to define responsibility, and to make accountable to the state the new means of organizing industrial activity to produce a greater wealth.

When forms of business organization were personal—partnerships or proprietorships—there was no problem about defining business ethics. Business ethics were personal ethics, and the ethics of the person may be described by the one word—"love." "Have and do whatsoever thou wilt," was the commandment of St. Augustine, but he was not inviting anarchy. A true love would not infringe the rights of others, and this boundary to one's actions preserves community and freedom.

To command a corporation to love would be madness.

Commanding a corporation to love would be asking it to distribute its wealth, to commit suicide. On the other hand, the corporation cannot be concerned simply with itself; it cannot be the object of its existence. It can and must be forced to conduct itself so that its activities correspond with the aims of the community, with the state itself as the seat of power and elected spokesman of the people.

V

What Can Politics Do?

I have made great use of the commitments made at the Williamsburg conference by the leaders of the seven industrial nations relating to the common defense of the West and the need to achieve comergence—i.e., integration of economic policies, particularly in the monetary, fiscal, and exchange-rate fields. The summit statements are the clearest and most comprehensive description of what has been taking place in the West, the putting in place of an informal supranational authority which could integrate the foreign-policy posture, the defence contributions, and the economic policies of the Western powers.

To repeat the substance of the decisions, the leaders of the seven leading industrial nations agreed:

1. In the statement on arms control: "We shall maintain sufficient military strength to deter any attack, to counter any threat, and to ensure the peace." Also, "The security

of our countries is indivisible and must be approached on a global basis."

2. In the text on economic recovery: "To promote convergence of economic performance in our economies" and "focusing on near-term policy actions leading to convergence in the medium-term." This goal was to be reached by following a pattern of non-inflationary growth of the money supply, appropriate interest rates, discipline over government expenditures, and convergence of exchange rates.

Williamsburg gives the impression that a community of the West has been created with authority over the participating nation-states. In fact, the leaders could do no more than agree to follow certain lines of conduct that would contribute to national and group security and to follow this up with appropriate economic initiatives.

Williamsburg as an exercise in public relations may or may not impress the Russians with the display of solidarity, but no international legal organization was created that could strip away elements of national sovereignty and so provide the unification that exists in the Soviet bloc. Not one of the Western leaders would have dared to accept openly the limitations of their sovereignty spelled out in the agreed press releases if these limitations were to be enshrined in an international treaty. It is worth repeating that the legal sovereignty of a state is incompatible with the existence of a supra-national authority that has a power centre of its own. A legal space is a universal space, although sovereign nations may choose not to exercise their rights in given situations. To the self-limitation of its sovereignty, Canada has been particularly prone.

Williamsburg did do something, and that something was to

establish a political, but not a legal, power centre which integrated the military and economic strengths of all seven nations and directed this accumulation of power to the turning back of the Russian threat—the priority purpose of the informal, political union. This priority of the bloc immediately assumed pride of place over the internal needs of the individual member nations, whose citizens were counselled to lower their expectations and to bear the burdens of unemployment and inflation a little longer.

It is to be emphasized that the Williamsburg agreements are not binding on the nations involved, for the voluntary agreements can be reversed at any time that national interests may dictate. Nor are the Williamsburg agreements a step forward in the quest for world order and peace, because the conference did not bring forward that set of moral principles and postulates that might serve as the basis for a true international authority, founded on the sovereignty of nations that is limited only by their respect for the freedom and self-determination of other nations.

The unifying forces at Williamsburg were two: sixteen thousand nuclear warheads in the arsenal of the United States, and the material interest of the six satellites in keeping open the huge markets of the United States. To possess power is to wield it, openly, and brutally or quietly, but firmly. Canada has the sovereign right to refuse to test the Cruise, but our political leaders know the economic costs and recoiled before the consequences. For the Europeans, the economic sovereignty lost is deemed a small price to pay for the security of the nuclear umbrella and the American pledge to safeguard the security of Western Europe as its own. Given the growing demonstrations against the deployment of the nuclear missiles in Europe, the summit leaders may yet find the cost in political instability to be very high.

It is not in the American interest to keep the impassioned rhetoric alive—the evil of the East and the goodness of the

West—thus creating the conditions of uncertainty and fear that will accelerate the pace of economic integration, and build a new Western economy composed of the resources of North America, Europe, and Japan with free movement of factors into and out of the United States heartland. So sweeping a unification of the Western economies, for the purpose of accumulating military and productive power, leads to the frustration of a constantly receding parity with an equally determined foe. There is no national security for either side in numbers, for parity at the level of a nuclear holocaust existed when each side possessed a thousand nuclear warheads. When today each side possesses sixteen thousand missiles, there is still parity and still the threat of holocaust—two republics of insects and ash.

For Canada the agreements reached at Williamsburg are simply more of the same. The three most sensitive areas for a nation jealous of its sovereignty are bound to be the areas of its relations with foreign countries, its defence arrangements, and its control of its money and credit. In all three areas, Canada agreed to follow the policy directions laid down by President Reagan and so confirmed again, for all the world to note, our membership in the American empire.

Until the British conversion to Free Trade in 1846, the Canadian colonies were content to be suppliers of raw materials to the mother country. After the withdrawal of British preferences, Canada sought and was granted reciprocity with the United States in 1854. When the treaty lapsed in 1865, Canada remained a supplier of resources and importer of manufactured goods, an integrated member of the continent's economy. Canada did not so much lose her independence as choose not to exercise it.

Canadian independence would have required some show of control over our resources, the land, the people, and the capital arising therefrom as well as the markets for goods and services and the surpluses they yielded. But all this was as freely available to Americans as to Canadians. And similarly with American resources and markets which were as open to the initiative, imagination, and drive of young Canadian entrepreneurs as to their own citizens. There were tariffs, but these were no more than excises, inland duties collected to finance railways and industrial expansion. From the beginning of Confederation, Canada was part of an economy in which the factors of production moved freely and goods did so with a slight surtax, an economic union that has just stopped short of full political unification.

As for defence, the Monroe doctrine applied to Canada as much as to any other nation in the Americas—at least as far as the United States was concerned, and that was all that counted. When it came to foreign affairs, we were taken for granted by foreign powers, who rightly assumed that we would follow the policies either of the motherland or the rich neighbour to the south. To most nations, friendly as they were, we were considered passive, even faceless, and seldom with a contribution to make. Canada did not have a minister of external affairs until 1946, a condition that served to emphasize our slow maturing as a nation.

I take the Williamsburg economic declaration for what it is, a clear and unequivocal request that Canada integrate its economic policies with those of the United States and adapt its resources to operate in a unified market system. Accepting this demand means that we make U.S. purposes and goals our purposes and goals, and their priorities our priorities. We give up the possibility of providing a framework in which a free and independent Canadian society may be built. If we are forced to accept as our own the objectives of other nations pursuing military superiority and nuclear supremacy, we have no right to call ourselves a nation. I prefer to believe that we are a nation, that we can follow a more independent course, and that we have the objective of greater employment for our people and an improved standard of living for the less fortunate in our nation.

Canada is at a crossroads. Our major market, the United States, can no longer afford free trade. If the United States operated in a fully free-trade environment, their trade deficit would be well beyond the $70 billion projected for this year. Worse, basic industries such as steel, heavy equipment, cars—the very core of a defence posture—would quickly collapse. Since this is unthinkable, it is obvious that the U.S. will become increasingly protectionist and press down more heavily on export markets such as our own.

Canadian history is a story of long-lived reliance on the export of natural resources. New sources in South America and Africa, with lower labour costs, are the competitors that are closing down our mines and refineries. As well, many of these nations have no other means of paying down their huge debts and interest charges than by increasing the volume of raw-material exports to the industrial West, thus earning the foreign exchange necessary to meet their commitments.

It is obvious that new directions are being imposed on us as the foundations of traditional economic policy, resource exploitation, and capital imports are crumbling beneath us. The decisions that we make in the eighties will make us a satellite economy operating on the fringes of the American empire unless we take stock of ourselves, our institutions, our human and material resources and resolve to put in place the political and economic structures that will provide us with the means and time to effect an evolving self-transformation.

It is time that Canada affirmed her independence as a sovereign state. We are not an accident of geography, nor are our traditions, culture, and languages to be written off in the alleged efficiency of a global economy. Nor can we yield control of our markets and means of production to others in the pursuit of some pseudo-internationalism.

I am not arguing against the possibility and hope in a great human family. I am simply saying that such an achievement, if it does come, will be an affair of the heart, the mind, and the spirit, not the result of organizing production on a world scale that maximizes skyscraper wealth, corporate cathedrals, and capital accumulation, leaves labour alone in the market place, and ends in the global homogenization of consumption and cultural patterns. The promise by globalists of a greater gross world product that would provide a rising standard of living for all people is an illusion and thoroughly dishonest.

Every nation must, if it is to satisfy the desires and needs of its citizens, have control of its economy. If the resources and the revenues from markets and production accrue largely to others, then the nation becomes dependent and vulnerable. An economy as a support system must also provide the non-exchange activities of a community, the universities, hospitals, cultural and social purposes, the spiritual elements that define a state as resting, not on material power alone, but on a system of moral values, intellectual freedom, and social responsibility.

A nation must believe in itself, or the worth of its people will never be realized. A nation must take, as its fundamental priority, responsibility for the welfare and standard of living of its people. We cannot accept the optimism and belief of the nineteenth century in a natural order built upon the creativity and enterprise of the individual. Nor can we believe that the vast conglomerates of the twentieth century have anything other than their own accumulations of power and wealth as goals.

As it applies to Canada, the Williamsburg continental integration signifies not only the placing of all our resources, physical and human, at the disposal of the American heartland, but would force the subordination of Canadian policies and interests to the objectives of the Western bloc. Military security in a nuclear world demands alliances and formal agreements. It does not require the subordination and subjugation of friends and allies. Canada's sovereignty demands that she be treated as an ally, not a satellite.

The nation-state is not through as an economic unit nor is it in decline because of the revolution in transportation and communication facilities. The so-called family of nations is a noble idea, but it is not, as Hegel pointed out, a reality. For centuries past, nations have been sensitive to the possible accession to power of the military forces and religious systems that even now control many parts of the world. The democratic nations of the West, however, have avoided these threats, which bring to power an authoritarian militarism or an unyielding fanaticism.

And yet we in the West are witnessing—quietly at first but now with an accelerating pressure—the increasing dominance and power of the commercial and industrial giants over our political institutions, a condition that will inevitably lead to a dictatorship of the left or right. A General Eisenhower warned of it, a Prime Minister Trudeau admits it.

The disarray in modern society comes from the argument that the sovereignty of the nation-state restrains the growth and efficiency of the corporation. Therefore the corporation must be freed from the control of the state, for only in this fashion can it take advantage of its true potential, size, economies of scale, and extended horizons.

It is clear that the nation-state and the corporation are operating on different levels. The corporation maximizes its own future, its own growth. For the nation-state, the heart of the economic system must be the distribution of what is produced in the nation, the power of the society to consume equalling its power to produce. The logic of the corporation is to grow, the responsibility of the state is to achieve a fair distribution. And so the conflict continues, because there is no moral consensus on what is fair, only the illusion that all nations must encourage bigness if they are to share in tomorrow's alleged plenty—for the love affair with bigness is the sentiment that the future will be better.

It is as Uncle Ernst says in *Howards End:* "It is the vice of a vulgar mind to be thrilled by bigness, to think that a thousand square miles are a thousand times more wonderful than one square mile, and that a million square miles are almost the same as heaven. That is not imagination. It kills it."

To think that a world is better than a hundred nation-states—or a thousand—is an illusion. There could be no single, most efficient application of the world's resources unless there were a single interest, but there is no single goal, or set of goals, to which such an application may be divided. The goals and aims of people are as varied and diverse as there are regions and communities and coalitions within the nation. In other words, choices and allocations are made through the processes of politics, which is the market place through which infinite needs and wants are given their priority and importance. In a democratic society, it is the political decision that, for better or for worse, ends the bureaucratic quibbling, silences the squalling screams for privilege and preference, and alone can provide the order and stability which will protect the individual in a world of conflicting claims and incessant struggles for power.

The nation-state is not in decline. It remains rooted in the soil and the hearts of its people. For a period after the Second World War there was an excessive internationalism that saw the rise of bureaucratic organizations such as NATO, OECD, GATT, and the United Nations itself, which sought to practise sovereignty without the basic element of authority, the power to enforce. Thus the United States ignores the condemnation of GATT for its DISC program, France pulls its forces out of NATO, and members are blandly indifferent to the boring nostrums of the OECD. These organizations can fulminate, they can recommend, but they have no power of their own.

For a generation, Canada has accepted the limitation of its sovereignty by these international organizations in the interests of establishing firm standards of international conduct. When all goes well, there is a disposition to accept the costs, but when unemployment soars and the claims of international bodies erode the sovereignty of the nation-state, the period of self-limitation of state powers is bound to come to a close.

National sovereignty and international authority cannot exist together. The danger of Williamsburg is that Canada accepts informally—for reasons of economic retaliation, political pressures, or balance-of-power tactics—what cannot be put into place legally. There can only be one legal order in Canada that may be flouted by a dominant and brutalizing neighbour. But there cannot be two legal bodies occupying the same space.

Let us be clear on this. Canada is sovereign, but we can be craven because we fear the economic sanctions and the loss of affluence that we now enjoy. This fear may have a foundation in reality. On the other hand, it is at least possible that what we fear is merely fear itself.

In any event, Canada has no choice. It cannot maintain the role of purveyor of raw materials for the simple reason that too many less-developed nations are taking over our markets with lower costs. We simply have to enlarge and diversify our industrial strength. There can be no question that the multinational corporation must adapt to the priorities and policies of the nation in which it operates as developer of resources, processor of goods, and supplier to markets. National policies do not conform to the motivations and objectives of the corporations that the state has admitted to the economy; it is the other way around. And this applies to domestic as well as multinational companies.

In a world in which the pressure on resources is growing from the two directions of, on the one hand, increasing demand with growing populations and rising standards of living and, on the other hand, the significant exhaustion of resources, it becomes evident that the private sector, motivated by its own growth, cannot be the final arbiter and allocator of resources between the corners of the earth, between consumption for today or investment for tomorrow, between the poor and the rich nations.

Limited sovereignty is not sovereignty at all. Hence, no nation can permit the corporation, domestic or multinational, to operate beyond the legal reach of its law. The sovereignty of the state demands that it maintain and secure the control of its own economy, the life-support system of its citizens. Canada has surrendered the value of too large a percentage of its lands, resources, and markets to corporations that have demanded the rights and privileges of absolute ownership as a condition of investment.

As the United States becomes increasingly protectionist, Canada will become increasingly isolated. In fact, it will become not only isolated but vulnerable, as Canadians realize that imported technology and ideas do not create new comparative advantages and that tariff protection does not foster an improved standard of living or allow infant industries time to grow.

Similarly, the emphasis on the export of natural resources before the competition of new nations financed by flows of foreign, including Canadian, capital. It is time that we left the field to the new arrivals of the third world.

New economic policies intend a change in direction, the switch from former ways into new paths. The costs become immediately apparent as change forces adaptation, offends the pride of policy makers, and disrupts ancient investment patterns. The benefits are in the future, but the costs are here and now—individually, corporately, and politically.

The new policies must come down hard on the old failures. Foreign capital never claimed to be a panacea for all our weaknesses. It was we who thought so. We forgot that foreign capital could not make up for the sale and export of our wealth and the emigration of our youth. We did not have enough control of ourselves or our economy to realize that, first and above all else, capital must be made and must be retained at home. By giving away the value of our resources, we never could accumulate the surpluses that would have enabled us to finance and invest in the balanced growth of the Canadian economy.

What can politics do? first, it must accept the responsibility of sovereignty and the supremacy of politics in deciding the allocation of resources and the directions of future development. Let the economists decide the application and costs of the directions chosen. Secondly, Canada can grow and be of value to the world and to itself only by being an independent, sovereign state, and it can do this only by the control of its own economy and politics.

The ultimate norms directing Canadian policies cannot be the interests of other nations, no matter how powerful, or the fear of their reprisals. Our aims will be truly Canadian when they arise out of the hearts and minds of our people, not when they are dictated at summit conferences or by ambassadorial pressures.

Our political leaders have much to work with. Not only the lands and people which we have always had, but the same burning desire that led so many Canadians to look for challenge elsewhere exists in today's generation. We have all the means to create a viable and gainful economy if we can find the leadership to put it all together.

A nation has an inner structure and vitality that imposes a pattern on its environment. Understanding and having confidence in the spirit and capacity of a people is an essential quality of sound political leadership.

Rene Dubos, in his book *A God Within: A Positive Philosophy for a More Complete Fulfillment of the Human Potential*, quotes Michelangelo expressing his feelings on looking at a block of marble:

The best of artists has that thought alone,
Which is contained within the marble shell.
The sculptor's hand can only break the spell,
To free the figures slumbering in the stone.

The potential and the capacity of Canadians to do great things in and for the world is there. It needs the political leadership and a belief in ourselves to break the spell.

The challenge facing our political leaders is to establish a clear and distinct Canadian identity as an independent state, a worthy ally, but an unwilling satellite.

An identity is clear when our policies, whether in the fields of trade and commerce, external affairs and defence, work in the same direction; an identity is independent when we have control of our own economy, money and credit; it is distinct when Canadian national interests and objectives, with full regard for the interests and choices of others, alone determine our attitudes.

| APPENDIX A |

SUMMIT STATEMENT ON ARMS CONTROL
Joint Communique
Williamsburg, Virginia—May 29, 1983

1. As leaders of our seven countries, it is our first duty to defend
   the freedom and justice on which our democracies are based.
   To this end, we shall maintain sufficient military strength to
   deter any attack, to counter any threat, and to ensure the peace.
   Our arms will never be used except in response to aggression.

2. We wish to achieve lower levels of arms through serious arms
   control negotiations. With this statement, we reaffirm our
   dedication to the search for peace and meaningful arms reductions. We are ready to work with the Soviet Union to this
   purpose and call upon the Soviet Union to work with us.

3. Effective arms control agreements must be based on the principle of equality and must be verifiable. Proposals have been put forward from the Western side to achieve positive results in various international negotiations: on strategic weapons (S.T.A.R.T.), on intermediate-range nuclear missiles (INF), on chemical weapons, on reduction of forces in Central Europe (MBFR), and a conference on disarmament in Europe (CDE).

4. We believe that we must continue to pursue these negotiations with impetus and urgency. In the area of INF, in particular, we call upon the Soviet Union to contribute constructively to the success of the negotiations. Attempts to divide the West by proposing inclusion of the deterrent forces of third countries, such as those of France and the United Kingdom, will fail. Consideration of these systems has no place in the INF negotiations.

5. Our nations express the strong wish that a balanced INF agreement be reached shortly. It is well known that should this not occur, the countries concerned will proceed with the planned deployment of the U.S. systems in Europe at the end of 1983.

6. Our nations are united in efforts for arms reductions and will continue to carry out thorough and intensive consultations. The security of our countries is indivisible and must be approached on a global basis. Attempts to avoid serious negotiation by seeking to influence public opinion in our countries will fail.

7. We commit ourselves to devote our full political resources to reducing the threat of war. We have a vision of a world in which the shadow of war has been lifted from all mankind, and we are determined to pursue that vision.

SUMMIT STATEMENT ON ECONOMIC RECOVERY
Joint Communique announced by President Reagan
Williamsburg, Virginia—May 30, 1983

Our nations are united in their dedication to democracy, individual freedom, creativity, moral purpose, human dignity and personal and cultural development.

It is to preserve, sustain and extend these shared values that our prosperity is important.

The recession has put our societies through a severe test, but they have proven resilient. Significant success has been achieved in reducing inflation and interest rates, there have been improvements in productivity and we now clearly can see signs of recovery.

Nevertheless, the industrialized democracies continue to face the challenge of insuring that the recovery materializes and endures, in order to reverse a decade of cumulative inflation and reduce unemployment, we must all focus on achieving and maintaining low inflation and reducing interest rates from their present too high levels. We renew our commitment to reduce structural budget deficits, in particular by limiting the growth of expenditures.

We recognize that we must act together and that we must pursue a balanced set of policies that take into account and exploit relationships between growth, trade and finance in order that recovery may spread to all countries, developed and developing alike.

In pursuance of these objectives we have agreed as follows:

1. Our governments will pursue appropriate monetary and budgetary policies that will be conducive to low inflation, reduced interest rates, higher productive investment and greater employment opportunities, particularly for the young.

2. The consultation process initiated at Versailles will be enhanced to promote convergence of economic performance in our economies and greater stability of exchange rates on the lines indicated in an annex to this declaration. We agree to pursue closer consultations on policies affecting exchange markets and on market conditions. While retaining our freedom to operate independently, we are willing to undertake coordinated intervention in exchange markets in instances where it is agreed where such intervention would be helpful.

3. We commit ourselves to halt protectionism and, as recovery proceeds, to reverse it by dismantling trade barriers. We intend to consult in appropriate existing fora on ways to implement and monitor this commitment. We shall give impetus to resolving current trade problems. We will actively pursue the current work programs in the General Agreement on Tariffs and Trade

(GATT) and Organization for Economic Cooperation and Development, including trade in services and high technology products. We should work to achieve further trade liberalization negotiations in the GATT with particular emphasis in expanding trade with, and among, developing countries. We have agreed to continue consultations on proposals for a new negotiating round in the GATT.

4. We view with concern the international financial situation and especially the debt burdens of many developing nations. We agree to a strategy based on effective adjustment and development policies by debtor nations, adequate private and official financing, more open markets and world wide economic recovery. We will seek ratification of the increases in resources for the International Monetary Fund and the general agreements to borrow. We encourage closer cooperation and timely sharing of information among countries and the international institutions in particular, between the International Monetary Fund (IMF), the International Bank for Reconstruction and Development (IBRD), and the GATT.

5. We have invited ministers of finance in consultation with the managing director of the IMF to define the conditions for improving the international monetary system and to consider the part which might, in due course, be played in this process by a high level, international, monetary conference.

6. The weight of the recession has fallen very heavily on developing countries and we are deeply concerned about their recovery. Restoring sound economic growth while keeping our markets open is crucial. Special attention will be given to the flow of resources, in particular, official development assistance to poorer countries, and for food and energy production, both bilaterally and through appropriate international institutions. We reaffirm our commitments to provide agreed funding levels

for the International Development Agency. We welcome the openness to dialogue which the developing countries evinced at the recent conferences of the non-aligned movement in New Delhi and the Group of 77 in Buenos Aires and we share their commitment to engage with understanding and cooperation in the forthcoming meeting of the United Nations conference on trade and development in Belgrade.

7. We are agreed upon the need to encourage both the development of advanced technology and the public acceptance of its role in promoting growth, employment and trade. We have noted with approval the report of the Working Group on Technology, Growth and Employment, which was set up at Versailles last year and commend the progress made in the eighteen cooperative projects discussed in that report. We will follow the implementation and coordination of work on these projects and look forward to receiving a further report at our next meeting.

8. We all share the view that more predictability and less volatility in oil prices would be helpful to world economic prospects. We agreed that the fall in oil prices in no way diminishes the importance and urgency of efforts to conserve energy, to develop economic alternative energy sources, to maintain and where possible improve contacts between oil-exporting and importing countries, and to encourage the growth of indigenous energy production in developing countries which at present lack it.

9. East-West economic relations should be compatible with our security interests. We take note with approval of the work of the multilateral organizations which have in recent months analyzed and drawn conclusions regarding the key aspects of East-West economic relations. We encourage continuing work by these organizations as appropriate.

10. We have agreed to strengthen cooperation in protection of the environment, in better use of natural resources and in health research.

Our discussions here at Williamsburg give us new confidence in the prospects for a recovery. We have strengthened our resolve to deal cooperatively with continuing problems so as to promote a sound and sustainable recovery, bringing new jobs and a better life for the people of our own countries and of the world.

We have agreed to meet again next year and have accepted the British Prime Minister's invitation to meet in the United Kingdom.

ANNEX
Strengthening economic cooperation for growth and stability

I. We have examined in the light of our experience the procedures outlined in the undertakings agreed at Versailles last year which seek to ensure greater monetary stability in the interest of balanced growth and progress of the world economy.

II. We reaffirm the objectives of achieving non-inflationary growth of income and employment, and promoting exchange market stability through policies designed to bring about greater convergence of economic performance in this direction.

III. We are reinforcing our multilateral cooperation with the International Monetary Fund in its surveillance activities, according to the procedures agreed at Versailles, through the following approach:

A. We are focusing on near-term policy actions leading to convergence of economic conditions in the medium term. The overall medium-term perspective remains essential, both to ensure that short-term policy innovations do not lead to divergence and to reassure business and financial markets.

B. In accordance with the agreement reached at Versailles, we are focusing our attention on issues in the monetary and financial fields including interaction with policies in other areas. We shall take fully into account the international implications of our own policy decisions. Policies and objectives that will be kept under review include:

(1) Monetary Policy. Disciplined non-inflationary growth of monetary aggregates, and appropriate interest rates, to avoid subsequent resurgence of inflation and rebound in interest rates, thus allowing room for sustainable growth.

(2) Fiscal Policy. We will aim, preferably through discipline over government expenditures, to reduce structural budget deficits and bear in mind the consequences of fiscal policy for interest rates and growth.

(3) Exchange Rate Policy. We will improve consultations, policy convergence and international cooperation to help stabilize exchange markets, bearing in mind our conclusions on the exchange market intervention study.

(4) Policies Toward Productivity and Employment. While relying on market signals as a guide to efficient economic decisions, we will take measures to improve training and mobility of our labour forces, with particular concern for the problems of youth forces, with particular concern for the problems of youth unemployment, and promote continued structural adjustment, especially by:

— Enhancing flexibility and openness of economies and financial markets.

— Encouraging research and development as well as profitability and productive investment.

— Continued efforts in each country, and improved international cooperation, where appropriate, on structural adjustment measures (e.g., regional, sectoral, energy policies).

IV. We shall continue to assess together regularly in this framework the progress we are making, consider any corrective action which may be necessary from time to time, and react promptly to significant changes.

|Appendix C|

Eric Kierans resigned as Federal Minister of Communications in April, 1971, citing many of the points he discusses in the Massey Lectures. Below are the texts of his resignation and Prime Minister Trudeau's reply.

Ottawa, April 28th, 1971

My dear Prime Minister:

I appreciate very much our lengthy discussion yesterday in which I expressed my concern about the economic problems, particularly employment, facing Canada in the seventies. Challenges which did not exist ten years ago now present themselves and demand a total re-examination of all elements of our economic policy. The rise of the international corporation, for example, is leading some economists and businessmen to talk in terms of gross world production as a better index of economic growth than the sum of national products. This may be, although

I sense no similar concern with the distribution of that product. One can detect, however, the implicit assumption that Canada is to be assigned the role of supplier of resources presumably because we have them and also because we do not have a sufficient domestic market to justify their conversion into finished or semi-finished products here at home.

Economic policy is put together from a variety of elements, but the overriding objective of all nations in the seventies must be the attainment of full employment, however defined, as the best guarantee of political, social, and economic stability. To this end, all elements of policy—monetary, fiscal, commercial, energy and resources, agricultural, regional development—must be interconnected to ensure that they do not work at cross purposes and at the expense of overall objectives.

It is in this realm of ideas and policy that I wish to concentrate my efforts. Economic growth is not unlimited. Even with an exponential increase in capital and population—three billion now, six billion people by the year 2000—a diminishing supply of non-renewable resources will restrain world growth. Canada is fortunate in its resource base and can insist on exports with a higher labour content. Tax concessions that force the pace of our raw material exports or favour the over-employment of capital, which we have to import, at the expense of labour which is in surplus would not be consistent with long-run Canadian growth and employment objectives. If Canada is to be an industrial force in the 1980s, we must be prepared now to husband our resources and to select those areas in which we can be internationally competitive and to manage and invest in the resources, physical and human, that will give us a compelling position.

To challenge openly long-established policies and practices would be embarrassing to my colleagues and to you, and unfair, if I were to remain in the Cabinet. Therefore, I ask you to accept my resignation as Minister of Communications, effective immediately. I leave with real regret.

I fully support the national unity policies of the government and I am certain that these will achieve a better and a united Canada. In my own sphere of activity, I have greatly enjoyed the challenge that you entrusted to me as Minister of Communications.

With my warmest personal regards, I am

Sincerely yours,

(signed) ERIC KIERANS.

Ottawa, April 29, 1971.
Dear Eric,

It was with regret that I received your request to resign as Minister of Communications and it is with reluctance that I shall recommend to the Governor General that it be accepted.

I fully share your concern about the economic future of Canada as do all your colleagues. While your own views have not always prevailed in the frequent discussions the Cabinet has had on this subject, they have nevertheless added a dimension that has helped provide the broad perspective within which our decisions have been made. It is not only I, but all of your colleagues who will miss your contribution.

As Minister of Communications, you have played a most important role in defining the problems and helping to shape Canada's course in this difficult and challenging field.

I would also like to express my thanks for all the other contributions that you have made to the government and to the people of Canada.

While you will no longer be participating in Cabinet, as a member of the Liberal Caucus your views on all matters will still command the government's attention.

I appreciate the courtesy you have shown and the spirit you have exhibited in handling the difficult personal dilemma that has faced you.

With warmest personal regards,

Yours sincerely,

(Signed) P. E. TRUDEAU

| Notes |

The Underdeveloped Country
by John Kenneth Galbraith

Chapter 1: *Underdevelopment and Social Behavior*
1. Stern traditionalists in the service of the United States still insist
   on this form. Cf. an interview with Mr. Thomas Mann, Undersecretary of State for Economic Affairs, *New York Times*, May 9,
   1965.
2. Albert O. Hirschman. *The Strategy of Economic Development*.
   New York. Yale University Press. 1958. Pp. 11 et seq.

Chapter 3: *Cause and Classification*
1. Cf. Jacob Viner, "The Economics of Development," in *The
   Economics of Underdevelopment*. A. N. Agarwala and S. P. Singh.
   (Bombay. Oxford University Press.) P. 13. Also Bernard Okun
   and Richard W. Richardson, *Status in Economic Development*

(New York. Holt, Rinehart and Winston) p. 236. "The size of per capita income is used by most writers as the criterion for differentiating between advanced and underdeveloped countries."

2. Henry J. Bruton, "Growth Models and Underdeveloped Economies," *Journal of Political Economy*, 1955. Reprinted in Agarwala and Singh. Op. cit. pp. 219-220.

3. Cambridge. (Cambridge University Press), 1960.

4. *Ibid.*, p. 36 et seq.

5. Simon Kuznetz, "Notes on the Take-Off." Paper presented before International Economic Association, September, 1960.

6. Professor Rostow states that India, along with China, launched its take-off during the 1950's. (Op. cit., p. 9.) He later cautions (p. 38) that it is still too soon to judge whether the effort will be successful—a suggestion of an otherwise unexplored notion that the stages of growth may be somewhat reversible. (He then concludes that as in China "the commitment . . . to modernization appears too deep to permit more than temporary setbacks") (p. 48). The near certainty is that only heroic efforts, including a continuation of extensive provision of food from abroad, will prevent a deterioration of per capita income in India in coming years.

7. I have drawn heavily, and gratefully, on seminar and class discussion of this classification. I first presented it at the Third Rehovot Conference in Israel in August, 1965. I have also benefited from that discussion.

8. Elliot J. Berg. "Socialism and Economic Development in Tropical Africa." *The Quarterly Journal of Economics*, November, 1964, pp. 560-561. (Mr. Berg argues with much effect that this shortage of qualified talent has not prevented—and has possibly encouraged—a number of these countries to commit scarce administrative resources to demanding experiments in socialism and planning at heavy cost to themselves.)

9. Ernest Lefever. *Crisis in the Congo*. The Brookings Institution, 1965. P. 9.

10. Frederick Harbison and Charles A. Myers, *Education, Manpower and Economic Growth*. New York. McGraw-Hill, 1964. P. 38. I am indebted to Richard S. Sharpe for a useful discussion of these figures in "The Manpower Gap in Middle Africa," an unpublished seminar paper, Harvard University.

11. Cf. George H. Kimble. *Tropical Africa*, Volume II, "Society and Policy." New York. Doubleday, 1962. Pp. 469 et seq.

CHAPTER 4: *Cause and Classification (Continued)*

1. "Basically, the problem [of Chilean agriculture] is lack of economic opportunities—resulting from the lack of employment alternatives, lack of knowledge and skills, and lack of collective power among workers." *An Open Letter to Chilean Landowners*. By Peter Dorner. Mimeographed, May, 1965. Professor Dorner of the University of Wisconsin has recently spent a number of years studying Chilean agricultural and tenure problems.

2. In 1949, 20 per cent of the population in Canada and the United States was in agriculture as compared with 60 per cent in South America. Production per person was something over five times as great. In 1947/48 output per person was 143 per cent of pre-war levels in North America (including Central America) and 83 per cent of pre-war in South America. United Nations Department of Economic Affairs. "Land Reform: Defects in Agrarian Structure and Obstacles to Economic Development." New York, United Nations, 1951. Data are from the Food and Agriculture Organization of the United Nations.

3. In certain philosophical or political contexts, this may be held to be true of the armed forces of any country. They are said to serve the wrong foreign policy, be part of the wrong defense

strategy, serve only the arms race, or whatnot. But the armed forces are seriously in the service of the disapproved philosophical or political goals. In Latin America no serious observer supposes that the armed services are seriously important for national defense, territorial integrity or any other military or foreign policy objective. Their role is exclusively related to domestic politics and income.

4. This is a matter of much practical importance, especially as regards the armed forces. Generally in the United States there has been recognition of the bearing of a regressive or feudal land system on economic development. That *caudillo* government, either by itself or in association with other non-functional groups, can be equally inimical has not been so readily seen. As a consequence, conservative, or more often simplistically traditionalist, officials regularly turn up defending army dictatorships in Latin America. And, in the past, military aid funds have regularly gone to support armies, which were a source of political power, at the same time that economic assistance was being given to development or even (hopefully) to land reform. It would be difficult to find a policy with a greater element of self-contradiction and this is not lessened by the tendency of those who espouse support to the Latin American military to assume that pragmatism, professionalism and even an element of righteousness are on their side.

5. Francis N. Schott. "Inflation and Stabilization Efforts in Chile, 1953-1958." *Inter-American Affairs*, Winter, 1959. Reprinted in *Leading Issues in Development Economics*, by Gerald M. Meier. New York. Oxford University Press, 1964. P. 221.

6. Venezuela also has rich income from oil but may gradually be breaking the hold of a regressive social structure which for a long time led to the dissipation and waste of this revenue.

7. Although not in all categories of teachers or with a sufficient willingness to serve in rural villages.

8. The army is not without political power in Pakistan. However, it is not a recognized avenue to political power and economic advantage as in Latin America. And the armed coup which brought President Ayub Khan to power in 1959 (like his subsequent administration) bore little or no resemblance to the Latin American phenomenon.

CHAPTER 5: *A Differential Prescription*

1. They constitute more than one-third of all degree-holding secondary teachers in Ghana and teach over 20,000 secondary students in that country. In Malawi, they provide over one-third of all secondary teachers and have helped to double the secondary school enrollment. In Sierra Leone, they provide over one-half of all qualified teachers. In Liberia, the Peace Corps furnished 90 per cent of all degree-holding teachers. In Nigeria, 25 per cent of all graduate teachers in secondary schools are Peace Corps Volunteers who teach 40,000 students, representing 35 per cent of the total enrollment of secondary students. In Ethiopia and West Cameroon, 40 per cent of all qualified secondary teachers are Volunteers. Sharpe, op. cit. in my third lecture, p. 30.

2. In Laos, in the 1950's, it was United States policy, when in doubt as to what should be done, to provide more money. The Eisenhower administration, with a warm respect for pecuniary values, naturally assumed that money must do good. In fact, in widening the economic difference between the city recipients and the countryside, and proving the feasibility of winning wealth without effort, it probably did a certain measure of damage.

3. The idea of a Teachers Corps in the United States, a proposal with which I have been identified, has similar provenance. The poor school districts need not money, which they often spend incompetently, but highly qualified and motivated talent which

they cannot buy. It is hoped that the Teachers Corps will provide such talent.

4. Cf. Berg. Op. cit. in my third lecture, p. 30.

5. This conclusion is argued by Celso Furtado in an important forthcoming paper, "Development and Stagnation in Latin America: A Structuralist Approach," Yale University, Economic Growth Center, which he has been good enough to let me read.

6. Professor A. O. Hirschman has drawn attention to other such policy rhythms, derived from a tendency to look with favor on any alternative to what is presently being done, in the field of exchange control, fiscal policy and development administration. *Economic Development and Cultural Change*. University of Chicago Press. 1957. I have been impressed by the same tendency and attribute much of it to optimistic newcomers, both indigenous and foreign, in the field of economic development. Along with extremely important enthusiasm they bring a strong tendency, on seeing something wrong, to assume that any change must be for the better. They cannot easily be persuaded either that present policy is the result of similar previous convictions or that the alternative policy had an earlier and equally unsatisfactory incarnation.

7. A case that has been argued in a different context by my colleague, Alexander Gerschenkron. "Economic Backwardness in Historical Perspective" in *The Progress of Underdeveloped Areas*. Edited by B. F. Hoselitz. Chicago. University of Chicago Press, 1952.

8. It will be the view of any close student of United States policy in Latin America, I believe, that more is to be feared from political innocence than political reaction. It has been extensively influenced in the past by a generation of professional diplomats who had no experience with the liberal leavening of domestic politics and the discovery that Negroes, the unemployed, farmers, trade

union members were not automatically enamored of the status quo and what best suited respectable and well-to-do white Anglo-Saxon Protestants of good family and education. Nor were they especially informed on the academic currents of liberal economic and political thought. At the same time, they drew on undoubted and lengthy experience in Latin America. This experience was all but exclusively with the elite; it led to an almost automatic identification with this point of view and a deep, self-confident and at times self-righteous conviction that the masses in Latin America did not count. These attitudes are not identified with any serious economic interest of the United States although they are, of course, applauded by American conservatives. It is for this reason that one properly associates them with innocence rather than reaction. Although sophistication is unquestionably increasing, these attitudes have not disappeared, at least from among the older generation of officers. They had an unhappy initial influence on recent policy toward the Dominican Republic; only gradually were more liberal and sophisticated attitudes brought to bear.

9. Technical assistance in industrial, educational and agricultural fields is, at best, of marginal importance in the Model. However, it is my feeling that in countries such as India, it has, in fact, been overemphasized. It can be useful in specific areas where, despite the ample cultural base, specific technical or other intellectual resources are limited.

Canadian Cities and Sovereignty Association
by JANE JACOBS

CHAPTER 1: *Emotions and a Tale of Two Cities*
1. David Cameron, *Nationalism, Self Determination, and the Quebec Question*, Toronto: Macmillan of Canada, 1974.
2. Garth Stevenson, *Unfulfilled Union*. Toronto: Macmillan, 1979.
3. Statistics Canada.
4. Statistics Canada, figures on mother-tongue of Montreal population.
5. Personal communication with Public Information Officer at the Toronto Stock Exchange.
6. Statistics Canada.
7. Statistics Canada.

CHAPTER 2: *The Separation of Norway from Sweden*
8. This and all subsequent history of Norway and Sweden come from the following books:
   T. K. Derry. *A History of Modern Norway 1814-1972*. Oxford: Clarendon Press, 1973.
   John Midgaard. *A Brief History of Norway*. Oslo: Johan Grundt Tanum Forlag, 1969.
   Karen Larsen. *A History of Norway*, Princeton, N.J.: Princeton University Press, 1948.

CHAPTER 3: *Some Paradoxes of Size*
9. Larry Grossman, Ontario's current Minister of Industry and Tourism.
10. Government of Canada, Department of Industry, Trade and Commerce; Western Europe Division.
11. Ibid.

12. Statistics Canada, Imports and Exports between Norway and Canada for years 1976-1978.

13. Gunnar Jerman (ed.). *Norway 79*. Oslo: Export Council of Norway, 1979.

14. Statistics Canada, Imports and Exports between Norway and Canada for years 1976-1978.

15. Ola Veigaard (ed.). *Facts About Norway*, 15th edition. Oslo: Aftenposten, 1975.

16. *Norway 79*, op. cit.

17. Gunnar Jerman (ed.). *New Norway*. Oslo: Export Council of Norway, 1973.

18. J. J. Brown. *Ideas In Exile*. Toronto: McClelland and Stewart, 1967.

19. George Gibb and Evelyn Knowlton. *History of Standard Oil*, vol. 2. New York: Harper, 1956.

20. Personal communication with the Chairman of the Ontario Hostelry Directorship Institute.

21. Iona and Peter Opie (eds.). *Oxford Dictionary of Nursery Rhymes*. Oxford: Clarendon Press, 1952.

22. F. H. Pritchard (ed.). *The World's Best Essays*. New York: Albert and Charles Boni, 1932.

23. Personal communication.

24. Statistics Canada, Federal Government Employment.

CHAPTER 4: *Sovereignty-Association: Connectors*

25. René Lévesque. *My Quebec*. Toronto: Methuen, 1979.

26. Government of Quebec. "Quebec-Canada: A New Deal—The Quebec Government proposal for a new partnership between equals: sovereignty-association." Tabled in the Quebec National Assembly, 1 November 1979.

27. Statistics Canada, Manufacturing and Primary Industries Division.

28. Personal communication.
29. Bank of Canada, Toronto.

Chapter 5: *Sovereignty-Association: Separateness*

30. Personal communication.
31. This and all others, except where noted, are from Lévesque, *My Quebec*, op. cit.
32. David Cameron, op. cit.
33. Stephen Jay Gould. "Dreamer," a review of Freeman Dyson's *Disturbing The Universe*. *New York Review of Books*. 11 October 1979.
34. A. O. Lovejoy. *The Great Chain of Being*. New York: Harper Torchbook, 1963.
35. Quebec, Le Ministre d'Etat au development culturel. "Towards a Scientific Research Policy for Quebec," as summarized in *Agenda*, a quarterly bulletin of the Science Council of Canada, vol. 2 number 3, 1979.
36. Morrison Renfrew, project manager for Ontario's Urban Transportation Development Corporation, quoted in the Toronto *Globe and Mail*, 25 July 1979.
37. Letter to the Editor from Shinji Nakamura, Head HSST System Engineering Group, Tokyo, in the Toronto *Globe and Mail*, 1 September 1979.
38. Virginia Woolf. *Between The Acts*. London: Hogarth Press, 1941.

ACKNOWLEDGMENTS
I am deeply indebted to Diane Rotstein for research and editorial assistance, to Max Allen for directing and editing the broadcast lectures, to Geraldine Sherman for arranging for them, and to all three for their advice, taste and the enjoyment of working with them.

I thank Decker Butzner, Stephen Clarkson, Kari Dehli, Robert,

James and Burgin Jacobs, Douglas Manzer, Doris Mehegan, Alan Powell and the staffs of the Norwegian Trade Commission, the Swedish Trade Commission and the Toronto Public Library for their various contributions of assistance.

My deepest gratitude is for a fact: that even when the subject is as contentious as the one I have chosen, Canada's government-owned broadcasting corporation can serve free speech without hint or taint of censorship.

Globalism and the Nation-State
by ERIC W. KIERANS

FOREWORD
1. Such concerns also appear in Professor Kierans' resignation from the Federal cabinet; see Appendix C.

CHAPTER 1: *The Meaning of Williamsburg*
1. The complete text is printed in Appendix A.
2. The complete text is printed in Appendix B.

About the Lectures and the Lecturers

The Massey Lectures were created in honour of the Right Honourable Vincent Massey, former governor general of Canada, and were inaugurated by the CBC in 1961 to enable distinguished authorities to communicate the results of original study or research on a variety of subjects of general interest. The Massey Lectures are today co-sponsored by CBC Radio, House of Anansi Press, and Massey College in the University of Toronto.

The Underdeveloped Country is the text of the fifth annual series of Massey Lectures, broadcast on CBC Radio during the fall of 1965. The series was arranged by Robert McCormack and produced by Lynn Higgins of the CBC Department of Public Affairs.

John Kenneth Galbraith (1908–2006) was a Canadian-born American economist, public servant, and writer. Born in Iona Station, Ontario, he earned a B.Sc. degree (1931) from the

Ontario Agricultural College at Guelph and an M.Sc. degree (1933) and a Ph.D. degree (1934) from the University of California, Berkeley, and later studied in England at Cambridge University. He became a U.S. citizen in 1937 and would serve in the Roosevelt, Truman, Kennedy, and Johnson administrations. During and after World War II, he was deputy administrator of the Office of Price Administration, director of the U.S. Strategic Bombing Survey, and director of Economic Policy with the U.S. Department of State. He was also Paul M. Warburg Professor of Economics at Harvard University, where he taught for many years, a U.S. ambassador to India (1961–63), and the author of many books on economics, including *American Capitalism*, *The Great Crash*, *1929*, *The Affluent Society*, *The New Industrial State*, and *Economics and the Public Purpose*, as well as hundreds of essays, a memoir, and a number of novels. He was awarded numerous honorary degrees, twice received the Presidential Medal of Freedom, in 1946 and in 2000, and was made an officer of the Order of Canada in 1997.

The Moral Ambiguity of America is the text of the sixth annual series of Massey Lectures, broadcast on CBC Radio during the fall of 1966. The series was arranged by Robert McCormack and produced by Del MacKenzie of the CBC Department of Public Affairs.

Paul Goodman (1911–1972) was an American writer, teacher, and social critic. Born in New York, his formal education was in philosophy and literature. He taught English, sociology, and city planning at the University of Chicago (where he obtained his Ph.D.), New York University, and the University of Wisconsin; at Sarah Lawrence College, in Bronxville, NY; at the experimental college of Black Mountain; and at the "free university" organized by students of San Francisco State College. He was an editor of *Liberation* magazine, an associate of the Institute for Policy Studies in Washington, D.C., a co-founder of the New York Institute for Gestalt Therapy, and a fellow of the Institute for Gestalt Therapy in Cleveland. The author of books on social themes (including *People or Personnel*, *Compulsory Mis-Education*, *Utopian Essays and Practical Proposals*, *The Society I Live in Is Mine*, *The Politics of Being Queer*, and *Growing Up Absurd*), he was also co-author (with Frederick Perls) of *Gestalt Therapy* and (with his brother Percival) of *Communitas*, a work on community planning. He also wrote literary criticism (*The Structure of Literature*, *Kafka's Prayer*), novels (including *Empire City* and *Making Do*), numerous short stories, plays, and several books of poetry.

Conscience for Change is the text of the seventh annual series of Massey Lectures, broadcast on CBC Radio during the fall of 1967. The series was arranged by the Ideas unit of the CBC Department of Public Affairs, with Janet Somerville as program organizer and production by Del MacKenzie.

Martin Luther King, Jr. (1929–1968) was a Baptist minister and a key leader in the American civil-rights movement. He was co-pastor, with his father, of the Ebenezer Baptist Church in Atlanta, GA, and president and one of the founders of the Southern Christian Leadership Conference. An eloquent advocate of achieving civil rights through non-violent means, he was awarded the Nobel Peace Prize in 1964. He was selected by *Time* magazine as one of the ten outstanding personalities of 1957 and was named its "Man of the Year" for 1963. Born in Atlanta, he obtained a B.A. degree at Morehouse College in 1948, a B.D. degree from Crozer Theological Seminary in Chester, PA, in 1951, and a Ph.D. degree in Systematic Theology from Boston University in 1955. He was awarded more than twenty honorary degrees by colleges and universities in the United States and abroad. He lectured extensively at academic institutions and authored a number of books, including *Stride Toward Freedom*, *Strength to Love*, *Why We Can't Wait*, and *Where Do We Go From Here: Chaos or Community*. Assassinated in Memphis, TN, on April 4, 1968, he was posthumously awarded the Presidential Medal of Freedom in 1977. Martin Luther King Day was established as a U.S. holiday in 1986.

Canadian Cities and Sovereignty-Association is based on the eighteenth annual series of Massey Lectures, broadcast on CBC Radio during the fall of 1979. The series was produced by Max Allen.

Jane Jacobs (1916–2006) was an urban activist and writer. Born Jane Butzner in Scranton, PA, she moved to New York City and became a freelance writer, later working for the Office of War Information and marrying the architect Robert Hyde Jacobs. She attended Columbia University's extension school, where she studied subjects as diverse as zoology, economics, and law. In 1962 she chaired the Joint Committee to Stop the Lower Manhattan Expressway, helping prevent the expressway from being built. She helped block the Lower Manhattan Expressway again in 1968, and was arrested during a demonstration. In part due to her anti–Vietnam War stance, that same year Jacobs moved to Toronto, where she would remain. There she helped stop the Spadina Expressway, and influenced the successful regeneration of the St. Lawrence neighbourhood. She also advocated for the city of Toronto to become its own Canadian province. Her books include *The Death and Life of Great American Cities*, *The Economy of Cities*, *Cities and the Wealth of Nations*, *Systems of Survival*, *The Nature of Economies*, and *Dark Age Ahead*. A Canadian citizen from 1974, she was named an officer of the

Order of Canada in 1996. The Rockefeller Foundation created a Jane Jacobs Medal in her honour in 2007.

Globalism and the Nation-State is based on the twenty-first annual series of Massey Lectures, broadcast on CBC Radio during the fall of 1983. The executive producer was Robert Prowse.

Eric W. Kierans (1914–2004) was a Canadian economist, business leader, politician, and writer. Born in Montreal and educated at Loyola College and McGill University, his career included that of president of the Montreal and Canadian stock exchanges, extensive business experience, director of the McGill School of Commerce, as well as the political offices of minister of revenue for Quebec, minister of health for Quebec, president of the Quebec Liberal Federation, candidacy for the federal leadership (Liberal) in 1968, and federal cabinet minister in Pierre Elliott Trudeau's first government with the positions of postmaster general and minister of communications. After resigning from the cabinet in 1971, he returned to teaching, as professor of economics first at McGill and later at Dalhousie University, and continued lecturing, writing, and serving as a consultant and in other senior positions for financial and government institutions across Canada. His books include *Challenge of Confidence: Kierans on Canada* and his memoirs, *Remembering*. In the 1980s and 1990s he was a member, along with Stephen Lewis and Dalton Camp, of a popular weekly political panel on CBC Radio's *Morningside* with Peter Gzowski. Eric Kierans was made an officer of the Order of Canada in 1995.

The Underdeveloped Country was first published in 1965 by the Canadian Broadcasting Corporation.

The Moral Ambiguity of America was first published in 1966 by the Canadian Broadcasting Corporation.

Conscience for Change was first published in 1967 by the Canadian Broadcasting Corporation.

Canadian Cities and Sovereignty Association was first published in 1980 by CBC Merchandising for the Canadian Broadcasting Association.

Globalism and the Nation-State was first published in 1984 by CBC Enterprises / les Entreprises Radio-Canada, a division of the Canadian Broadcasting Corporation.

Permission is gratefully acknowledged to reprint text from the following:

(pp. 1–53) *The Underdeveloped Country* by John Kenneth Galbraith (Toronto: Canadian Broadcasting Corporation, 1965). Used by permission of the estate of J. K. Galbraith.

Every reasonable effort has been made to contact the holders of copyright for materials quoted in this work. The publishers will gladly receive information that will enable them to rectify any inadvertent errors or omissions in subsequent editions.

Cover design: Bill Douglas at The Bang
Cover illustration: Thomas Del Brase/Getty Images
Text design and typesetting: Laura Brady, Brady Typesetting & Design

We acknowledge for their financial support of our publishing program the Canada Council for the Arts, the Ontario Arts Council, and the Government of Canada through the Book Publishing Industry Development Program (BPIDP).

Printed and bound in Canada